AF633467

AICPA® & CIMA®

MULTISTATE INCOME TAX

By Andrew Johnson, CPA

Notice to readers

Multistate Income Tax is intended solely for use in continuing professional education and not as a reference. It does not represent an official position of the American Institute of Certified Public Accountants, and it is distributed with the understanding that the author and publisher are not rendering legal, accounting, or other professional services in the publication. This course is intended to be an overview of the topics discussed within, and the author has made every attempt to verify the completeness and accuracy of the information herein. However, neither the author nor publisher can guarantee the applicability of the information found herein. If legal advice or other expert assistance is required, the services of a competent professional should be sought.

ISBN 978-1-11975-647-7 (Paper)
ISBN 978-1-11975-745-0 (ePDF)
ISBN 978-1-11975-744-3 (ePub)
ISBN 978-1-11975-746-7 (oBook)

Course Code: 732476001
Revised: **August 2019**
MIT GS-0419-0B

SKY10019824_072120

Table of Contents

Overview

Course objective

The overriding course objective is for the participant to gain the skills necessary to understand and prepare multistate corporate returns. To that end, the course covers when a business must file a state's return, modifications to taxable income, apportionment and allocation of state taxable income, and combined or "unitary" filing. The goal is to enable the participant to identify issues such that proper tax planning and preparation are ensured.

Introduction

Forty-seven states and the District of Columbia impose some type of income or franchise tax on corporations. Nevada, South Dakota, and Wyoming do not impose corporate income taxes, although South Dakota does have a franchise tax on financial institutions. Although they do not have a corporate income tax, Ohio, Texas, and Washington do have a gross receipts tax, called the Commercial Activity Tax (CAT) in Ohio, the Texas Margin Tax (TMT) in Texas, and the Business and Occupation Tax (B&O) in Washington. Most other states "piggyback" off federal taxable income. Unfortunately, while the concepts of dividing a company's taxable income among the states in which it is doing business are few in number, the application and methods of applying those concepts are varied and often contradictory.

The state approach to taxing multinational corporations differs from the federal approach. The latter generally uses a "separate accounting" approach that requires that income be allocated to a specific jurisdiction based on complex transfer pricing and sourcing rules. States apportion a multistate or multinational corporation's income based upon a formula intended to reflect the company's presence and income in each state. The formula traditionally has relied on factors such as sales, property, and payroll.

The basic outline of state income tax begins with federal taxable income, adds and subtracts certain state modifications and allocable nonbusiness income, and then multiplies the apportionable income based on some combination of sales, property, and payroll factors. The tax formula on page Overview-5 illustrates the basic computation.

Why a national multistate income tax course?

Multistate corporate income tax courses are not widely available in colleges or other institutions of higher learning. It is only recently that undergraduate textbooks have begun to include chapters on multistate taxation. In addition, multistate income tax courses continue to be difficult to find at the local level. Although no two states are identical in their treatment of corporations doing business in a multistate tax environment, a general multistate income tax course seems appropriate for a variety of reasons.

First, states rely on a limited number of concepts in applying their corporate income tax laws. For instance, most states distinguish between business and nonbusiness income and use some variation of the traditional three-factor method (sales, property, and payroll) for apportioning business income.

Second, given the rapid technological changes in e-commerce, more small businesses are doing business in a multistate environment. State tax administrators, for example, continue to press for authority to tax any out-of-state business that does only online sales in their state. In some states, simple participation in a trade show by an out-of-state business will create a filing obligation with the hosting state. A simple misstep by even the smallest of "Mom and Pop" businesses can result in thousands of dollars of tax, penalties, and interest.

After taking this course, you should be alerted to situations where there are potential multistate income tax-saving opportunities. In each situation, you will need to review the appropriate rules, regulations, and practices of the particular jurisdiction to see what options and alternatives may be available.

In summary, the national multistate income tax course is intended to make the reader aware of the pertinent issues, potential liabilities, and opportunities in doing business in more than one state.

Who should take this course?

This course is intended to be an introduction to the basic concepts of multistate corporate income tax. CPAs, chief financial officers, attorneys, and other professionals will benefit from this course.

This course addresses issues pertinent to public practitioners as well as accountants in industry or other nonpublic positions. The examples in the chapters illustrate issues and principals that apply to companies in a variety of industries and recur time and again in multistate taxation.

How your business or practice will benefit

In light of the competitive business environment that includes not only public accounting, but virtually all businesses, this course should assist you or your business in reducing costs, generating additional revenues, and creating goodwill with clients or superiors.

As mentioned previously, many businesses unwittingly incur significant state income tax liabilities. This course will familiarize the participant with the basic concepts of multistate corporate income so that potential liabilities and tax savings may be identified.

The basic teaching included in this course can assist you, whether you are dealing with a state department of revenue, or when negotiating a fee with an outside expert. For example, the ability to negotiate a settlement has its obvious benefits. Having a basic knowledge of the multistate income tax will enable you to approach, discuss, and perhaps even negotiate more effectively and with more confidence.

Federal taxes have always been the mainstay for tax advisers. The focus has been so heavy on federal taxes that, until recently, state tax planners have had little competition. This is changing quickly, making the state and local tax arena an exciting and competitive field.

An expertise in multistate tax can offer both employees and practitioners a higher profile in their company or community. Obviously, these taxes can have a drastic effect on a company's bottom line, and the field is rich with planning opportunities.

Tax formula for multistate corporate taxpayers

	Federal taxable income (Form 1120, line 28 or 30)	$
Plus or minus	State modifications	$
Equals	State tax base	$
Minus	Allocable nonbusiness income	$
Equals	State apportionable income or (loss)	$
Times	State's apportionment percentage	%
Equals	State apportioned income or (loss)	$
Plus	State's allocable nonbusiness income	$
Equals	State taxable income (loss)	$
Times	State tax rate	%
Equals	Tax liability before credits	$
Less	State tax credits	$
Equals	Net state income tax liability	$

The majority of states begin with federal taxable income and then add or subtract a variety of modifications such as accelerated depreciation, interest income on federal obligations, state income taxes, and interest on state and municipal obligations to arrive at the state's taxable base.

The state tax base is then divided into two separate buckets — business income and nonbusiness income. Business income is apportioned among the states based on a variety of factors including sales, property, and payroll. Nonbusiness income, however, is specifically allocated to a particular state. Thus, nonbusiness income is initially subtracted from the tax base, leaving business income to be apportioned and then added back to the apportioned income. If the nonbusiness income is to be allocated to that specific state, it arrives at the state's taxable income or loss.

The following simplified example illustrates the basic multistate calculation.

The Rocky Mountain Corporation does business in two states, North Dakota and Kansas. Its federal taxable income for the year was $1,900,000, which included interest on U.S. obligations of $26,000. During the year, the company made estimated tax payments of $50,000 to North Dakota and $20,000 to Kansas. The company's sales, property, and payroll by state were as follows:

	North Dakota	Kansas	Total
Sales	$ 38,000,000	$ 12,000,000	$ 50,000,000
Property	6,000,000	3,000,000	9,000,000
Payroll	1,200,000	800,000	2,000,000

Rocky Mountain's modified state taxable income is $1,874,000 ($1,900,000 – $26,000). The company's North Dakota apportionment factor is 67.56% making its North Dakota taxable income $1,266,074 ($1,874,000 × .6756).

Using the North Dakota figures, our tax formula for North Dakota looks like this:

	Federal taxable income (Form 1120, line 28 or 30)	$ 1,900,000
Plus or minus	State modifications	26,000
Equals	State tax base	$ 1,874,000
Minus	Allocable nonbusiness income	–
Equals	State apportionable income or (loss)	$ 1,874,000
Times	State's apportionment percentage	67.56%
Equals	State apportioned income or (loss)	$ 1,266,074
Plus	State's allocable nonbusiness income	–
Equals	State taxable income (loss)	$ 1,266,074
Times	State tax rate	5.00%
Equals	Tax liability before credits	58,619
Less	State tax credits	(50,000)
Equals	Net state income tax liability	$ 8,619

The company's Kansas apportionment factor is 32.44%, making its Kansas taxable income $607,926 ($1,874,000 ×.3244).

Using our tax formula, the Kansas numbers look like this:

	Federal taxable income (Form 1120, line 28 or 30)	$ 1,900,000
Plus or minus	State modifications	26,000
Equals	State tax base	$ 1,874,000
Minus	Allocable nonbusiness income	–
Equals	State apportionable income or (loss)	$ 1,874,000
Times	State's apportionment percentage	32.44%
Equals	State apportioned income or (loss)	$ 607,926
Plus	State's allocable nonbusiness income	–
Equals	State taxable income (loss)	$ 607,926
Times	State tax rate	4.00*
Equals	Tax liability before credits	24,317
Less	State tax credits	(20,000)
Equals	Net state income tax liability	$ 4,317

*For purposes of this example, a flat rate of 4% has been used.

Please note that the apportioned income comes out to exactly 100% (67.56% for North Dakota and 32.44% for Kansas). The chances of this happening in the real world are highly unlikely. For example, let us say that North Dakota decided to adopt single sales factor apportionment. Then, the company's apportionment factor would be 76% (38,000,000/$50,000,000), and now Rocky Mountain is apportioning more than 100% of its income. In fact, it is apportioning 108.44% of its income (76% + 32.44%). This is not good. However, just the opposite could happen as well. Suppose Kansas, instead of North Dakota, adopted a single sales factor. The Kansas factor would then be 24% (12,000,000/50,000,000) and Rocky Mountain would now be apportioning only 91.56% of its income (24% + 67.56%). The fact is that given the differences among the states in how they define the tax base and the apportionment factors, it would be downright miraculous if a company ever ended apportioning exactly 100% of its income.

In this course we will study the elements of this formula in detail. The topics we will cover will include the required and allowable modifications to federal taxable income, what constitutes business and nonbusiness income, and a detailed examination of the factors (property, payroll, and sales) of the apportionment formula and the different weight that is often given to the sales factor.

Irregular corporate tax structures

There are a handful of states with unique tax structures that are beyond the scope of this course. They include Michigan's new Business Tax (MBT), Ohio's CAT, the Texas' TMT, and Washington's B&O. The following is a snapshot of those taxes.

Michigan (prior to tax years beginning January 1, 2012)

To the dismay of tax software programmers everywhere, the Michigan legislature once again rewrote that state's tax structure. Effective January 1, 2012, the business income tax and the modified gross receipts tax that were part of the MBT were replaced by a more traditional corporate income tax (CIT).

The CIT rate is 6% and it is applied to regular C corporations, but not pass through entities such as partnerships, limited liability companies, and S corporations. The CIT base begins with federal taxable income followed by several modifications (additions and subtractions of taxes, interest, dividends, and the like) that are typical of other states. The CIT nexus standard is similar to the MBT, and combined filing is still mandatory with apportionment based upon a single sales factor using a Finnigan approach. (See chapters 3 and 5.)

The following rules apply to the Michigan corporate tax structure for years prior to January 1, 2012.

Michigan's Single Business Tax (SBT) was repealed effective December 31, 2007 and replaced with the MBT. Applicable to almost all business entities including C corporations, S corporations, limited liability companies, partnerships, and sole proprietorships, the new tax is composed of two parts. The first part, the Business Income Tax (BIT), is imposed on business income at a rate of 4.95%. The second part, the Modified Gross Receipts Tax (GRT), is imposed at the rate of 0.8%. Most taxpayers will pay both taxes. Certain industries, specifically insurance companies and financial institutions, pay special taxes rather than the MBT. Insurance companies will pay a premiums tax of 1.25% on gross direct premiums and financial institutions will pay a franchise tax on the net capital at a rate of 0.235%. Businesses with gross receipts of less than $350,000 are exempt from the MBT and a credit phase-in is available to businesses with gross receipts between $350,000 and $700,000.

The nexus standards for the two elements of the MBT are different. The BIT applies to any taxpayer whose activity in the state exceeds the safe harbor provisions of Public Law 86-272. (See chapter 1 for a discussion of nexus and P.L. 86-272.) The GRT applies to any taxpayer who (*a*) has physical presence in the state for more than one day during a tax year; or (*b*) actively solicits sales in Michigan and who has gross receipts sourced to the state of more than $350,000. The state defined "active solicitation" in Revenue Administrative Bulletin (RAB) 2007-6, 12/28/07 to mean solicitation through

- the use of mail, telephone, and email;
- advertising, including print, radio, internet, television, and other media; and
- maintenance of an internet site over or through which sales transactions occur with persons in Michigan.

The examples of active solicitation provided by RAB 2007-6 include "sending mail order catalogs; sending credit applications; maintaining an internet site offering online shopping, services, or subscriptions; and soliciting through media advertising, including internet advertisements." It is clear from these examples that the nexus standard for the GRT is really more of an "economic presence" rather than a "physical presence" test.

Unlike Michigan's previous SBT, both taxes are applied on a unitary basis. (See chapter 3 for a discussion of the unitary concept) using a single sales factor (see chapter 5 for a discussion of the sales factor.)

A unitary group is defined as

- a group of U.S. persons, other than a foreign operating entity, one of which owns or controls, directly or indirectly, more than 50% of the ownership interest with voting rights of the other U.S. persons, and whose business activities has a flow of value between or among persons included in the unitary group that are integrated with, are dependent upon, or contribute to each other. [See S.B. 94 Section 117(6).]

A foreign operating entity is a U.S. person that has substantial operations outside the United States and has at least 80% of its income characterized as active foreign business income as that is defined in IRC Section 861(c)(1)(b).

The Michigan Department of Revenue recently released guidance on the first part of the unitary definition, the control test, but not the relationship test. See Michigan Revenue Administrative Bulletin 2010-1, 02/05/2010. The Bulletin provides examples and details of how to apply the control test to parent-subsidiary, brother-sister, and combined controlled entity groups.

Business income tax

The business income tax base for the BIT begins with federal taxable income followed by several modifications, including

- add back federally exempt interest and dividends from non-Michigan sources, net of any expenses to generate that income.
- add back any net income taxes deducted in arriving at federal taxable income.
- add back any net operating losses deducted to arrive at federal taxable income.
- add back any loss attributable to another entity subject to the BIT, to the extent included in federal taxable income.
- add back any royalty, interest, or other expenses paid to a related person for the use of an intangible asset, if that person is not included in the unitary group.
- subtract interest income from U.S. obligations, to the extent included in federal taxable income.
- subtract any deduction taken for net earnings from self-employment of the taxpayer, partner, or member of a limited liability company. (This provision will put sole proprietors, for example, on a level playing field with corporations.)
- subtract any net operating loss, after allocation and apportionment, incurred after 2007. (Business losses may be carried forward 10 years.)

Please note also that effective January 1, 2008, Michigan decoupled from the federal taxable income by excluding any bonus depreciation [IRC Section 168(k)] and the domestic production activities deduction (IRC Section 199).

The taxable base, after the preceding modifications, is then apportioned or allocated based on a single sales factor. The sales factor is the percentage derived from dividing total sales in Michigan by total sales everywhere. For a unitary group, Michigan sales will include sales in Michigan by each member of the unitary group regardless of whether that member has nexus with Michigan. (See the discussion of the "Finnigan rule" under the sales factor in chapter 5.)

Sales of tangible personal property are based on ultimate destination, while sales of services rely on the market approach. Service sales under the prior SBT were sourced based upon cost of performance coupled with an all-or-nothing approach to services provided in more than one state. Service sales under the new MBT will not only be included in the jurisdiction of the recipient of the services, but will be prorated to the extent the service is provided in more than one state. The MBT also provides extensive guidance for sourcing sales for various industries such as investment, brokerage, oil and gas, and telecommunication companies.

Modified gross receipts tax

The GRT is assessed on the taxpayer's "modified gross receipts tax base," which is defined as "gross receipts less purchases from other firms before apportionment." Gross receipts is defined much like it was under the prior SBT as "the entire amount received by the taxpayer from any activity whether in intrastate, interstate, or foreign commerce carried on for direct or indirect gain, benefit, or advantage to the taxpayer or to others." [See S.B. 94 Section 111(1).] The rate for the GRT is 0.8%.

"Purchases from other firms" includes inventory, materials, supplies, assets, and compensation costs paid to staffing firms and construction companies.

Michigan surcharge

In 2007, Public Act 145 instituted an MBT surcharge of 21.99% of a taxpayer's MBT liability after allocation and apportionment, but before any tax credit. The surcharge is capped at $6 million for all taxpayers, except for financial institutions. For financial institutions, the MBT is currently 23.4%. The MBT surcharge was eliminated on January 1, 2017. Insurance companies are not subject to the surcharge, nor are taxpayers who qualify for the state's Small Business Alternative Credit. Taxpayers must factor in the surcharge in their calculation of estimated tax credits. Although the surcharge was the key element of PA 145, the provision made additional changes that are beyond the scope of this text, but included such items as reductions and caps on various credits and changes in taxpayer refund opportunities.

Needless to say, many questions remain and controversies are sure to ensue. Fortunately, the Michigan Department of Revenue has helpfully issued roughly 380 Frequently Asked Questions (FAQ) covering administrative matters, and questions regarding nexus, apportionment, unitary groups, and many other topics.

Ohio

Beginning in 2005 and ending in 2009, Ohio phased out its traditional income tax and replaced it with the CAT. The CAT was fully phased in for the 2010 tax year.

The CAT is a tax on the privilege of doing business in Ohio, and is not measured by net income, but rather by taxable gross receipts. As a privilege tax, the tax is on the person receiving the gross receipts, such as the vendor, not the purchaser. "Person" is widely defined and includes individuals, corporations, partnerships, limited liability companies, trusts, indeed, almost any combination of individuals in any form. Thus, the tax applies to all types of businesses including retailers, contractors, manufacturers, and service providers such as accountants, doctors, and lawyers. That said, the tax does not apply to financial institutions, public utilities, or insurance companies.

The tax base is gross receipts, and includes amounts received from sales, services, and exchanges including "the total amount realized by a person, without deduction for the cost of goods sold or other expenses incurred . . . the fair market value of any property and services received, and any debt transferred or forgiven as consideration." Excluded items include interest, dividend, and capital gain income, repayment of principal, contributions to exempt organizations, life insurance proceeds, tax refunds, damage awards, gifts, and certain excise taxes.

Receipts from the sale of tangible personal property are sourced to Ohio, if the property is received by the purchaser in the state. Service sales are sourced according to where the benefit is received, and rents and royalties are sourced based on the location or use of the underlying property.

Nexus for the CAT exists if a taxpayer owns or uses capital in Ohio, holds a certificate of compliance to do business, or has a "bright line presence" in the state. A bright line presence is established if a taxpayer meets any one of the following tests:

- Has more than $50,000 in property in the state
- Has more than $50,000 in payroll in the state
- Has gross receipts of $500,000 or more in the state
- Has 25% or more of its total property, payroll, or sales in the state
- Is domiciled in Ohio for any other business purpose

Under these nexus standards, a taxpayer who has no presence or connection with the state other than online sales will have a filing obligation if the sales into Ohio exceed $500,000. The Ohio legislature specifically said that the CAT was not an income tax and thus the safe harbor provisions of P.L. 86-272 (see chapter 1) do not apply. In addition, the state revenue department does not believe that physical presence, required for sales tax nexus, applies to the CAT. In other words, you do not have to have physical presence in the state to have nexus for the CAT. Economic presence is sufficient. (Please note that a state legislature's opinion regarding the application and interpretation of a federal law carries no more authoritative legal weight than your own.) The state's economic presence standard was sustained in three court cases: *Newegg Inc. v. Testa*, No. 2012-234 (Ohio Bd. Tax App. Feb. 26, 2015); *Crutchfield, Inc. v. Testa*, Nos. 2012-926, 2012-3068, 2013-2021 (Ohio Bd. Tax App. Feb. 26, 2015); and *Mason Companies, Inc. v. Testa*, Nos. 2012-1169, 2012-2806 (Ohio Bd. Tax App. April 20, 2015).

There have already been constitutional challenges to the CAT. The Ohio Court of Appeals ruled that the CAT, when applied to certain food sales, was an unconstitutional excise tax on food. See *Ohio Grocers Association v. Ohio*, 178 Ohio App3d, 897 NE2d 188 (Ohio 2008). The case was appealed to the Ohio Supreme Court, which reversed the Appeals Court decision on September 17, 2009 [*Ohio Grocers Assn. v. Levin*, 916 NE2d 446 (Ohio 2009)]. The Ohio Supreme Court held that the CAT was a permissible tax on the privilege of doing business and not a tax triggered by the sale of food. Although the CAT falls upon sellers of food, it is not the case that it necessarily falls upon the sale or purchase of food.

The tax rate for the CAT is a flat $150 on the first million dollars of taxable gross receipts with a rate of 0.26% of taxable gross receipts over $1m.

The CAT's reporting period is quarterly (annually for taxpayers with gross receipts of less than $1m).

An affiliated group of corporate taxpayers may elect to file a consolidated return. The election is binding for two years (specifically eight calendar quarters) and allows the intercompany sales of the group to be excluded from the taxable gross receipts of the group. However, the consolidated group must include all commonly owned entities (80% or more), even if the entities do not have nexus with the state. Any taxpayers with common ownership of more than 50% must file a combined return. Combined groups may not exclude intercompany receipts, but may exclude the receipts of any member of the group that does not have nexus with Ohio.

The Ohio Department of Revenue is regularly releasing new guidance on the CAT. Nonetheless, there are many unanswered questions and the CAT imposed some difficult problems during the transition period with respect to various issues with net operating losses, consolidated and combined filing, and FASB ASC 740, *Income Taxes*.

Texas

Through 2006, Texas' taxpayers calculated their corporate franchise tax based on "net taxable earned surplus" and "net taxable capital" and paid the greater of the two. Texas' "net taxable earned surplus" was basically a corporation's federal taxable income, plus an add-back of compensation paid to officers and directors. "Net taxable capital" was the corporation's stated capital plus surplus. Surplus was the net assets of the corporation minus its stated capital. S corporations and limited liability companies were also subject to the Texas franchise tax.

Texas replaced the state's franchise tax with a modified gross receipts tax that has come to be called the TMT or the Revised Texas Franchise Tax. The formula for the margin tax is as follows:

Start with:	Total revenue from combined business entity or group
Less:	The greater of:
	1. Cost of goods sold
	2. Compensation
	3. **$1,000,000**
Equals:	Margin tax base (but not to exceed 70% of total revenue)
Times:	Texas apportionment percentage
Equals:	Margin tax base apportioned to Texas
Less:	Other deductions
Equals:	Taxable margin
Times:	Tax rate of 0.95% (or 0.475% for wholesalers or retailers) for reports due in 2015. For reports due beginning January 1, 2016, the rates are 0.75% and 0.375%, respectively.
Equals:	Texas tax liability
Less:	Tax credits
Equals:	Texas tax due

Businesses that must pay the margin tax include partnerships, limited liability companies, business trusts, corporations, banks, savings and loans, joint ventures, and other professional and business associations. General partnerships having only individuals as partners and sole proprietorships are not subject to the margin tax.

Total revenue is taken from an entity's federal tax return. For example, a corporation will start with the amount from line 1c of its form 1120 and add the amounts from lines 4 through 10. A partnership will start with line 1c of form 1065 and add the amounts from lines 4 through 7.

Exclusions from revenue include dividends and interest from federal obligations, Schedule C dividends, foreign royalties, and dividends under IRC Sections 78 and 951-964.

The margin tax also has specific definitions for cost of goods sold and compensation. For example, cost of goods sold has a separate calculation different from the federal calculation for cost of goods sold. Compensation will include wages, tips, healthcare contributions, retirement benefits, and stock options deductible for federal taxable income, but is capped at $300,000 per individual per year. The cap is adjusted for each even-numbered year beginning January 2010, and is based on the percentage increase or decrease in the consumer price index. The cap for 2018 and 2019 is $370,000 per person.

The cost of goods sold calculation has generated a significant amount of controversy and confusion. For example, a movie chain has been allowed to deduct its exhibition costs, and a service company has been allowed to deduct its acquisition and processing activities to acquire seismic data. [See *American Multi-Cinema, Inc. v. Hegar*, No. 03-14-00397-CV, (Tex. Ct. App., April 30, 2015) and *Hegar v. CGG Veritas Services, Inc.*, No. 03-14-00713-CV (Tex. Ct. App., March 9, 2016).]

After the calculation of total revenue, cost of goods sold, and compensation, the tax base is apportioned based on gross receipts. The apportionment calculation is similar to the calculation made previously under the state's franchise tax. There are differences, however. For example, there are no throwback sales under the margin tax.

A taxable entity with total revenue of $10m or less may elect to pay the franchise tax by multiplying total revenue times its apportionment factor times 0.331% (0.00331). Taxable entities with annualized revenue of $1m or less do not owe any tax, but must still file a return.

Texas is a combined reporting state. (See chapter 3.) Taxable entities that are part of an affiliated group engaged in a unitary business must file a combined report. An affiliated group is a group of taxable entities in which a controlling interest is owned by a common owner, or by one or more of the member entities. A combined group must include eligible entities, even if those entities do not have nexus with the state. Unlike most other combined reporting states, partnerships and other flow-through entities are taxable entities for purposes of combined filing. (Most states use the federal definition of an affiliated group under IRC Section 1504(a), generally 80% or more common ownership, which excludes noncorporate entities from being part of an affiliated group.) Some states use 50% or more common ownership for their combined reporting requirement. Partnerships, limited liability companies taxed as partnerships, S corporations, and disregarded entities are all taxable entities subject to combined filing.

There is an ongoing debate over whether the margin tax is an income tax or a gross receipts tax for purposes of deduction and nonresident individual tax credits (see chapter 2, the section on state income taxes). Since the margin tax was passed in May 2006, the state has issued a series of explanations, clarifications, and rulings. These can be found at the state's website at www.window.state.tx.us/taxes/.

Many questions remain and changes in the application of the new tax should be expected.

Washington

The state of Washington does not have an individual or corporate income tax. Instead it has the B&O gross receipts tax that is levied for the privilege of doing business in the state. Gross receipts include proceeds from the sale of services and goods largely to Washington customers. Sales of tangible personal property are sourced according to their shipping destination, and service sales are sourced to where the services are performed.

As a gross receipts tax, generally there are no deductions for wages, materials, or other costs of doing business. Other than returns and allowances, bad debts, advances, and casual sales, there are few exemptions or deductions. The law also provides a few credits against the tax for rural county employment, high technology investment, small business, and most importantly, a multiple activities credit that mitigates paying the B&O tax twice on the same product or transaction under different categories. Finally, unlike a sales tax, a sale does not have to occur to be subject to the B&O. For example, manufacturing items for your own use is subject to the B&O. Like a sales tax, however, returns are filed monthly, quarterly, or annually depending on your annual tax liability.

Washington adopted new rules regarding nexus in 2010, and the state is particularly aggressive in asserting nexus.

Prior to October 1, 2018, a taxpayer is deemed to have nexus if the taxpayer is a nonresident individual or business entity that is organized or commercially domiciled outside Washington, and in any calendar year has (*a*) more than $57,000 of payroll or property in Washington; (*b*) more than $285,000 of receipts from Washington; or (*c*) at least 25% of its total property, total payroll, or total receipts in Washington. For a recent decision in Washington regarding nexus see *Lamtec Corp. v. Washington*, 246 P.3d 788 (Wash. 2011). Please note that this economic presence standard does not apply to out-of-state taxpayers making sales of tangible personal property into Washington at retail or wholesale, and who otherwise have no contact with the state. For those taxpayers, the bright-line physical presence test still applies. (See chapter 1.) After September 30, 2018, Washington implemented a new economic nexus program for its taxes. If an out-of-state seller has more than $100,000 in gross sales in a 12-month period or 200 separate transactions, then they will have nexus with Washington.

The B&O tax applies to all types of businesses including corporations, partnerships, limited liability companies, and sole proprietorships. The B&O tax rate varies depending upon the business type. The five primary types and their rates include the following:

B&O classification	Rate
Retailing	0.00471
Extraction	0.00484
Manufacturing	0.00484
Wholesaling	0.00484
Services	.015

In addition, Washington has numerous specialized classifications including manufacturing aircraft, aluminum, solar energy, processing meat at wholesale, gambling and services such as travel agents, tour operators, boarding homes, and manufacturing microchips among others. (For a complete list go to https://dor.wa.gov/find-taxes-rates/business-occupation-tax/business-occupation-tax-classifications.)

A business may be subject to tax under more than one classification. For example, selling building materials to a homeowner is a retail sale while the same transaction to a custom builder could be a wholesale sale. Nonretail businesses making less than $28,000 per year are not required to file returns.

The following material is a brief description of the major B&O tax classifications adapted from the state's publication on its B&O tax.

Retailing

Businesses that sell products and specified services to consumers are retailers. Taxable retail services include the following:

- Construction
- Repair

- Certain personal services, including the following:
  - Turkish and steam baths
  - Dating and escort services
  - Tattooing
- Specialized activities, including the following:
  - Lawn mowing, tree and shrub pruning, and trimming
  - Insect spraying
  - Guided tours
  - Renting equipment with operators

Wholesaling

Wholesalers sell goods and services to persons who will resell them to others. The B&O tax is calculated on the wholesale selling price. If you are a wholesaler, you must keep a resale certificate on file from each buyer to document that the transaction was not a retail sale. Retail sales tax is not collected on wholesale transactions. Blanket resale certificates for frequent wholesale customers must be renewed every four years.

Manufacturing

The manufacturing B&O tax classification is used by firms that produce items in Washington, regardless of where that item is sold. Thus, products sold and delivered out of state are still subject to the manufacturing B&O. Manufactured products that are used by the manufacturer, but are not sold (or are used prior to sale), are also subject to tax under the manufacturing classification. The manufacturing B&O tax is based on the value of the products. In cases where there is no sale, the value is the selling price of similar products.

Financial services

Businesses that provide financial services including banking, securities and/or investment management, investment advising, and similar activities are subject to the B&O tax under this classification.

Service and other activities

Businesses that provide personal and professional services (such as doctors, hairdressers, consultants, and software programmers) are generally subject to B&O tax under this classification. This classification includes services that are not subject to the retailing B&O tax, or the financial services B&O tax classifications. Also, any business that is not described under a particular classification of the B&O tax must report under this catch-all category. For example, garbage collection services and janitorial services are taxed under this classification. Commission income is also subject to tax under this classification.

In addition to the major B&O classifications, the state provides many specialized classifications. Some of these include rates for insurance agents, printers, publishers, warehousing, radio and television broadcasting, and government contracting (0.00484); manufacturing and selling aircraft (0.002904); extraction and manufacturing of timber (0.002956); travel agents, tour operators, manufacturing computer chips (0.00275); processors of meat, soybeans, wheat, seafood, fruit, vegetables and dairy products (0.00138); and gambling contests (0.015 or 0.0163 depending on the amounts).

Farming, federal credit unions, governments, sales of real estate, and certain not-for-profit activities are not subject to the B&O tax. Cities and towns may also have a local B&O tax not to exceed 0.02%. However, keep in mind that there is no necessary connection between the state and local B&O taxes.

Capital stock and franchise taxes

There are several states that have more than one element to their corporate income tax. For example, New York and Pennsylvania each have a capital stock calculation.

New York corporations calculate their tax using four different measures — a tax measured by net income, a tax measured by the company's capital base, a tax measured by the minimum taxable income tax, and a fixed dollar minimum base. (To calculate the tax on capital, a company must divide its capital into several components — investment capital, business capital, and subsidiary capital.) The corporation must pay the highest of the four taxes. In addition, the state imposes a tax on subsidiary capital allocated to New York.

Pennsylvania has a capital stock or franchise tax in addition to its corporate net income tax. The capital stock tax is a property tax imposed on the capital stock value of domestic corporations. The franchise tax is imposed on the capital stock value of foreign corporations doing business in the state. The Pennsylvania capital stock or franchise tax has been eliminated for tax years beginning January 1, 2016 and after.

Obviously, this brief thumbnail sketch cannot do justice to the exclusions, exemptions, modifications, and other complexities of these unusual or irregular tax structures. This course, instead, will focus on the key themes of nexus, state modifications, allocable and apportionable income, and the makeup of the sales, property, and payroll factors common to the majority of states.

Conclusion

This manual is designed to be a permanent reference tool. Nevertheless, it is no substitute for researching a state's specific tax statutes, regulations, and case law. We hope your reading of this manual enriches your professional learning experience.

Note: We use the terms he and she alternately throughout the course (except when a particular person is mentioned), because both sexes are well represented throughout the profession.

Chapter 1

Interstate Activity and Nexus

Learning objectives

- Identify nexus issues.
- Distinguish between income tax and sales tax nexus.
- Recognize the constitutional issues that drive nexus decisions.
- Identify the limitations of Public Law 86-272.

Introduction

Nexus is the beginning issue in any multistate activity. Unless you are doing business in, or have nexus with, a political jurisdiction, there is no obligation to file a return with that jurisdiction.

The word *nexus* comes from the Latin word *nexum* referring to obligations between contracting parties. More simply, in the state and local tax context it refers to both the quantity and quality of contacts, links, or connections between a taxpayer and a political jurisdiction sufficient enough to subject the taxpayer to the jurisdiction of the state. Or to put it even more simply, are you doing business in __________ (fill in the blank: town, county, or state)?

The nexus issue is becoming increasingly volatile and complex in light of the states' attempts to broaden their tax base and increase their tax collections. States are pressing out-of-state companies, with the most slender of connections to the state, to file returns and pay sales tax and income tax. The rapid growth of e-commerce and the internet has added to this complexity, making proper tax planning in this area more critical than ever. Even though this is a class on multistate corporate income tax, we discuss both sales tax nexus and income tax nexus in this chapter. The principles behind nexus for both taxes overlap and, as a consequence, there is a lot of confusion over the distinction between sales tax and income tax nexus. It is critical to understand both nexuses and the differences between the two.

Knowledge check

1. The volatility of the nexus issue for purposes of state income taxes has

   a. Lessened.
   b. Become less complex.
   c. Increased.
   d. Stopped completely.

Nexus defined

Nexus is the contact that must be established with a taxing jurisdiction before that jurisdiction can require a business to collect its tax, or otherwise subject it to its taxing authority. Generally, states extend their taxing authority as far as constitutionally possible. Consequently, it is with the U.S. Constitution that we must begin our discussion of nexus.

Please note, however, that nexus may be different for different taxes. In analyzing income tax issues, be careful not to confuse nexus for sales and use tax purposes with nexus for income tax purposes. For instance, most businesses are concerned with three types of nexus when doing business in surrounding states or states outside their domicile's taxing jurisdiction. Most common are nexus for sales and use tax purposes, nexus for income and franchise tax purposes (if this tax applies in a state), and nexus for purposes of registering or qualifying with the Secretary of State's office to do business in a state. Nexus conditions for all three of these are generally different.

The two clauses of most importance in the U.S. Constitution for defining the taxing jurisdiction of states are the Due Process and Commerce Clauses.

Due process

The Fourteenth Amendment to the Constitution prohibits states from denying any person "life, liberty, or property, without due process of law." Because taxation is regarded as depriving someone of their property, a state cannot exact such tolls without due process of law.

Due process relates essentially to questions of fundamental fairness, to "traditional notions of fair play and substantial justice." "That test is whether property was taken without due process of law, or if we must paraphrase, whether the taxing power exerted by the state bears fiscal relation to protection, opportunities and benefits given by the state. The simple but controlling question is whether the state has given anything for which it can ask return." (*Wisconsin v. J.C. Penney Co.*, 311 U.S. 435)

The Due Process Clause of the Fourteenth Amendment imposes four hurdles a state must overcome before it can impose a tax.

- There must be a minimum connection between the taxpayer and the state.
- There must be "some definite link, some minimum connection, between a state and the person, property, or transaction it seeks to tax." *Quill v. North Dakota*, citing *Miller Brothers v. Maryland*, 347 U.S. 340, 344-345 (1954).
- There must be some rational relationship requirement between the taxpayer and the state.
- The "income attributed to the State for tax purposes must be rationally related to 'values connected with the taxing State.'" *Quill* at 306, citing *Moorman Mfg. Co. v. Bair*, 437 U.S. 267, 273 (1978). If property is taken, or responsibilities are imposed on the taxpayer, the government must have sufficient jurisdiction over the taxpayer, or due process is not served (*Wisconsin v. J.C. Penney*, 311 U.S. 435 (1940); *National Bellas Hess v. Illinois Dept. of Revenue*, 386 U.S. 753

(1967)). (The *National Bellas Hess* decision seemed to combine both the Commerce Clause and the Due Process Clause analyses.)

For many years, it has been fairly clear that the Due Process Clause is not really a serious hurdle. Why? Because the Supreme Court has ruled that the due process hurdle is cleared whenever a company purposefully directs it business activity or solicitation toward a state's residents. The minimum connection for a company need be no more than "purposefully avail[ing] itself of the benefits of an economic market in the forum State," or engaging "in continuous and widespread solicitation of business within a State." In other words, the Due Process Clause does not require physical presence. Thus, a mail-order company, whose only contacts with a state were catalogs and goods sent through the U.S. mail, satisfied the nexus standard for due process (see *Quill Corp. v. North Dakota*, 504 U.S. 298,306 (1992)).

Commerce clause

The second applicable constitutional provision is the Commerce Clause, which provides for congressional regulation of interstate commerce. The Commerce Clause of the Constitution provides that "Congress shall have the power to regulate Commerce with foreign Nations, and among the several states, and with the Indian tribes." (*U.S. Constitution, Art. I, Section 8, Cl. 3*)

The Commerce Clause has been interpreted as not only conferring power on the national government to regulate commerce, but also as limiting the states' power to interfere with commerce even where Congress has not acted. Under this dormant Commerce Clause principle, taxes that have been found to unduly burden interstate commerce have been declared unconstitutional. However, the crux of the Commerce Clause analysis is not necessarily that states are prohibited from imposing any burden on interstate commerce, but rather whether the tax discriminates against interstate commerce, either by providing a direct commercial advantage to local businesses, or by creating multiple taxation on interstate commerce. In short, states can tax interstate commerce so long as they meet the four-prong test of *Complete Auto Transit*.

In *Complete Auto Transit*, the Supreme Court provided a four-prong test for determining whether a state tax on interstate commerce is constitutional. A state tax will be deemed constitutional if

- the tax is applied to an activity with substantial nexus with the taxing state.

For sales and use tax purposes, substantial nexus has historically been defined as requiring at least a minimal physical presence. See *Quill v. North Dakota*, 504 U.S. 298 (1992). However, the recent *Wayfair* decision has added economic thresholds as a means of creating nexus. See *South Dakota v. Wayfair*, 585 U.S. (2018).

- The tax is fairly apportioned.

The Supreme Court has stated that fair apportionment requires that the tax meets both an internal and external consistency test. "Internal consistency is preserved when the imposition of a tax identical to the one in question by every other State would add no burden to interstate commerce that intrastate commerce would not also bear." *Oklahoma Tax Comm'n v. Jefferson Lines*, 514 U.S. 175, 185 (1995).

In short, if every state adopted the same test as the one before the court, and the income tax would be no more than 100%, then the internal consistency test is met.

External consistency is "the economic justification for the State's claim upon the value taxed, to discover whether a State's tax reaches beyond that portion of value that is fairly attributable to economic activity within the taxing State." *Oklahoma Tax Comm'n v. Jefferson Lines*, 514 U.S. 175, 185 (1995). In short, external consistency requires that the formula or methodology used be a fair or reasonable reflection of how the income is earned in the state.

Most of the debate over the fair apportionment test has been over the formulas used by states in apportioning and allocating the income of a multistate business.

- The tax does not discriminate against interstate commerce.

A state may not "impose a tax which discriminates against interstate commerce . . . by providing a direct commercial advantage to local business." *Northwestern States Portland Cement Co. v. Minnesota*, 358 U.S. 450, 458 (1959).

- The tax must be fairly related to services provided by the taxing state.

The "fourth criterion asks only that the measure of the tax be reasonably related to the taxpayer's presence or activities in the State." *Complete Auto Transit, Inc., v. Brady*, 430 U.S. 274 (1977). Generally, if the sale takes place in the state and is measured by its purchase price, there will be no violation of this fourth test.

In sum, state taxes may be imposed on interstate commerce, but they will be justified only if the taxes are designed so that the interstate business bears a fair share of the cost of the government entity whose protection it enjoys [*Complete Auto Transit, Inc.* U.S. 274 (1977); *Western Livestock v. Bureau of Revenue,* 303 U.S. 250 (1938); *McGoldrick v. Berwind-White Coal Mining Co.,* 309 U.S. 33 (1940); *Northwestern States Portland Cement Company v. State of Minnesota,* 358 U.S. 450 (1959)].

It is important to note that the nexus requirements for the two constitutional hurdles, Due Process and the Commerce Clause, are not the same; a point emphasized by the U.S. Supreme Court in *Quill*. "[North Dakota] contends that the nexus requirements imposed by the Due Process and Commerce Clauses are equivalent and that if, as we concluded previously, a mail-order house that lacks a physical presence in the taxing State nonetheless satisfies the due process 'minimum contacts' test, then that corporation also meets the Commerce Clause 'substantial nexus' test. We disagree. Despite the similarity in phrasing, the nexus requirements of the Due Process and Commerce Clauses are not identical." (*Quill Corp. v. North Dakota*, 504 U.S. 298 (1992))

Knowledge check

2. The right to impose tax on an out-of-state business rests upon

    a. The U.S. Constitution.
    b. State law.
    c. Local taxing authority.
    d. The Supreme Court.

3. The Due Process Clause defines nexus as __________, and the Commerce Clause definition requires __________.

    a. Fair apportionment; rational relationship.
    b. Substantial nexus; minimal contacts.
    c. Minimal contacts; substantial nexus.
    d. Fair apportionment, minimal contacts.

4. The Commerce Clause requires all but

    a. Minimal nexus
    b. Nondiscrimination
    c. Fair apportionment
    d. Some relation to services provided

In summary, the Due Process Clause requires only (1) minimum contacts (physical presence not necessary), and (2) a rational relationship between the income and the state. The Commerce Clause requires (1) substantial nexus, (2) nondiscrimination, (3) fair apportionment, and (4) some relation to the services provided.

We can look at an example to see how the preceding case law and rules work in practice.

For example, Crystal City Computers has one small store in Denver, Colorado, but sells most of its computers and peripherals over the internet and through catalogs. It has no employees, sales representatives, or facilities other than the Denver store. A farm girl from Kansas, named Dorothy, orders one of the company's computers over the internet. Crystal City ships a computer to Dorothy by common carrier. Crystal City does not exceed any economic nexus threshold in Kansas. Crystal City does not have any obligation to collect sales or use tax from Dorothy on the sale because it does not have nexus with the state of Kansas. Nor does Crystal City have any obligation to file an income tax return with Kansas.

Would our answer be any different if Crystal City has maintenance agreements with several Kansas computer service repair shops that provide warranty repair in case Dorothy's computer fails? Perhaps. Many states have adopted a rule asserting that warranty repair services provided by third-party independent contractors will create nexus for a remote vendor. Suppose Crystal City delivers the computer in its own truck rather than using a common carrier. Would that create nexus? If the deliveries were infrequent and sporadic, the seller might not have nexus. However, if the deliveries are significant in number, most states will claim that sales tax (but not income tax) nexus has been created between itself and the remote seller.

Suppose Crystal City had one sales person who made only two trips into Kansas during the past 18 months. Would the physical presence of the salesperson create a filing obligation on the part of

Crystal City? Perhaps not. It is not enough physical presence for some states. However, Washington recently held that two visits to the state were sufficient to create a filing obligation (see *Lamtec Corp. v. Washington*, 246 P.3d 788 (Wash. 2011)).

The questions about deliveries, the extent of physical presence, and the actions of agents are part of the continuing debate over nexus. But before we look at those issues, it is important to stop for a moment and distinguish sales tax nexus from income tax nexus. People often confuse the two.

Sales tax nexus

There are three key U.S. Supreme Court cases that define the test for sales tax nexus: *National Bellas Hess, Inc. v. Illinois*, 386 U.S. 753 (1967), *Quill v. North Dakota*, 504 U.S. 298 (1992), and *South Dakota v. Wayfair, Inc.* In the first two instances the Court ruled that physical presence is the bright-line test for sales tax nexus, and subsequently added an additional economic presence standard that could be met with the third.

National Bellas Hess was a landmark decision in the sales and use tax nexus area. In this 1967 case, the seller was a Missouri mail-order house with no presence or activity in Illinois, except for catalogs and flyers that were mailed to its customers twice a year. Any products sold in Illinois were delivered by common carrier. Illinois required that National Bellas Hess register to collect sales and use tax, asserting it had nexus with the State of Illinois. Illinois believed that Bellas Hess was doing business in the state because its "large-scale, systematic, continuous solicitation and exploitation is a sufficient 'nexus' to require Bellas Hess to collect" Illinois use tax. The U.S. Supreme Court held that Bellas Hess did not have a filing obligation with Illinois. In fact, the court held that a taxpayer must have physical presence in a state before incurring a sales or use tax filing obligation. The court was sensitive to the fact that the thousands of sales taxing jurisdictions in the United States posed a considerable impediment to interstate commerce.

The court decided that the activities of National Bellas Hess in Illinois were strictly in interstate commerce. Accordingly, there was not sufficient nexus for National Bellas Hess to be liable for Illinois use tax on sales to Illinois residents. The court determined that requiring the seller to collect sales and use tax in Illinois would violate the company's rights under both the Due Process and Commerce Clause of the U.S. Constitution. In short, the sales were clearly a matter of interstate commerce; the company did not have any physical presence in the state and, thus, had no obligation to collect the state's tax.

Given the significant changes in technology, including computers, fax machines, mobile phones, and the internet, since the Bellas Hess decision in 1967, it was no surprise that state tax administrators believed the physical presence test to be archaic and wanted to revisit the issue. North Dakota did just that in Quill in 1992.

The *Quill* case was similar factually to the *National Bellas Hess* decision. Quill Corporation, a non-North Dakota business, had no physical presence or employees in North Dakota. Quill sold business equipment and supplies in North Dakota only through catalogs, flyers, and by telephone. The post office or common carriers delivered all sales in North Dakota.

The opinions of the lower courts involved in the *Quill* cases were varied. The North Dakota trial court found *Quill* indistinguishable from *National Bellas Hess* and, accordingly, ruled in favor of Quill. The North Dakota Supreme Court, however, overruled the trial court in favor of the state citing that changes in the economy and the law, in essence, outdated *National Bellas Hess.* The North Dakota Supreme Court embraced an economic presence test versus a physical presence test and held that Quill's economic presence in the state was sufficient nexus to require Quill to collect the use tax. After all, reasoned the court and its supporters, with fax machines, mobile phones, satellite transmissions, and the beginning of the internet, a company no longer had to be physically present in a state to do business there.

Nevertheless, the U.S. Supreme Court reversed the decision of the North Dakota Supreme Court, but agreed with it on some grounds. With respect to the due process analysis, the court held that a physical presence was not required. The court's due process analysis was based on whether a multistate business's contacts with a state made it reasonable to require it to defend a lawsuit in the state. The Supreme Court reasoned that Quill's continuous and widespread activity within North Dakota was sufficient warning that its activities may subject it to the taxing jurisdiction of the state. It is important to note that this finding differed from the court's position in *National Bellas Hess*. One of the Supreme Court justices indicated that in the 25 years between the *National Bellas Hess* ruling and the *Quill* ruling, there were enough changes in law and in technology that the due process analysis of *National Bellas Hess* was no longer applicable.

The U.S. Supreme Court held that while requiring *Quill* to collect North Dakota's sales or use tax was not a due process violation, it would still place an unconstitutional burden on interstate commerce. The court found that the physical presence requirement is still a valid requirement under the Commerce Clause analysis and, in that regard, it refused to overrule *National Bellas Hess*'s reasoning. It also reaffirmed that the Complete Auto Transit four-part test was an adequate test under the Commerce Clause. In essence, the decision maintained the status quo, yet sent a strong message to Congress that Congress is not only better qualified to resolve this issue, but that it also has the ultimate power to do so.

In summary, the *Quill* decision holds that a taxpayer has established nexus for sales and use tax under the Due Process Clause where the taxpayer's activity is limited to purposefully directing its economic activities to the state's residents. Thus, a retailer whose only activity in a state is limited to the mailing of catalogs has probably created nexus for purposes of the Due Process Clause. In other words, a company need not be physically present in a state to create a filing obligation for purposes of the Due Process Clause.

The Commerce Clause, however, still offers significant protection to remote sellers. First, a state cannot interfere with the regulation of the national economy. Second, a state can only assert jurisdiction over businesses where there is substantial nexus with the state. The U.S. Supreme Court disagreed with the North Dakota Supreme Court's assertion that the technological and economic business changes since *Bellas Hess* would justify totally overruling that decision. Physical presence is still one of the easier means to identify if nexus has been created. But, nexus has been greatly expanded by the recently decided *South Dakota v. Wayfair, Inc.* case.

Forget Nexus. Let's try "notice and reporting."

There is another trend happening now that could have great impact. Even with the *Wayfair* decision, notice and reporting is still alive and well. Failure to comply with what some call the "Notice and Reporting" rules have some egregious penalties.

Colorado was the first state to enact this new "Amazon law." Their approach was to say, "Okay, if we can't force out-of-state sellers to collect our use tax because of *Quill*, what if we can make it really expensive not to collect it by imposing very expensive record-keeping and onerous reporting requirements? If we do that maybe we can 'convince' sellers to 'choose' to collect the tax."

It was enacted in 2010 but immediately challenged. As enacted, Colorado's use tax notification requirement applies to out-of-state businesses that sell taxable goods to Colorado residents but don't collect Colorado sales or use tax. It requires noncollecting businesses making at least $100,000 in total gross annual sales to

1. inform Colorado customers they may be subject to Colorado use tax;
2. send an annual purchase summary to Colorado customers who purchase more than $500 in taxable goods in one year, along with a reminder of their use tax obligation; and
3. provide the Colorado Department of Revenue with annual customer information (names, addresses, and amount of purchases).

The Direct Marketing Association (DMA) immediately challenged the policy because it discriminates against interstate commerce and unduly burdens out-of-state businesses. The DMAs lawsuit in *Direct Marketing Association v. Brohl* is what prompted the opinion by Justice Kennedy mentioned previously.

DMA lost

The original DMA case created a stir because of the comments by Kennedy as have already been discussed. After the original case was remanded back to the state court for a rehearing on the merits, the state court upheld the legality of the notice and reporting requirements. That was a shame for businesses because those requirements are so onerous. When that second State court ruling was then re-appealed to the U.S. Supreme Court, they declined the case, letting the lower court's ruling and the onerous Colorado laws stand.

Penalty for not reporting

The taxpayer might be tempted to just ignore this requirement in Colorado. Do so at your peril though, because the penalties could be devastating:

- There is a $5-per-transaction penalty for each failure to inform Colorado customers that they may be subject to Colorado use tax.
- There is a $10 penalty per each failure to send an annual purchase summary to Colorado customers who purchase more than $500 in taxable goods in one year, along with a reminder of their use tax obligation.

That's how Colorado decided to bully out-of-state sellers to comply. These requirements may seem like an unconscionable burden on retailers, but this is the current law of the land in Colorado. Colorado's success in the courts prompted Louisiana and Vermont to pass similar notice and reporting laws. More states are likely to follow. In fact, the state of Washington recently passed its own version, effective January 1, 2018.

Before *Wayfair*, this approach seemed like the easiest path for a state to take to make people register to collect tax. If a client is selling in Colorado and facing these penalties, they will quickly realize it is way more expensive to comply with the notifications rules and file these reports than just to get registered in Colorado and collect the tax. That is exactly what Colorado was hoping for, and pre-*Wayfair* it seemed likely many more states would adopt the same approach. In fact many other states did pass similar legislation including Louisiana, Pennsylvania, Rhode Island, Vermont, and Washington, and others are expected to jump in. Each state has its own version of the law. The following are the sales thresholds in each state that would subject a taxpayer to these new laws:

State	Threshold
Colorado	$100,000
Louisiana	$100,000
Oklahoma	$10,000
Pennsylvania	$10,000
Rhode Island	$100,000 or 200 transactions
Vermont	None mentioned
Washington	$10,000

The penalties are onerous. Here's what they are in each of the preceding states:

State	Penalty
Colorado	$5 to $10 per item missed
Louisiana	Unknown
Oklahoma	Lesser of $20,000 or 20% of sales
Pennsylvania	Lesser of $20,000 or 20% of sales
Rhode Island	None stated
Vermont	$5 to $10 per item missed
Washington	$20,000 maximum

Because of *Wayfair*, economic nexus is now in force, but physical presence also creates nexus. The question around physical presence has always been "How much physical presence is necessary?" In brief, the physical presence standard since *Quill* has generally revolved around three questions:

- How much physical presence is sufficient to create substantial nexus? (Or is physical presence in and of itself substantial nexus?)
- Can nexus be attributed to the seller through the physical presence of the seller's agent or affiliate?
- Is there a physical presence test for income tax?
- How much physical presence?

The U.S. Supreme Court has stated (and this statement has not been changed by the *Wayfair* case) that physical presence must be more than the slightest presence to rise to a standard of constitutional nexus. *National Geographic Soc'y v. California Bd. of Equalization*, 430 U.S. 551, 556 (1977). For example, in *Quill* the court held that Quill's ownership of some floppy disks and the licensing of the accompanying software in North Dakota did not create sales and use tax nexus in the state. The disks, while owned by Quill, were software used by its customers to place orders and check current inventories and prices. Despite the court's reference to a slightest presence and Quill's software in the state, it is not uncommon for auditors to take the position that any physical presence is, by definition, substantial nexus.

That said, it is difficult to say with certainty how much physical presence will create the necessary substantial nexus to satisfy the Commerce Clause. Prior to *Quill*, in *Miller Bros. Co. v. Maryland*, 347 U.S. 340 (1954), the U.S. Supreme Court ruled that occasional deliveries, in its own trucks by a Delaware retailer into Maryland, did not create nexus for sales and use tax. After *Quill*, the court had an opportunity to revisit the delivery issue in *Brown's Furniture, Inc. v. Wagner*, 171 Ill. 2d 410, cert. denied, 519 U.S. 866 (1996) but declined. The Illinois Supreme Court held that Brown's Furniture had nexus in Illinois by virtue of its advertising in the state coupled with 942 deliveries in its own trucks over a 10-month period. Such activity created nexus, the court said, because it was more than incidental, occasional, or sporadic, but instead it was regular and frequent. More recently, the Illinois Appellate Court ruled that 30 furniture deliveries over a 26-month period was enough physical presence to be substantial nexus for sales and use tax (*Town Crier, Inc. v. Illinois*, 315 Ill. App. 3d 286, 733 N.E.2d 780 (2000)). In Maine, a company whose advertising and solicitation were specifically directed toward the state, and who made 180 deliveries in its own trucks into Maine, had sufficient physical presence to constitute the substantial nexus necessary to create a filing obligation to the state (*John Swenson Granite v. State Tax Assessor*, 685 A.2d 425 (Me. 1996)).

The trend initiated by Illinois continues today. In 2014, Colorado ruled that using a contract carrier rather than a common carrier triggers a filing obligation because the contract carrier "is an agent of the shipper." (Colo. Information Letter GIL-14-015 (5/29/2014)) Texas ruled that a Louisiana retailer delivering furniture in its own trucks into Texas established nexus in the state (Texas Comptroller Decision No. 107,751 (7/23/2014)). Finally, and not surprisingly, Washington held that an Oregon fuel distributor who made 1,675 deliveries to 40 different customers in Washington during the three-year audit period established nexus in the state (*Space Age Fuels, Inc. v. Washington*, 315 P.3d 604 (Wash. Ct. App. 2013)). On the other hand, a Washington County Superior Court held that an out-of-state taxpayer who regularly shipped goods to a single customer in the state using leased railcars did not have a filing obligation with the state (*Washington v. Sage V Foods*, Dkt. No. 12-2-01893-3 (8/20/2013)). It is uncertain, but the difference between the two cases seems to depend on the fact that the latter's activities did not help to create and maintain a market for its goods in the state.

State courts have also differed on whether occasional or sporadic visits by employees are sufficient physical presence to constitute substantial nexus. New York has held that visits by an out-of-state retailer's employees exceeded the state's slightest physical presence test, thereby creating nexus. In one case, the visits were to 19 wholesalers, four times a year, and in another, there were 41 visits over a three-year period. According to the New York court, an out-of-state company's presence need not be substantial; it need only be more than the slightest presence. *Orvis Co. v. Tax Appeals Tribunal*, 86 N.Y.2d

165, 654 N.E.2d 954, *cert. denied,* and *Vermont Info. Processing, Inc. v. Tax Appeals Tribunal*, 86 N.Y.2d 165, 654 N.E.2d 954, *cert. denied,* 516 U.S. 989 (1995). In a holding to the contrary, the Kansas Supreme Court ruled that 11 visits by an out-of-state seller to install card readers did not create nexus, because the visits were isolated and sporadic [*In re Appeal of Intercard, Inc.*, 270 Kan. 346, 14 P.3d 1111 (2000)]. The Arizona Court of Appeals held that a company had nexus with the state whose only activity during a three-year period was one visit per year by a salesperson, coupled with 21 days of customer training (*Care Computer Systems v. Arizona*, 4 P.3d 469 (Ariz. 2000)).

More recently, the Washington Supreme Court held that two or three visits per year were sufficient to trigger a filing obligation for the state's B&O tax. The court added that the physical presence test in *Quill* was irrelevant because that case was limited to a sales tax, and the issue before the court was a gross receipts tax (*Lamtec Corp. v. Washington*, 246 P.3d 788 (Wash. 2011)). Furthermore, P.L. 86-272 was not applicable because the B&O is not an income tax, but a gross receipts tax. (See the discussion of P.L. 86-272 that follows.)

The harsh result in *Lamtec* should be compared to a Utah private letter ruling that held that an out-of-state entertainment company's annual presence at a 10-day film festival did not trigger an income tax filing obligation with the state. [See Utah Private Letter Ruling 08-013, (05/04/2009).] Inconsistency between jurisdictions continues to abound. The Oregon Tax Court recently held that a franchisor did not have an income tax filing obligation with the state because it found in-state inspections of the company's seven franchisees coupled with a three- to five-day training did not rise to the level of substantial nexus (*Rent-A-Center, Inc. v. Oregon*, Dkt. No. 111031D (Ore. Tax Ct., 2014)).

The physical presence need not be that of an employee or independent contractor. North Carolina attempted to hold a company responsible for sales, corporate income, and franchise taxes, whose only connection with the state is the selling and renting of VHS videotapes through the mail. Educational Resources, Inc. (ERI), a South Carolina company, sells and rents videotapes about workplace safety. Between 1990 and 1995 it made 219 sales and 906 rentals into North Carolina totaling $201,304 and $99,521, respectively. ERI did not have any employees in North Carolina or any other contacts with the state except for the tapes that it sold and rented to North Carolina customers through the mail. The tapes rented for $150 to $200. Customers would keep rented tapes between 5 and 30 days before mailing them back to ERI.

The North Carolina Department of Revenue audited ERI and assessed them for sales, income, and franchise taxes. North Carolina argued that the presence of the rented tapes, which were ERI's property, created nexus with the state. The Superior Court ruled in favor of ERI stating that "the Court finds and concludes that, under the Commerce Clause of the United States Constitution as interpreted in *Quill* . . . , and other cases, there is not a 'substantial nexus' justifying the state's attempts to collect the use tax, corporate income tax, and franchise tax in these cases." (*Educational Resources, Inc. v. Tolson*, Nos. 00CVS14723 and 14724, Wake County, (North Carolina Superior Court, Feb. 20, 2003)) As the reader may recall, the U.S. Supreme Court ruled in *Quill* that the licensing of its software in the state along with the presence of a few floppy disks did not constitute substantial nexus. Compare North Carolina's actions with a recent decision in Alabama. In Alabama, an administrative law judge has ruled that an out-of-state leasing company was not doing business in the state despite the fact that the company's lessee was using the company's property in the state (*Union Tank Car Co. v. Alabama Dep't of Revenue*, Admin. Law Div., Dkt. No. Corp. 04-247 (1/11/05)).

The most disconcerting ruling of 2014 was issued by Texas. The court ruled that the licensing of software downloaded over the internet established nexus for sales and use tax. A Utah taxpayer sold computer programs and digital content online. The taxpayer retained all rights in title to and ownership of the downloaded software. Because it did so, and because the state contends that computer software downloaded electronically is tangible personal property, the taxpayer had a sales and use tax filing obligation with Texas (Texas Comptroller's Decision No. 106,632 (9/19/2014)). This ruling seems inconsistent with the *Quill* decision in which the Supreme Court dismissed the fact that Quill licensed software to its customers in North Dakota. The court held that while the presence of a few floppy disks in the state "might constitute some minimal nexus," it did not rise to the level of substantial nexus as required under the Commerce Clause. Texas acknowledged this in its decision, but held that in *Quill* it was unclear as to what rights Quill retained to the software, and that in any case, the record established that the taxpayer's software in Texas "generated fees [that] cannot be dismissed as not establishing a substantial physical presence in Texas." This is a bold ruling, but fortunately it is only an administrative level decision, carrying no precedential authority and is likely to be overruled if a similar case ever goes to court.

Sporadic visits and trade show nexus

The landmark case with respect to trade shows is *Share International, Inc. v. Florida*, 676 So.2d 1362 (Fla. 1996); *cert denied*, 117 S.Ct. 685 (1997). Share International was a Texas corporation in the business of manufacturing and distributing chiropractic supplies primarily through direct mail solicitation. It did not have any offices or employees in Florida. However, the company did attend a three-day seminar in Florida every year at which it displayed and sold some of its products. Share registered with Florida and collected and remitted sales tax on the seminar sales, but not on its mail order sales. Florida argued that the seminar presentation and sales created the sufficient nexus with the state that obligated Share to collect and remit sales tax on all of its Florida sales, including its mail order sales. The Florida Supreme Court disagreed, holding that Share's physical presence at the seminars was not sufficient to rise to the standard of substantial nexus.

In light of the Share decision and coupled with pressure from business and economic development groups, several states have backed away from asserting trade show nexus. For example, California regulations provide that out-of-state retailers may receive up to $100,000 in sales at up to 15 days of trade shows, seminars, or conventions without incurring any sales or use tax collection responsibilities for the retailer's remote sales (Sales tax must be remitted, however, on any sales made at the trade show) (Cal. Code Regs. tit. 18, Section 1684). Connecticut's trade show legislation is restricted to 14 days per year and trade show activities are limited to displays and promotion. No sales are allowed (see SB 1232, Laws 2005.) Connecticut's exemption also appears to be limited to trade shows within its designated convention centers (see Sec. 12-407(a)(15)(D).) Minnesota also provides a similar, but more restrictive safe harbor of 3 days over 12 months (Minnesota Revenue Notice 00-10). Maine's law is simpler — merely attending trade shows or conventions does "not constitute a substantial physical presence." (36 MRS Section 1754-B(1)(G)(2).) Many states, however, do not provide such exemptions or safe harbors and aggressively pursue taxpayers for use tax collection with any physical presence in the state. For example, Alaska, Georgia, Indiana, Iowa, and Ohio have indicated that trade show attendance for fewer than even 14 days a year may create a tax filing obligation. Other states such as Illinois have provided mixed signals. Some of Illinois' early letter rulings indicated that any participation in a trade show triggered nexus. Illinois retracted that position in the mid-90s, but recently seemed to have reversed themselves (see ST 94-0126-GIL; PLR 87-003; PLR 86-0170; ST 95-0089-GIL; ST00-0089-GIL; and ST01-0049-GIL). Kansas holds that any trade-show participation where sales orders are taken triggers nexus, while Colorado, which initially held that participation did create nexus (Colo. DOR InforEmail June 27, 2008), reversed that position in May 2014. (Colo. Information Letter, GIL -14-015 (5/29/2014); see Kansas Dept. of Opinion Letter No. 0-2009-011.) Massachusetts provides for three-day trade show protection. New Mexico held in 1997 that attending a trade show and exhibiting or promoting triggers a filing obligation (Rev. Rul. 480-97-01) as has Tennessee in 1996 (PLR No. 96-16) and Texas (PLR 200006394L). Washington recently held that attending a trade show four times a year over a seven-year period triggers nexus for both sales and use tax and the state's Business and Occupation tax (Washington Tax Determination No. 13-0213, 33 WTD 64 (7/15/2014)). However, a recent safe harbor was enacted to allow for a single day of attendance per year at a trade show if sales were not made there (Sec. 82.32.531, Rev Code of Wa.)

Arguments continue between tax practitioners, revenue officials, and other commentators over whether the substantial nexus test for purposes of the Commerce Clause means substantial physical presence.

Printer's nexus

A company may trigger nexus with a state in which it contracts with a printer, particularly if the company stores printed material at the printer's warehouse or makes frequent or routine visits to the printer to supervise or inspect the printed material. It may be that the visits would be de minimis, but the threat is real enough that many states, at the behest of local printers, have passed safe harbor laws exempting such activity from triggering any filing obligations. States that have passed such legislation include Connecticut, Florida, Georgia, Illinois, Indiana, Kentucky, Maine, Ohio, Oklahoma, Pennsylvania, South Carolina, Tennessee, Utah, Virginia, and Wisconsin. Some of the state provisions provide a safe harbor for both sales and income tax, but several states limit their provisions to only sales tax or income tax, but not both.

Fulfillment centers, public warehouses, and distribution centers

Printers have not been the only industry to successfully lobby for nexus safe harbor provisions. Because engaging a fulfillment center to take orders or engage in telemarketing and storing inventory at a public warehouse may often provide the substantial nexus to trigger a filing obligation, several states have passed protective legislation in these areas as well. Some of the states that exclude contractual arrangements with fulfillment service providers from nexus include Connecticut, New Mexico, New York, Ohio, and South Carolina. Unfortunately, most of these states limit the safe harbor to sales tax nexus. Even among those states, the varying qualifications, the activities covered, the time involved, and the specific nuances of each state's statute make generalizations nearly impossible. Nevertheless, like printers nexus legislation, it is important to note that it may be available and, therefore, specific state research is in order.

Servers and websites

Advertising via the internet through a website should be no different than advertising on national television or providing 1-800 numbers. Absent any other activity, it is an interstate communication activity protected by the Commerce Clause. It should not trigger nexus. Nevertheless, there is no specific prohibition blocking states from trying to tax a company that maintains a website on a server in the state. The state may argue that the server itself is sufficient property to trigger nexus, or it may argue that the service provider hosting the website is an agent acting on behalf of the out-of-state company. As with printers and fulfillment centers, some states have specifically provided, either through statute or rule, that owning or operating an in-state server will not create nexus. That said, given the ever-evolving technology of the internet, states have begun to closely study the various types of marketing appearing online, such as eBay, craigslist, and so on. For example, do website linking arrangements constitute a physical presence, local solicitation, or intangible property in the state? Maybe they do, according to New York (who, in 2008 began requiring online retailers, who pay commissions or other compensation to New York businesses for customer referrals, whether by a link on an internet website or other manner, and who generate sales into the state over $10,000 for the past four quarters, to register with the state and begin collecting state and local taxes on all the retailer's sales into the state). Rhode Island, North Carolina, California, and a large number of other states have also passed similar legislation, and it is being considered in other states. Some states, like Pennsylvania, have reinterpreted existing statutes to cover compensated customer referrals. Each state that has passed these statutes has a slightly different tweak to it, so that a program that forms nexus in one state may not in another.

Several states have issued policy positions, revenue determinations, and letter rulings addressing this issue, but the rulings are often inconsistent and so factually specific that it is difficult to ascertain the underlying rule. In fairness to state tax administrators, the rapid technological changes have made defining nexus in these circumstances akin to flying your plane while building it.

Affiliation, attribution, and agency

In addition to the continuing debate over physical presence, there is a question as to whether the physical presence of a third party will create substantial nexus for an out-of-state taxpayer. The fact that the third party is an independent contractor is usually irrelevant. What is at issue is the nature of the contractor's activities. As long ago as 1960, the U.S. Supreme Court held that independent contractors could create sales tax nexus for an out-of-state retailer. According to the Supreme Court: "The test is simply the nature and extent of the activities" in the state. Where there is "continuous local solicitation," and the independent contractors are performing the same role and function as sales employees by establishing and maintaining a market in the state for the remote seller, the out-of-state seller has nexus with the state. (See *Scripto v. Carson*, 362 U.S. 207, 208 (1960) and *Tyler Pipe Industries, Inc. v. Washington Dept. of Revenue*, 483 U.S. 232 (1987)). Often, the key problem is in defining an agency relationship.

If a third party acts as an agent for an out-of-state seller, that agency relationship may create nexus for the seller. A series of cases involving high school book club sales is illustrative: *Scholastic Book Clubs v. State Board of Equalization,* 207 Cal. App. 2d 734 (1st Dist. 1989) (out-of-state book club is deemed to have nexus because teachers collected money from the schoolchildren); *Pledger v. Troll Book Clubs Inc.,* 871 S.W.2d 389 (Ark. 1994) (teachers are not agents for the out-of-state bookseller); *Scholastic Book Clubs v. Michigan Department of Treasury,* 567 N.W.2d 692 (Mich. Ct. App. 1997) (taxpayer does not have nexus, because teachers, lacking the authority to bind Scholastic, are not agents of Scholastic); and *In re Scholastic Book Clubs, Inc.,* 920 P.2d 947 (Kan. 1996) (Kansas Supreme Court holds that Scholastic has nexus, because an agency relationship exists with the schoolteachers); *Scholastic Book Clubs, Inc. v. Farr, Tenn. Ct. of App.*, No. M2011-01443-COA-R3-CV (January 27, 2012) (Scholastic's connections with Tennessee are sufficient to establish nexus because the taxpayer has created a de facto marketing and distribution network through Tennessee teachers and schools); *Scholastic Book Clubs, Inc. v. Alabama Department of Revenue*, Alabama Tax Tribunal, No. S. 14-374, Mar. 25, 2016.) In an eminently more reasonable opinion, the Connecticut Superior Court recently ruled that the teachers were simply not representatives of the book seller because they were not in the same class as salesmen, canvassers, or solicitors. Although their administrative functions were important to Scholastic, those functions did not rise to the level of a sales force (*Scholastic Book Clubs Inc. v. Commissioner of Revenue*, Dkt. Nos. CV 07 4013027 S; CV 07 4013028 S, Superior Court of Connecticut Judicial District of New Britain, (April 9, 2009)). Although the differing conclusions of these cases sometimes indicate the importance of a state's specific interpretation of its laws on agency, the cases remain troubling because substantial nexus can be created by a third party in absence of a formal contract or compensation.

In any event, Scholastic eventually failed in both Connecticut and Tennessee. The Connecticut Supreme Court overturned the lower Superior Court's decision holding that because the teachers acted as representatives for Scholastic, the company had nexus and a sales tax filing obligation in the state. Scholastic appealed both the Connecticut and Tennessee decisions to the United States Supreme Court who declined to review them. (See *Scholastic Book Clubs v. Farr*, Tenn. Ct. App. at Nashville, Dkt. No. M2011-01443-COA-R3-CV, 01/27/2012, *petition for cert denied,* U.S. S.Ct., Dkt. No. 12-374, 11/26/2012.) and *Scholastic Book Clubs, Inc. v. Commissioner of Revenue Services*, Conn. S. Ct., Dkt. No. SC 18425, 03/27/2012, 304 Conn 204, 38 A3d 1183 (2012), *petition for cert. denied*, U.S. S.Ct., Dkt. No. 11-1532, 10/09/2012.))

A secondary issue related to the use of independent contractors and the law of agency is whether activities unrelated to sales or solicitation will also constitute substantial nexus. For example, will the performance of post-sale services by independent contractors create nexus for an out-of-state seller? The Multistate Tax Commission's Nexus Program Bulletin 95-1 (MTC 95-1) generated considerable discussion when it was issued, because it asserted that warranty repair services provided by third-party independent contractors created sales tax nexus for an out-of-state seller (remember, services are not protected by P.L. 86-272; so, arguably, warranty work triggers income tax nexus as well). More than 20 states have adopted the Bulletin. New York has held that an independent third party engaged by an out-of-state seller to diagnose and repair computers sold in-state by the seller created nexus for the seller (TSB-A-00 (42) S (N.Y. Dep't of Taxation Fin. Oct. 13, 2000)).

Dell Computer has litigated the issue of whether sales tax nexus is created by a third-party independent contractor, performing warranty repair services in Connecticut, Louisiana, and New Mexico. In all three states, Dell contracts with BancTec, an independent contractor, to perform repairs and warranty work with respect to the company's catalog and internet computer sales. Dell won its case in Connecticut and at the District Court level in Louisiana [*Dell Catalog Sales v. Commissioner*, 834 A2d 812 (Super. Ct. 2003) and *Louisiana Dep't of Revenue v. Dell Catalog Sales*, LP, No. 456,807 (La. Dist. Ct., May 25, 2004)]. However, Louisiana's Court of Appeal has rejected the District Court's decision to grant summary judgment and has instructed the lower court to determine if there existed an agency relationship between Dell and BancTec, and whether the latter helped to establish and maintain a market for Dell's computers in the state (*Louisiana v. Dell International Inc.*, Dkt No. 2004 CA 1702 (Feb. 15, 2006)). Dell suffered another setback in New Mexico when the state Court of Appeals ruled that the company had nexus in the state because BancTec helped to "establish and maintain a market" in the state for Dell's computers. (See *Dell Catalog Sales, LP. v. New Mexico*, 189 P.3d 1215 (N.M. Ct. App. 2008)). In short, BancTec's relationship with Dell was sufficient substantial nexus to subject Dell to New Mexico's gross receipts and compensating tax. Because BancTec provides similar services to other computer retailers such as Toshiba and Compaq, these cases were closely watched.

MTC 95-1 is typical of many states' approach to agency. In brief, the states are extending the agency argument from one of true agency to a "but for" argument, such as; but for some unrelated party, the taxpayer could not do business in the state, and therefore by helping the taxpayer to create and maintain a market for its goods in the state, that relationship is a nexus-creating activity. The use of the "but for" argument is misleading if not clearly a logical fallacy, but nevertheless difficult to contest.

Most states have been routinely unsuccessful in arguing that the physical presence of an out-of-state seller's affiliate creates nexus for the out-of-state taxpayer. Generally, the states have tried to argue that the affiliate had an agency relationship with the out-of-state vendor, because the two entities shared the same business names, trademarks, and logos, engaged in cross advertising, or were in similar lines of business. For example, Bloomingdale's had different affiliated corporate entities conducting sales in Pennsylvania: one through in-state retail stores, the other through mail-order catalog. Pennsylvania argued that the mail-order company had nexus, because its corporate affiliate's in-state stores sold many of the same goods, shared advertising campaigns, and on two occasions accepted merchandise returns of items purchased by catalog. The Pennsylvania Commonwealth Court found for the taxpayer, rejecting the state's argument that nexus existed because of an agency relationship between the affiliated corporations (*Bloomingdale's By Mail, Ltd. v. Department of Revenue*, 567 A.2d 773 (Pa. Commw. Ct. 1989), *aff'd without opinion,* 591 A.2d 1047 (Pa. 1991)). The courts came to similar conclusions in two cases with Saks Fifth Avenue. *SFA Folio Collections Inc. v. Bannon*, 217 Conn. 220 (1990), 585 A.2d 666 (Conn. 1991); *SFA Folio Collections Inc. v. Tracy*, 652 N.E.2d 693 (Ohio 1995). The Ohio case is of particular interest because the state attempted to use the income tax unitary doctrine to assert substantial nexus for sales tax.

California is one of the state leaders in asserting nexus through agency and affiliation, and where an agency relationship can be established, the state has been successful in asserting nexus.

Borders Online Inc. operated a website through which it sold primarily books, CDs, and DVDs. It is a separate corporate entity affiliated with the traditional bricks and mortar Borders Inc. bookstores. Borders Inc. bookstores routinely accepted returns from its patrons, regardless of whether the item was purchased at Borders Inc., Borders Online Inc., or one of Border's competitors. If the item was purchased from a competitor, Borders Inc. would give the purchaser store credit. If the item was purchased from Borders Online, the store would provide a cash refund.

The SBE determined that the refunding of cash for returned goods made Borders Inc. the authorized representative of Borders Online. In addition, the SBE held that the refunding of cash for returns was a key element of the selling process and, in and of itself, constituted selling in California under California Revenue & Taxation Code (CRTC) Section 6203.

The decision was roundly criticized at the time by the tax community, who argued that Borders's return policy was nothing more than good customer service, rather than an action taken as a representative on behalf of Border's Online. Furthermore, critics said, the SBE decision did not adequately address the principle articulated in *Scripto* and *Tyler Pipe* that an in-state representative creates nexus only through actions that purposefully establish and maintain a market in the state for the remote seller (*Scripto Inc. v. Carson*, 362 U.S. 207 (1960) and *Tyler Pipe Industries Inc. v. Washington*, 483 U.S. 232 (1987)). The key to the court's decision may be that Borders Online directed customers on its website to return online purchases to its local brick and mortar stores for returns or exchanges. This policy, according to the court, indicated that the stores were acting on behalf of the online affiliate.

One year after its ruling in Borders Online, the SBE held that the online subsidiary of Barnes & Noble Booksellers, Inc. (B&N) had nexus in California because B&N distributed discount coupons that could be redeemed with its online affiliate Barnes & Noble.Com (B&N.C). As in the Borders decision, the SBE determined that B&N acted as B&N.C's representative, through their joint marketing effort whereby B&N.C, paid to have printed coupons inserted into the shopping bags of B&N customers. The SBE rejected the taxpayer's argument that the discount coupons inserted into shopper's bags were simply advertising akin to coupon inserts in magazines and newspapers (*Barnes & Noble.com*, No. 89872 (Cal. State Bd. Equal., Sept. 12, 2002)).

On September 7, 2007, the California Superior Court overruled the SBE holding that B&N.C did have nexus through its brick and mortar sister corporation, B&N. According to the Court, B&N did not act as B&N.C's agent or representative. Distributing coupons or bags with advertising logos, the court said, was akin to somebody on the street corner passing out flyers or coupons. Agency requires much more, and because the state did not provide a useful definition of agency, the Court looked to general principles. The essential principle of agency is that the agent must have authority to bind the principal and B&N did not have that authority. In addition, there was no evidence that common management or control existed between the two companies. For example, neither company had any common directors or officers. (See *barnesandnoble.com, LLC. v. SBE*, Calif. Super. Ct. (San Francisco County), Case No. CGC-06-456465, 9/7/2007.) Despite the win at Superior Court, on May 29, 2008, Barnes & Noble agreed to a settlement with the SBE, paying $9 million of the original assessment of $17.7 million. The settlement covered all taxes, penalties, and interest through November 1, 2005: the date barnesandnoble.com began voluntarily collecting the state's sales and use taxes.

Louisiana has also argued that barnesandnoble.com had nexus in that state as well. Unlike California, however, Louisiana focused its argument on certain key facts; arguing that those facts alone met the substantial nexus hurdle required of states under the Commerce Clause. (See St. Tammany Parish Tax Collector v. barnesandnoble.com, U.S. Dist. Ct., Eastern District, LA, Dkt. No. 05-5695 (3/22/2007)). The facts included a common membership program, gift card exchange, advertising, preferential treatment on returns, and commissions. The federal district court found the facts were either misplaced or insufficient to create substantial nexus. The common advertising was limited and the commissions, membership program, and gift cards were common to all booksellers, including competitors. Although the return policy was a bit more generous for barnesandnoble.com than others, it was not sufficiently so. In brief, Louisiana's argument was reduced to holding that the close corporate relationship between the companies, similar company names, and brand identity itself was sufficient to establish substantial nexus. The court simply disagreed.

The New Mexico Supreme Court upheld the appellate court's decision that an online bookseller had nexus because the many intercompany activities, such as gift card promotions, sharing of customer data, common loyalty programs, and shared use of trademarks and logos were significantly associated with the online bookseller's ability to establish and maintain a market in the state for its goods (New Mexico Taxation & Revenue Department v. Barnesandnoble.com LLC,2012-NMCA-063, 283 P3d 298 (2012)).

Other states followed California and Louisiana's lead, and in April 2005, the Multistate Tax Commission proposed a new affiliate nexus standard, entitled "Proposed Model Affiliate Sales Tax Nexus Proposal." The proposed standard provides that an out-of-state business has nexus with an in-state business if they (1) are related (members of the same federal controlled group, or there exists a 50% ownership), and (2) they use "an identical or substantially similar name, trade name, trademark or goodwill to develop, promote, or maintain sales," or (3) the in state business "provides services to, or that inure to the benefit of, the out-of-state business related to developing, promoting, or maintaining the in-state market."

Instead of litigation, other states have simply passed legislation providing that companies are taxable in the state for sales and use tax through affiliation. Effective January 1, 2002, a remote seller affiliated with an Arkansas retailer has nexus with the state for the purposes of sales and use tax. The out-of-state or remote seller will have to collect and remit Arkansas use tax on sales into the state, if the seller is affiliated with an Arkansas retailer and "the vendor sells the same or substantially similar line of products . . . under the same or substantially similar business name, or the facilities or employees of the Arkansas retailer are used to advertise or promote sales by the vendor to Arkansas purchasers." (Ark. Code Ann. Section 26-52-117 (2011)).

Like Arkansas, Minnesota has amended its statutes to require that an affiliated remote seller of an in-state retailer must collect the state's use tax. An out-of-state retailer or remote seller is an affiliate of an in-state entity if "the entity uses its facilities or employees in this state to advertise, promote, or facilitate the establishment or maintenance of a market for sales of items by the retailer to purchasers in this state or for the provision of services to the retailer's purchasers in this state, such as accepting returns of purchases for the retailer, providing assistance in resolving customer complaints of the retailer, or providing other services." (Minn. Stat. Section 297A.66(4)). Other states to enact attributional or affiliate nexus statutes include Alabama (Ala. Code Section 40-23-190); Colorado (C.R.S. Section 39-26-102(3)); Georgia (Ga. Code Section 48-8-2(3)); Idaho (Idaho Code Section 63-3611); Illinois (35 ILCS 105/2 and 35 ILCS 110/2); Indiana (Ind. P.L. 81-2004 (H.B. 1365, effective July 1, 2004)); Kansas (Kan. Stat. Section 79-3702); Kentucky (Kentucky Rev. Stat. Section 139.340); New Jersey (N.J. Stat. Section 54:32B-2); New York (N.Y. Tax Law Section 1101(b)(8)(i)(I)); Oklahoma (Okla. Stat. Section 1401(9); South Dakota (see S.B. 147 effective July 1, 2010); Texas (Tex. Tax Code Section 151.107(a)(4)); Utah (Utah Code Section 59-12-107)); and Wisconsin (Wis. Stat. Section 77.51(13g)(d)).

Yet another approach states have taken recently to encourage remote sellers to charge and collect the state's use tax is to require that any vendors doing business with any state or local agencies register and collect the state's sales and use tax. California initiated such a requirement effective January 1, 2004. Other states with similar requirements include Connecticut, Hawaii, Illinois, Missouri, North Carolina, Oklahoma, South Dakota, Virginia, and Wisconsin. Critics have charged that the practice is illegal and a violation of the Commerce Clause. They claim that while states may have the right to establish their purchasing requirements, such requirements violate the Constitution when their participation in the market becomes an attempt to regulate the interstate market.

Federal legislation

The Multistate Tax Commission (MTC) and state supporters have continued each year to introduce the Commission's single standard nexus proposal. In brief, the proposal provides that any company whose activity in a state exceeds (1) owning $50,000 of property; or (2) $50,000 of payroll; or (3) $500,000 of sales has nexus for both income and sales tax. Under the proposal, a remote seller whose only contacts with the state are either through the internet or catalog sales would have nexus in the state if those sales exceeded $500,000. With the *Wayfair* decision having been issued now approving lower economic thresholds than the MTC and its member states had been requesting, we do not expect the MTC to continue to ask for these higher thresholds any more.

The Amazon wars and click-through nexus

One of the triggering developments in sales tax nexus for online sellers (and ultimately leading to the *Wayfair* decision) was ignited by legislation passed by New York in spring 2008 that required online retailers, who paid commissions or other compensation to New York businesses for customer referrals, whether by a link on an internet website or other manner, and who generated sales into the state over $10,000 for the past four quarters, to register with the state and begin collecting state and local taxes on all the retailer's sales into the state (New York Senate Bill 6807, Chapter 57, N.Y. Laws of 2008).

The New York legislation was particularly significant at the time because it said that a taxpayer need not have had physical presence in New York to be subject to the state's sales tax. This was clearly contrary to the U.S. Supreme Court's decisions in both *National Bellas Hess* and *Quill* discussed previously. Thus, it was no surprise that Amazon.com and Overstock.com filed suits immediately after the New York law was passed, challenging the legislation as invalid, illegal, and unconstitutional because it violated the Commerce, Due Process, and Equal Protection Clauses of the U.S. and New York constitutions. In 2013, New York's highest court, the New York Court of Appeals found that the state's click-through nexus statute did not facially violate the Due Process and Commerce Clauses of the U.S. Constitution. (Whether the law violated the Constitution in practice was not addressed by the court.) The two businesses appealed the decision to the U.S. Supreme Court, but in December 2013, the Court denied review. (The two cases were combined early in appeal.)

The importance of New York's legislation and the constitutional challenges it raised were pivotal in getting us to where we are today and cannot be overemphasized. Several other states attempted to follow New York's lead by adopting similar legislation. The legislation initially failed in Connecticut, Maryland, and Tennessee. However, it passed in California, Hawaii, and Minnesota, only to be vetoed by the governors of those states, partly in fear that the legislation was unconstitutional. Twenty-one states quickly enacted their own click-through nexus provisions.

Initially Amazon fought the state's assertion that they should be collecting tax quite vigorously. When they found very little success, they reversed their position entirely and as of this writing now collect tax on their own sales in every state in the United States. And today Amazon has become a vocal supporter of legislation requiring remote sellers to collect sales tax in other states. Such was the power of the New York decision.

Colorado's "notice and reporting" legislation in 2010 (discussed earlier) was inspired by New York's move. The Colorado legislation prompted the Direct Marketing Association, an association of businesses that uses catalogs, newspapers, and the internet to market products to consumers, to litigate the issue at both the federal district and Colorado district state courts. The U.S. Court of Appeals initially ruled that the federal courts did not have jurisdiction over the case because the federal Tax Injunction Act (TIA) prohibited federal courts jurisdiction over state tax controversies. (*Direct Marketing Association v. Brohl*, CA-10, 735 F.3d 904 (2013)). However, the U.S. Supreme Court unanimously reversed the Tenth Circuit's decision on March 3, 2015, holding that the TIA did not bar Direct Marketing's suit (*Direct Marketing Ass'n v. Brohl*, 135 S.Ct. 1124 (2015)). Justice Kennedy, in a concurring opinion, wrote that it was time to revisit the *Quill* decision, noting that with mobile phones and laptop computers, a taxpayer can be present in a state in a "meaningful way without that presence being physical." He went on to say that he viewed the *Quill* decision as "tenuous" and that given the increase in online sales, it was "inflicting extreme harm and unfairness on the States." The case has since been resolved. The Tenth Circuit Court of Appeals found that Colorado's notice and reporting requirements did not burden interstate commerce. In doing so, they declined to expand the holdings in *Quill* to nontax matters. The Supreme Court subsequently declined to review the case, establishing it as law in Colorado and precedent in the rest of the 10th circuit. Although this precedent is not binding on states residing in the other circuits, it will still tend to embolden other states to pass similar legislation (*Direct Marketing Association v. Brohl,* Dkt. 12-1175, 10th Cir 2016).

The ultimate challenge

Not surprisingly, states reacted quickly to Justice Kennedy's invitation to challenge the *Quill* decision. Alabama's Governor Robert Bentley issued Proposed Rule 810-6-2-.90.03 providing that remote sellers with no physical presence in the state will have nexus in Alabama if their sales in the state exceed $250,000 per year. The rule is effective January 1, 2016, and the governor made it quite clear that he welcomed Amazon.com or some other remote seller to challenge the law.

Tennessee also joined the fray early on. The Tennessee Department of Revenue promulgated Rule 1320-05-01-.129, effective January 1, 2017. The rule required out-of-state sellers to register with the state if they have substantial nexus with the state. The rule defines substantial nexus as being established through the regular and systematic solicitation of sales from Tennessee customers that result in more than $500,000 in gross sales during the prior 12-month period. Starting March 1, 2017, taxpayers meeting that threshold are required to register with the state and collect sales tax. However, this requirement was put on hold pending the outcome of a lawsuit ([see *Am. Catalog Mailers Ass'n v. Tenn. Dep't of Revenue*, Tenn. Ch. Ct., No. 17-307-IV (complaint filed March 30, 2017)] and further action from the Tennessee legislature.

South Dakota also answered the challenge with its own economic nexus statute. It passed Senate Bill 106, which added a new nexus standard. Any out-of-state business that does not otherwise have nexus with the state will acquire nexus if they either sell $100,000 of taxable goods, services, or electronically transferred goods into South Dakota, or sold taxable goods or services in 200 or more separate transactions (91st Session, S.D. Legis. (2016)). However, this act came with a unique twist. The act allowed South Dakota to file suit against any sellers who do not comply with the new ordinance. Although the first of these cases is pending, the act requires the state to file an injunction against itself that bars the Department of Revenue and other agencies from collecting or administering the tax in regard to remote sellers until a final resolution is made on the suit. The act specifically states that it is in direct contradiction of the *Quill* holding, and that a final holding by the courts (specifically, the U.S. Supreme Court) is required. This law is what generated the *Wayfair* court case that was decided on June 21, 2018 (*South Dakota v. Wayfair, Inc. et al.*, 585 U.S. ______(2018)).

Wayfair v. South Dakota — Economic nexus rising

By the nature of its design, the South Dakota law was accelerated through the state court system and landed at the U.S. Supreme Court. Both parties filed briefs, and over 40 interested parties filed amicus curiae briefs with the court on the matter. South Dakota pinned its argument on the meteoric growth in e-commerce, the increasing gap of uncollected sales tax, and the increasing ease with which software can provide solutions to tax rate and filing issues in the 45 states plus D.C. that impose a sales tax. They presented facts showing cheap compliance and steep tax losses. In addition, the state also argued that e-commerce has changed the landscape so much that stare decisis was no longer sufficient to keep the holdings in *Quill* and *National Bellas Hess*.

Wayfair and the other defendants, on the other hand, argued that tax filing was just a small portion of the cost. The company argued that taxability and legions of hungry sales tax auditors presented a grave threat to online sellers who in many cases tend to be small businesses. They presented a picture of expensive compliance costs, massive filing headaches, and a treacherous landscape for small businesses. In addition, the defendants also pointed out that the tax gap was already closing with Amazon, Inc. now collecting tax on its sales in every state.

During oral arguments, it was clear that the justices had read the litany of briefs presented and were well prepared with questions. In addition to the aforementioned arguments, the U.S. Solicitor General decided to join in and argue in favor of South Dakota.

After considering the arguments the Court voted 5–4 to overturn the limitations of *Quill* and *National Bellas Hess*. Justice Anthony Kennedy wrote the majority opinion, joined by Ginsburg, Thomas, Alito, and Gorsuch. The court reverted to the older Complete Auto Transit test (see *Complete Auto Transit v. Brady*, 430 U.S. 274 (1977)). In *Complete Auto*, a four-prong test was applied to determine if a tax was imposed in violation of the Commerce Clause. The *Wayfair* case specifically focuses on the first prong, whether or not there is a sufficient nexus with the taxing state. In its analysis, the Court found that continuous economic activity from an online seller could create a sufficient connection with the state. In an interesting twist, the court also found that the *Quill* decision was flawed from the outset, and did not comply with modern-day Commerce Clause jurisprudence.

After overturning *Quill*, the South Dakota law was then evaluated on its merits to see if it complied with *Complete Auto*. In analyzing the South Dakota statute, the court specifically noted some factors that aided in its finding of sufficiency. The South Dakota law included a minimum threshold of $100,000 in gross sales, or 200 individual transactions in a 12-month period. These figures could not be reached ". . . unless the seller availed itself of the substantial privilege of carrying on business in South Dakota" (see Wayfair, pp. 23). Specific mention was also made of the fact that South Dakota was a full member of the Streamlined Sales and Use Tax Agreement and had a single state taxing authority. This last part raises interesting questions as to the applicability of *Wayfair* to the so-called "Home Rule" states of Alabama, Arizona, Colorado, and Louisiana where the local governments can self-administer their own taxing schemes.

It is worth noting that the dissenting opinion in the case, written by Chief Justice Roberts, would not have upheld *Quill* on its merits. Instead, it would have held that the arguments were insufficient to overcome stare decisis in the face of a declining tax gap. The dissent felt that Congress was better suited to resolve the issue, and that the lessening tax gap of uncollected taxes had to be balanced against the added burdens to small businesses on the internet. This shows that none of the justices were in favor of the original logic behind *Quill*.

As of this writing, there are economic nexus provisions active or announced in Alabama, California (effective 4/1), Colorado, Connecticut, Washington, DC, Georgia, Hawaii, Illinois, Indiana, Iowa, Kentucky, Maine, Maryland, Massachusetts, Michigan, Minnesota, Mississippi, Nebraska, Nevada, New Jersey, New York, North Carolina, North Dakota, Ohio (cookie nexus), South Carolina, Tennessee (pending legislative action), Texas (effective 10/2019), Utah, Vermont, Washington, West Virginia, Wisconsin, and Wyoming.

Physical presence — not dead yet

In the wake of *Wayfair*, it is important to remember that physical presence is still enshrined in most states' nexus laws. Although economic nexus can create a sales/use tax responsibility, the old physical presence standard can do it just as easily. The new *Wayfair*-inspired laws do not replace physical presence as the doorway to nexus; they merely add a second doorway that can be used. Always be mindful of both factors when determining whether your business has nexus in a given state.

Knowledge check

5. In the *Wayfair* decision, the following 12-month sales dollar figure was approved as establishing nexus:

    a. $50,000.
    b. $100,000.
    c. $500,000.
    d. $200,000.

6. In the *Wayfair* decision, the following 12-month sales transaction amount was approved as establishing nexus:

    a. 1 transaction.
    b. 200 transactions.
    c. 500 transactions.
    d. 1,000 transactions

Income tax nexus

Although physical presence is the bright-line test for sales tax nexus, it does not determine income tax nexus. In fact, a company can have numerous employees in a state creating physical presence aplenty and yet not have an income tax filing obligation. That is because a federal law, Public Law 86-272, creates a safe harbor from income tax nexus, even where there is physical presence.

Public Law 86-272

Due process and interstate commerce are the constitutional hurdles. But there is also a bit of federal legislation, which adds yet another hurdle to establishing nexus, but only for income tax nexus. That legislation is Public Law (P.L.) 86-272.

Public Law 86-272 states that "No state . . . shall have the power to impose (an) income tax . . . if the only business activities within such state (are) the solicitation of orders . . . for sales of tangible personal property, which . . . are sent outside the State for approval or rejection, and, if approved, are filled by shipment or delivery from outside the State . . . "

In brief, P. L. 86-272 provides a safe harbor for certain activities with respect to income tax nexus. Essentially, physical presence alone will create a filing obligation for *sales tax*. So if your company has employees, property, even independent contractors in a state, it is likely that the company will have a sales tax filing obligation to that state. Note, however, that under P.L. 86-272 a company can have employees busy soliciting sales in the state and not create nexus for income tax. In the earlier Crystal City Computers example, the company could hire employees to sell their computers in Kansas (in fact, the employees could live in Kansas), and so long as those employees restricted their activities to the solicitation of sales of tangible personal property, and those sales orders were sent back to Colorado for acceptance and fulfillment, Crystal City would not have to file income tax returns with Kansas. New York recently ruled that the presence of an in-state representative working out of his office-in-the home, and provided with a company laptop, constituted protected activities under P.L. 86-272 (see NYS Dep't of Tax'n and Fin., TSB-A-05(7)(C) (4/4/05)).

Please pay particular attention to the fact that P.L. 86-272 applies only to net income taxes and the sales of tangible personal property. Some states (for example, Tennessee) impose combined franchise and excise taxes upon income and property, and the taxpayer may have to pay tax upon both calculations. These states have taken the position that P.L. 86-272 only applies to their *income base*, not their *capital base*. Thus, a taxpayer who may have only salespeople soliciting in the state would still be required to pay the state's franchise tax based on capital, but not income. The Texas Court of Appeals specifically ruled that the net worth component of the state's old franchise tax did not fall under the safe harbor provision of P.L 86-272 (see *INOVA Diagnostics, Inc. v. Compt'r*, 166 SW3d 394 (Tx Ct. of App. 2005)). Texas has since replaced its corporate franchise tax with a modified gross receipts tax called the Texas Margin Tax that the Texas legislature specifically stated did not fall under the safe harbor provisions offered by P.L. 86-272. Taxes measured by gross income or receipts are not covered by P.L. 86-272. As a consequence, there are different nexus standards for the state of Washington's B&O Tax and New Mexico's Gross Receipts Tax.

Knowledge check

7. Under federal law (P.L. 86-272), a business may be able to avoid

    a. Both income and franchise taxes.
    b. Income taxes, but not franchise taxes.
    c. Franchise taxes, but not income taxes.
    d. Neither income or franchise taxes.

Please note also that P.L. 86-272 applies only to the solicitation of sales of tangible personal property. Sales of services, for example, are not protected. Thus, if Crystal City Computers were to offer training seminars or computer classes in Kansas, these activities would not be protected and Crystal City Computers would have to begin filing Kansas income tax returns.

Finally, P.L. 86-272 leaves undefined what constitutes solicitation. The Supreme Court addressed the term in its decision in *Wisconsin Dept. of Revenue v. William Wrigley, Jr. Co.*, 112 S. Ct. 2447 (1992). Wrigley's activities within Wisconsin included the in-state recruitment, training, and evaluation of sales reps who solicited sales using company cars, and carried gum samples, display racks, and promotional literature with them. The court ruled these activities were protected under 86-272. The sales reps also supplied gum for a charge to retailers who installed new display racks and occasionally replaced stale gum. Despite the fact that the replacement of stale gum only represented 0.00007% of the company's total sales in Wisconsin, the court ruled that these activities went beyond solicitation. In brief, because one would have reason to replace stale gum apart from solicitation, it is not the volume, but the company practice itself that exceeds the safe harbor provisions of P.L. 86-272. The court wrote that the demarcation between protected solicitation and other activities is the "clear line . . . between those activities that are entirely ancillary to requests for purchase — those that serve no independent business function apart from their connection to the soliciting of orders — and those activities that the company would have reason to engage in any way but chooses to allocate to its in-state sales force."

There is one exception to the preceding rule: "Even if engaged in exclusively to facilitate requests for purchases, the maintenance of an office within the State, by the company or on its behalf, would go beyond the 'solicitation of orders.'" That said, for purposes of P.L. 86-272, the one key difference between an employee and an independent contractor is that the latter can have an office in the state.

The MTC offered its interpretation and an elaboration of the term solicitation in its "Statement of Information Concerning Practices of Multistate Tax Commission and Signatory States under Public Law 86-272" issued in January 1986. The statement has been revised and reissued in January 1993, July 1994, and July 2001. According to the MTC, the term solicitation includes (1) speech or conduct that explicitly or implicitly invites an order; and (2) activities that neither explicitly nor implicitly invite an order, but are entirely ancillary to requests for an order. "Ancillary activities are those that serve no independent business function for the seller apart from their connection to the solicitation of orders." If the seller would engage in an activity apart from soliciting orders, the activity is not ancillary. Even if the activity is not ancillary, it will still qualify for immunity if it is *de minimis*. "*De minimis* activities are those that, when taken together, establish only a trivial connection with the taxing state." Both the quantitative and qualitative nature of the activity will be considered, but not its economic importance. If the activity is conducted on a regular or continuous basis, it will not normally be considered trivial or *de minimis*.

The statement provides examples of minimal activities within a state that could establish nexus for income tax purposes, including the following:

- Repairs and maintenance
- Collections on accounts
- Credit investigations
- Installation and supervision of installation
- Nonsolicitation training
- Nonsolicitation technical advice
- Handling or processing customer complaints (except mediating customer complaints when the sole purpose is to ingratiate sales personnel with the customer)
- Approving or accepting orders
- Repossessing property
- Securing deposits on sales
- Picking up or replacing damaged or returned property
- Hiring, training, or supervising personnel other than those involved only in solicitation
- Using agency stock checks or any other instrument by which sales are made in the state by sales personnel
- Maintaining a sample or display room in excess of 14 days at any one location within the state during the tax year
- Carrying samples for sale, exchange, or distribution in any manner for value
- Owning, leasing, using, or maintaining a repair shop; parts department; warehouse; meeting place for directors, officers, or employees; stock of goods (other than samples for sales personnel or that are used entirely ancillary to solicitation); telephone answering service that is publicly attributed to the company or to the employee(s) or agent(s) of the company in their representative status; mobile stores; real property or fixtures of any kind; or any other office (other than a protected in-home office described subsequently)

- Consigning tangible personal property to any person
- Maintaining by any employee or other representative, an office or place of business of any kind (other than an in-home office located within the residence of the employee or representative that (i) is not publicly attributed to the company or the employee or representative in an employee or representative capacity, and (ii) so long as the use of such office is limited to soliciting and receiving orders from customers; for transmitting orders outside the state for acceptance or rejection; or for such other activities that are protected under P.L. 86-272)
- Any indication through advertising or business literature that the company or its employee or representative can be contacted at a specific address within the state, or a telephone or other public listing within the state for the company or its employee or representative in a representative capacity is normally considered an in-state office or place of business. However, the normal distribution and use of business cards and stationery that identify the employee's or representative's name, address, telephone and fax numbers, and affiliation with the company is not, itself, considered as advertising or otherwise publicly attributing an office to the company, its employee, or representative.
- The maintenance of any office or other place of business that does not qualify as an in-home office described previously will, itself, cause the loss of protection under P.L. 86-272. It is not relevant whether the company pays directly, indirectly, or not at all for the maintenance of such in-home office.
- Entering into or selling franchises or licenses; selling tangible personal property pursuant to such franchise or license agreements to in-state franchisees and licensees
- Any other nonprotected, nonancillary activity (even if such activity helps to increase purchases)

Activities that the MTC deems protected include the following:

- Soliciting orders for sales by any type of advertising
- Carrying samples and promotional materials for display only or for distribution without charge or other consideration
- Furnishing or setting up display racks and advising customers on display of products without charge or other consideration
- Providing autos to sales personnel for use in protected activities
- Passing orders, inquiries, and complaints to the home office
- Checking customers' inventories without charge (for reorder only)
- Maintaining a sample or display room for 14 days or less at any one location within the state during the tax year
- Soliciting orders for sales by an in-state resident employee or representative of the company, provided such person does not maintain an in-state sales office or place of business other than a protected in-home office
- Missionary sales activities (such as, the solicitation of indirect customers for the company's goods. For example, a manufacturer's solicitation of retailers to buy the manufacturer's goods from the manufacturer's wholesale customers would be protected if such solicitation activities are otherwise immune)
- Recruiting, training, or evaluation of sales personnel, including the occasional use of homes, hotels, or similar places for meetings of sales personnel
- Mediating direct customer complaints when the purpose is solely for ingratiating the sales personnel with the customer and facilitating requests for orders
- Coordinating shipment or delivery without payment and providing related information prior to or subsequent to placement of order
- Owning, leasing, using, or maintaining personal property for use in an in-home office or car that is used solely for protected activities

Physical presence and income tax

As the preceding discussion indicates, a taxpayer can have physical presence in a state and still avoid an income tax filing obligation if that presence is protected by P.L. 86-272. Please note, however, that any services are not protected under P.L. 86-272. As a consequence, employees that telecommute can trigger an income tax filing obligation. For example, the state of New Jersey successfully taxed TeleBright, a Maryland software company that allowed one of its employees to telecommute from her home in New Jersey. The employee, a software developer, moved from Maryland to New Jersey because her spouse changed jobs. Because she was a highly regarded and skilled employee, TeleBright proposed she work from home. According to the court, because the employee regularly received and carried out her assignments, began and ended her workday by checking in, and routinely received assignments from her supervisor either by email or phone, the corporation was doing business in the state under N.J.A.C. 18:7-1.9(b). (*Telebright Corp. v. New Jersey*, No. A-5096-09T2, N. J. Super. Ct. (March 2, 2012). See also Appeal of Warwick McKinley Inc., No. 489090, California State Board of Equalization, (January 11, 2012)).

However, the current debate over income tax nexus has focused not so much on P.L. 86-272, but on whether a taxpayer's economic presence in a state can create income tax nexus.

The U.S. Supreme Court has never addressed whether there exists a physical presence requirement for income tax nexus. In fact, more than one state Supreme Court has ruled that physical presence is not necessary for income tax nexus. The South Carolina Supreme Court ruled that a Delaware holding company, whose only presence in the state was the licensing of its trademarks, was subject to South Carolina's income tax. In brief, the state's argument was that physical presence is unnecessary for income tax nexus, due process is satisfied by the purposeful direction of business activity, and that P.L. 86-272 does not protect the licensing of intangibles: only the solicitation of the sale of tangible personal property. The South Carolina Supreme Court ruled in favor of the state and the U.S. Supreme Court denied cert. (*Geoffrey, Inc. v. South Carolina Tax Commission*, 437 S.E.2d 13, *cert. denied*, 114 S. Ct. 550 (1993)).

The *Lanco* decision, like the Geoffrey cases, involved an intangible holding company, a tax planning structure that is considered by some state tax administrators to be little more than a tax scam. That cannot be said, however, of the *MBNA American Bank* case. (See *West Virginia v. MBNA,* 640 S.E.2d 226 (W.Va. 2006)).

MBNA America did not have any employees, property, or other physical presence in West Virginia. Nonetheless, the company had $8 to $10 million in gross receipts from the state through the issuance and servicing of credit cards. The only contacts MBNA had with West Virginia were through mail and telephone solicitation. Nevertheless, the West Virginia Supreme Court ruled that the bank's "systematic and continuous business activity in [the State] produced significant gross receipts attributable to its West Virginia customers which indicate a significant economic presence sufficient to meet the substantial nexus prong of *Complete Auto*." In addition, an income tax imposition, unlike that of sales and use tax, imposed little burden on interstate commerce. In any case, the technological changes in commerce made "the application of a physical presence standard . . . a poor measuring stick of an entity's true nexus with the state." On March 9, 2007, MBNA filed a petition for certiorari with the U.S. Supreme Court. It was denied on June 18, 2007.

Not surprisingly, other states followed West Virginia's lead in targeting financial institutions via economic nexus. The Indiana Tax Court followed the reasoning of the West Virginia court in ruling that MBNA had substantial nexus in the state without physical presence (*MBNA America Bank v. Indiana Department of State Revenue*, Ind. Tax Ct., No. 49T10-0506-TA-53, Oct. 20, 2008). The Massachusetts Supreme Judicial Court came to the same conclusion based on the same reasoning as the West Virginia and Indiana courts (*Capital One Bank v. Massachusetts*, 899 NE2d 76 (Mass. 2009)). However, the New Jersey Tax Court recently rebuffed the state's attempt to adopt a significant economic presence test in determining nexus, for the simple reason that it had not been adopted by the state legislature. (See *AccuZIP, Inc. v. Director*, N.J. Tax, Dkt. No. 005744-2003, (08/13/2009) (unpublished)). Nevertheless, several other states, including California, Connecticut, Hawaii, Minnesota, and Tennessee, have indicated that they expect to adopt the economic nexus standard articulated in these recent cases. The decisions are unsettling, because given the basis for the courts' holdings in West Virginia, Indiana, and Massachusetts, there is no reason why such reasoning cannot be extended to any business whose presence in a state is limited to solicitation through the mail or over the internet. It is no exaggeration to say that the implications of *MBNA* and *Capital One* are enormous.

Financial institutions, however, are not the only industry that has been targeted by state tax administrators. Franchising has also become a primary target. On December 30, 2010, the Iowa Supreme Court ruled that Kentucky Fried Chicken's (KFC) licensing of intangibles in the state to its franchisees, was the "functional equivalent of 'physical presence' under *Quill*." Consequently, despite having no employees, property or other presence in the state, KFC had to pay tax on the royalties it received from its franchisees in the state. The court went on to say that even if the intangibles were not the functional equivalence of physical presence, it didn't really matter because *Quill* was limited to sales tax and inapplicable to income tax. (*KFC Corporation v. Iowa*, 792 N.W.2d 308 (Ia. 2010)). KFC appealed to the U.S. Supreme Court but their appeal was denied (*KFC Corp. v. Iowa Dept. of Rev.*, Iowa S. Ct., Dkt. No. 09-1032, 12/30/2010, 792 NW2d 308 (2010), *cert denied*, U.S. S. Ct., Dkt. No. 10-1340, 10/03/2011)). Iowa has continued to go after taxpayers whose only connection with the state is franchising fees. (*See Jack Daniels Properties, Inc. v. Department of Revenue*, Iowa Department of Inspections and Appeals, Dkt. No. 09DORFC002, (July 28, 2011)).

The state pursuit of nexus through intangibles has not always been wins for the states. In 2012 the West Virginia Supreme Court (yes, the same court that ruled in *MBNA*) held that an out-of-state subsidiary was not liable for corporation income tax on its royalty income, where it did no business in the state and was not created for tax avoidance purposes (*Griffith v. ConAgra Brands, Inc.*, 728 S.E.2d 74 (W. Va. 2012)). The Oklahoma Supreme Court came to a similar decision regarding an insurance company's receipts from intellectual property licensed to a related party's restaurant chain (*Scioto Insurance Co. v. Oklahoma Tax Commission*, 279 P.3d 782 (Okla. 2012)).

Nevertheless, the pattern seems clear. First, the states have targeted intangible holding companies, then banks, and now franchisors. With economic nexus tests now explicitly blessed by the Supreme Court in the wake of *Wayfair*, other taxes are open to a more expansive nexus setup. What will be next?

What we know and where to go from here

In brief, here is where we are. We know that physical presence and economic nexus are tests for sales tax nexus, but it is not clear how much physical presence must be involved, or under just what circumstances the physical presence of a third party can be attributed to the out-of-state taxpayer. Finally, we know that many states are using economic nexus in the wake of the *Wayfair* decision. Physical presence still creates nexus, but with *Wayfair* it is no longer the primary concern.

For income tax, we know that physical presence does not trigger an income tax filing obligation if the activities fall within the safe harbor provisions of P.L. 86-272. However, if a taxpayer's activities include services, or the licensing of intangibles, or any other activities not protected under 86-272, we know that several states have successfully asserted that the taxpayer has nexus, absent any physical presence. What isn't clear is whether economic presence in a state will necessarily trigger an income tax filing obligation in those states that have not specifically addressed the issue.

Nevertheless, what is certain is that states will continue to pursue a broad interpretation of what constitutes nexus.

Marketplace facilitator

Some states have gone the route of requiring large retailers who have platforms that facilitate commerce to collect and remit the sales and use taxes. Washington led the way, and has been joined by a number of states. Although some states may allow vendors selling only through facilitator channels to not register, others still require registration and filing. It is important to note that this facilitator may not cover all taxes, and nexus and a filing obligation may still exist. Washington's B&O tax is a prime example of this as those using the facilitator's service still need to file and pay this tax.

Offers in compromise (voluntary disclosures)

Many states provide for a formal offer-in-compromise program. Some companies may have had nexus for quite some time, but have refrained from filing because of ignorance or misunderstanding of the law, or have simply postponed fulfilling this obligation because of administrative constraints, or even because they "didn't want to bother."

Those companies may be willing to file prospectively, but fear that doing so would cause the taxing jurisdiction(s) to look back after receiving the application, and then propose a substantial (if not staggering) assessment. Note that, even where activity was rather limited, assessments could still be very significant, because the statute of limitations does not start running until a return is filed. Theoretically, states could go back indefinitely, although they usually will not do so. In fact, many states go back 7 to 10 years. In addition, the assessment would include significant penalties and interest.

These are the ideal circumstances in which an offer-in-compromise or voluntary disclosure agreement (VDA) may be appropriate. There are two primary advantages to a VDA. First, most states will waive penalties and some will even waive part of the interest due. Second, and perhaps more importantly, the state will limit the look-back period, usually to three or four years. Generally, the VDAs are proposed anonymously through the use of a tax professional. For effecting a satisfactory compromise, it may be best to ask an expert tax professional to contact the state(s) and determine whether a lump-sum settlement would be agreeable to bring the taxpayer current, or alternatively, whether the state might be willing to limit its review to just a few years (for example, three to five). VDAs are particularly useful in those situations where the nexus determination is ambiguous or in a particularly gray area of the law. For companies facing a FIN 48 issue, a VDA can be very helpful.

Making an offer could also be considered in conjunction with state amnesty programs. However, even if there is such a program, the taxpayer should act very cautiously, because the program might specifically limit the amnesty to specified periods or types of taxes. State amnesty programs should also be regarded with a healthy dose of skepticism for several reasons. Amnesty programs will usually offer a waiver of penalties, and often a partial waiver of interest. This can make them seem more appealing than the state's VDA program, which usually only waives penalties. However, most amnesty programs lack the ability to limit the lookback period that is the hallmark of VDA programs. When these amnesty programs are being considered, they should be compared to the applicable VDA program to see which is a better fit to a particular set of facts for a given taxpayer.

In addition to specific state programs, the MTC has a formal offer-in-compromise program through which taxpayers and their representatives can approach multiple states through a voluntary disclosure process. For more information, see the MTC website at www.mtc.gov.

Chapter 2

Calculation of State Taxable Income: Modifications

Learning objectives

- Identify the most common additions to federal taxable income.
- Identify the most common subtractions from federal taxable income.
- Distinguish deductible from nondeductible state income taxes.
- Recognize the limitations of the intergovernmental immunity doctrine.

Introduction

The majority of states piggyback off the federal corporate income tax base. Most state statutes specifically begin with federal taxable income although some states limit their adoption of the federal Internal Revenue Code (IRC) to a specific date. States that do not automatically follow federal taxable income must annually update their statutory adoption of the IRC. Requiring annual legislative adoption provides the state legislatures in those states an opportunity to review federal changes before adopting them. A few states are prohibited from automatically following changes in the federal tax code, because their judiciaries have ruled that such a delegation of legislative authority to the federal government is unconstitutional. Many states' tax bases, such as New York's, do not tie directly to federal taxable income. New York uses a taxpayer's entire net income as the beginning point for calculating state taxable income. As a consequence, foreign source income, which is often excluded in other states, can be part of New York's state tax base. (See *Reuters, Ltd. v. Tax Appeals Tribunal*, 623 N.E.2d 1145 (N.Y. Oct. 12, 1993) and *Matter of Schlumberger Limited*, No. 811620 (N.Y. Div. Tax App. Apr. 13, 2000)).

Although most states begin with federal taxable income as a starting point (either line 28 or line 30 from the federal form 1120), every state has certain additions or subtractions that must be made before arriving at state taxable income before allocation and apportionment. Naturally, state modifications vary by state, and in this chapter, we will cover the most commonly encountered adjustments. In practice, each state's modifications must be considered. In brief, state modifications fall into one of two categories — additions or subtractions. There are some items, such as interest from state obligations, that are not in federal taxable income and so must be added to it to arrive at the state tax base. There are other items, such as interest on U.S. obligations, that are in federal taxable income, but generally cannot be taxed by states, and thus must be subtracted from federal taxable income to arrive at the state income tax base. Some states, via their Franchise Taxes, however, will tax U.S. government bond interest (California, for example).

Keep in mind that additions will increase federal taxable income, and subtractions will decrease federal taxable income. Typical additions include state, local, and foreign income taxes, interest from state and local obligations, federal net operating losses (NOLs), excess depreciation, capital loss, and charitable contribution carryovers. Typical subtractions include dividends, interest on U.S. obligations, state income tax refunds, wages upon which the federal jobs credit was taken, subpart F income, and the federal income tax.

Knowledge check

1. Most States that do their own calculation of NOLs start out by referring to

   a. Line 28 of Form 1120.
   b. Line 30 of Form 1120.
   c. Line 32 of Form 1120.
   d. Line 34 of Form 1120.

2. California has recently changed its laws regarding NOLs by

   a. Allowing NOL carrybacks over a two-year period, starting in 2013.
   b. Allowing NOL carrybacks and carryforwards similar to the federal NOL rules, beginning in 2012.
   c. Phasing in the allowance of NOL carrybacks over three years, beginning in 2013.
   d. Allowing NOL carryback over a two-year period, starting in 2015.

Additions

Some of the more common additions to federal taxable income include the following items.

Decoupling from depreciation, depletion, and amortization

States first started decoupling from federal depreciation with the introduction of the Accelerated Cost Recovery System (ACRS) in 1981. Bonus depreciation, first introduced in 2002 with the Job Creation and Worker Assistance Act (JCWAA), prompted many more states to depart from the federal depreciation rules. State differences also exist with immediate expensing under IRC Section 179, depletion, and intangible drilling costs. For example, Iowa, Minnesota, Mississippi, Tennessee, and Wisconsin only allow cost, not percentage, depletion. What follows is a summary by federal legislation of the more common decouplings.

Tax Cuts and Jobs Act of 2017

The Tax Cuts and Jobs Act of 2017 (TCJA) has many areas where there are significant changes to federal tax law. Some states have rolling conformity, yet often will decouple from specific provisions. The most consistent response so far has been to decouple from the 100% depreciation afforded to businesses. Conformity is an area that is frequently in flux and is worth researching for your specific cases. As of this writing, seven states have yet to update their IRC conformity to the TCJA.

Foreign derived intangible income (FDII) global intangible low-taxed income (GILTI) IRC Section 250

These are both components of a deduction for taxpayers with foreign income. Many states have decoupled, or the basis for their starting point for taxable income, is not impacted by these deductions. The states that are the same as the federal return due to starting point for income calculation are Alabama, Colorado, Delaware, Florida, Georgia, Illinois, Iowa, Kansas, Maryland, Michigan, Missouri, Nebraska, Oklahoma, Vermont, Virginia, and West Virginia. Those that do not conform due to their starting point are Alaska, Connecticut, District of Columbia, Mississippi, Montana, New Mexico, Oregon, Pennsylvania, Rhode Island, Tennessee, and Utah. States with an addback include Idaho, Indiana, Kentucky, Louisiana, Maine, Massachusetts, New York, North Carolina, and North Dakota.

Contributions to the capital of a corporation IRC Section 118

The TCJA changed the way certain incentives from government entities to a corporation are treated. Now grant proceeds from civic groups or government entities are taxable unless the civic group or governmental entity is a shareholder. The states that allow subtractions for contributions of capital made by governmental entities and civic groups are California, Georgia, Minnesota, New Hampshire, South Carolina, and Tennessee.

Protecting Americans from Tax Hikes Act of 2015

The Protecting Americans from Tax Hikes Act of 2015 (PATH) made permanent several tax incentives including the research credit, and extended dozens of others including 50% bonus depreciation, and increased expensing under IRC Section 179. For states with "rolling" conformity, the PATH provisions are generally automatic. However, for those states that specifically adopt the IRC as of a certain date, further analysis will be needed. For example, Texas conforms to the IRC as of January 1, 2007 with modifications for its "margin" tax. New York and Illinois have rolling conformity with certain specific exceptions. California conforms to the IRC as of January 1, 2015. Unfortunately, given the late date at which the U.S. Congress has been passing federal legislation the past couple of years, states' coupling or decoupling acts have become an annual headache as well.

Tax Increase Prevention Act of 2014

The Tax Increase Prevention Act of 2014 (TIPA) extended the 50% bonus depreciation and the immediate expensing provision of IRC Section 179 for the calendar year 2014. States typically followed their past tradition (see other acts in the following) in either adopting or decoupling from TIPA. For example, conforming states for bonus depreciation included Alabama, Alaska, Colorado, Delaware, Kansas, Louisiana, Missouri, Montana, Nebraska, New Mexico, North Dakota, Oregon, Utah, and West Virginia. Conforming states for IRC Section 179 included Alabama, Alaska, Arizona, Colorado, Connecticut, Delaware, Georgia, Iowa, Idaho, Kansas, Louisiana, Maine, Massachusetts, Michigan, Mississippi, Missouri, Nebraska, New Mexico, North Dakota, Oklahoma, Oregon, Pennsylvania, Rhode Island, Tennessee, Utah, Virginia, and West Virginia.

The American Taxpayer Relief Act of 2012

The American Taxpayer Relief Act of 2012 (ATRA) extended many of the items from which states have decoupled, including 50% bonus depreciation and IRC Section 179 expensing. Other items extended by the ATRA include the following:

- The New Markets Tax Credit
- Certain Subpart F exceptions
- Seven-year life for motorsports facilities
- Employer wage credits for military reservists
- Enhanced deduction for food contributions
- Dividend treatment for regulated investment companies
- Special expensing provisions for the film and television industry
- Accelerated depreciation for property on Indian reservations
- Election to expense mine safety equipment

These are only a few of the items extended by ATRA that may be treated differently at the state level and for which adjustments must be made. For example, Minnesota has not adopted the accelerated depreciation for business property on Indian reservations, the enhanced deduction for food contributions, the special expensing provisions for the film and television industry, the expensing of mine safety equipment, or the seven-year life for motorsports entertainment complexes. On the other hand, Indiana recently recoupled to the IRC and for 2013 will allow the seven-year life for motorsports facilities, oil and gas well depletion deduction, and the expensing of mine safety equipment. Fortunately, most tax services include federal conformity charts that allow preparers to check each state's conformity with the IRC.

Tax Relief, Unemployment Insurance Reauthorization and Job Creation Act of 2010 (2010 Tax Relief Act)

The 2010 Tax Relief Act boosted bonus depreciation from 50% to 100% for qualified purchases made after September 8, 2010. Many states were decoupled from (or never conformed to) federal bonus depreciation in the past, and that tradition was upheld with this legislation. States decoupling from 100% bonus depreciation included Arkansas, Connecticut, Florida, Georgia, Hawaii, Iowa, Idaho, Kentucky, Massachusetts, Maryland, Maine, Michigan, Minnesota, Mississippi, North Carolina, New Hampshire, New Jersey, New York, Oregon, Pennsylvania, Rhode Island, South Carolina, Tennessee, Virginia, Vermont, Wisconsin, and the District of Columbia.

Many of the same states that decouple from bonus depreciation have also decoupled from immediate expensing under IRC Section 179. There are enough exceptions, however, so that no one can assume that if a state refuses to adopt one, it will also reject the other. States that have decoupled from IRC Section 179 include Arkansas, Arizona, California, Florida, Georgia, Hawaii, Indiana, Kentucky, Maryland, Maine, Minnesota, North Carolina, New Hampshire, New Jersey, Oregon, Rhode Island, Wisconsin, and the District of Columbia. States that conform to IRC Section 179 include Alaska, Alabama, Colorado, Connecticut, Delaware, Idaho, Illinois, Kansas, Louisiana, Massachusetts, Michigan, Missouri, Mississippi, Montana, North Dakota, Nebraska, New Mexico, New York, Oklahoma, Pennsylvania, Tennessee, Utah, Vermont, Virginia, and West Virginia.

In addition to the various decoupling rules, the key point to remember is that when an asset is sold, its federal tax basis will be different from its state tax basis. For example, ABC Company purchases a machine for $10,000, takes the 50% federal bonus depreciation, and depreciates it over five years. At the beginning of the second year, when its federal basis is $4,000 ($10,000 less $5,000 bonus depreciation less $1,000 MACRS ($5,000 × 0.20)), the company sells the machine for $6,000. For federal tax purposes, ABC Company has a $2,000 gain. However, if the state in which ABC is located has decoupled from bonus depreciation, the company has a $2,000 loss ($10,000 less MACRS of $2,000 ($10,000 × 0.20)), because its basis for state tax purposes is $8,000, while its basis for federal tax is $4,000.

Related party royalty and interest payments

In an effort to combat the use of intellectual holding companies or passive investment companies such as in the *Geoffrey* or *Lanco* cases, many states have passed legislation disallowing a deduction for royalties or interest paid to a related party. Because the states acknowledge that there may be many valid circumstances where such deductions are appropriate, the rules with respect to these add backs are often confusing and vary from state to state. There is no substitute for checking each state's specific rules and exceptions. That said, the states that have passed such add back legislation include Alabama, Arkansas, Connecticut, Georgia, Illinois, Indiana, Kentucky, Maryland, Massachusetts, Mississippi, New York, New Jersey, North Carolina, Ohio, Oregon, South Carolina, Tennessee, Virginia, and the District of Columbia.

The Multistate Tax Commission has adopted a model statute addressing related party add backs for intangible expenses and interest paid to a related member. The statute's language echoes the language used in several of the states that have already enacted add back legislation.

Intangible expenses include expenses, losses, or costs related to the acquisition, use, maintenance, or management of intangible property. Intangible property is defined to include trade names, patents, copyrights, trademarks, and trade secrets. A related member or entity includes component members defined in IRC Section 1563(e), a 50% or more stockholder, or a corporation or affiliate that is owned 50% or more by the taxpayer.

The intangible and interest expenses will not have to be added back if the related party's income is taxable in another jurisdiction at a rate within a certain percentage of the taxpayer's state rate. There are other exceptions as well. In any case, it is clear that the model statute is aimed at intangible holding companies such as those found in the *Geoffrey* case. Some states also require add backs for management fees or rent expense and some states have enacted enhanced penalties for those taxpayers failing to add back the required expenses. Finally, some states have provided a "subject to" exception to their add back provision that allows the expense so long as the related party is "subject to" tax in its own state on the income it receives. For an example and discussion of the "subject to" provision, see *Beneficial New Jersey, Inc. v. Director*, Tax Court of New Jersey, Dkt. No. 009886-2007, (August 31, 2010).

It will come as no surprise that the MTC's proposed model legislation and the add back legislation already passed by many states has met with serious criticism. Many commentators firmly believe the statutes to be unconstitutional. Unfortunately for those commentators and taxpayers, the Alabama Court of Civil Appeals recently rejected a corporation's attempt to argue that the state's addback statute was unconstitutional. In addition to rejecting the company's constitutional pleas, the Court rebuffed the taxpayer's argument that it met the two exceptions provided in the statute for add backs; specifically, that the income was taxable in another state and the state adjustment was unreasonable. (See *Surtees v. VFJ Ventures, Inc.*, 8 So.3d 950 (Ala. Ct. App. 2008)). The Alabama Supreme Court affirmed the Appeals court decision on September 19, 2008 stating that "in light of that thoughtful opinion, we see no need to explicate further." (*VFJ Ventures, Inc. v. Surtees*, 8 So.3d 983 (Ala. 2008)). A petition for certiorari was filed with the U. S. Supreme Court on January 21, 2009, but the court declined to review the decision on April 27, 2009. *VFJ Ventures*, however, is just the first salvo in what is likely to be a protracted battle for some time.

State and municipal interest income

State and municipal interest income is an example of income that is not taxable at the federal level, and accordingly, not included in the federal return. (See IRC Section 103.) Many states require that federal taxable income be increased by the amount of state and municipal interest income that had been excluded on the federal return. At the same time, if there were expenses related to this income that had been disallowed for federal purposes, those expenses can be offset against the add-back of interest income. Be sure that you do not add back interest income in those states that exempt that income received on their own, or their own political subdivisions and obligations. Most states, however, will tax other states' bond interest income while excluding their own.

Not all municipal interest is exempt. For example, interest on bonds issued to finance certain projects, such as industrial business parks or convention centers, should be included in federal taxable income, thus no add back is necessary. (See IRC Section 146.)

A couple from Kentucky recently challenged the constitutionality of the state's distinguishing between in-state and out-of-state interest income. Kentucky is one of 41 states that exempts from taxation interest income derived from bonds issued by the state or its subdivisions, while taxing the interest income from other states' obligations. The lower courts in Kentucky agreed with the taxpayers, holding that Kentucky's taxation of other states' bond interest was unconstitutional on its face because it violated the Commerce Clause by affording more favorable taxation treatment to instate bonds than it did to out-of-state bonds. The U.S. Supreme Court rejected this argument in a splintered 7 to 2 decision, holding that the issuance of state municipal bonds was a government function, not susceptible to Commerce Clause analysis. The opinion generated seven different opinions, but nevertheless held that Kentucky's position had been supported in amicus brief by the other 49 states (even states with no income tax). The court found that Kentucky was motivated by legitimate political objectives apart from economic protectionism banned by the Commerce Clause, and that the state's participation in the municipal bond market did not favor Kentucky taxpayers over other taxpayers, but simply aided the state government in making its bonds more marketable. (See *Kentucky Department of Revenue v. Davis*, 127 S.Ct. 2451 (2008)).

Knowledge check

3. In *Kentucky Department of Revenue v. Davis*,

    a. The Supreme Court held that Kentucky statutes violated the Commerce Clause.
    b. The lower court upheld the State of Kentucky's right to tax out of state bond interest.
    c. The courts ruled that Kentucky's participation in the municipal bond market did not favor Kentucky taxpayers over other taxpayers.
    d. The courts ruled that all interest income from Kentucky bonds is now taxable.

State income taxes

Just as the federal government does not allow a deduction for its own income tax, neither do most states allow deductions for their own income taxes. Thus, any state income taxes deducted on the federal return must usually be added back to arrive at state taxable income. Curiously enough, there are a few states, such as Alabama and Louisiana, which do allow a deduction for federal income taxes attributable to state sources. Iowa and Missouri allow a deduction for 50% of the federal income taxes paid. (See also *Kinney Shoe Corporation v. State*, 552 N.W.2d 788 (N.D. 1996).)

Care must be taken in considering just which types of state income taxes must be added back. For example, some states limit their add-back to state taxes based on or measured by net income. As a consequence, those states' tax deductions involving a franchise tax on capital may not have to be added back to federal taxable income. Franchise taxes are usually a tax on a company's book value, measured either by capital stock or net worth. Another state with a franchise tax element is New York.

Other state taxes that are not based on or measured by net income, and thus may not have to be added back, are Washington's Business and Occupation Tax, and Ohio's Commercial Activity Tax. There is some debate as to whether the new Texas Margin Tax (TMT) is an income tax or a gross receipts tax or both. The FASB concluded that the TMT was an income tax for purposes of Financial Accounting Standards ASC 740. Carole Keeton Strayhorn, the state comptroller at the time, claimed the TMT is an income tax, but Section 21 of H.B. 3 stated that the new margin tax "is not an income tax and P. L. 86-272 does not apply to the tax." The confusion arises because the taxpayer has one of four options in calculating the tax; specifically, the taxpayer can elect to subtract the larger of either (1) cost of goods sold; (2) compensation; (3) 30% of revenue; or (4) $1,000,000. Depending upon which election is made, the tax looks more or less like an income tax. In short, the confusion arises because the tax is a modified gross receipts tax with some deductions allowed.

Not surprisingly, state revenue departments have come to different conclusions about whether the TMT is an income tax. For example, Massachusetts, Minnesota, Pennsylvania, and Virginia have issued rulings holding that the TMT is not a tax based on net income, while Kansas, Missouri, South Carolina, and Wisconsin hold that it is a tax on income. (See Mass. Dep't of Revenue, Directive 08-7 (December 18, 2008); Minnesota Dep't of Revenue, Notice 08-08 (July 21, 2008); Pa. Dep't of Rev., Corp. Tax Bulletin 2008-05 (Dec. 1, 2008); Ruling of the Comm'r, PD 08-169 (Va. Dept. Tax'n, September 11, 2008); Cal. FTB Technical Advice Mem. No. 2011-03 (Apr. 13, 2011); Kansas Dep't of Revenue, Office of Policy and Research, Op. Ltr. O-2008-004 (September 2, 2008); Mo. Dep't of Revenue, Priv. Ltr. Rul. No. LR5309, (December 12, 2008); and Wisconsin Dep't of Revenue, Publication 125 (February 26, 2008).)

California declined to "provide a definitive characterization" of the TMT and held that "the characterization of this tax is dependent on the method used to calculate it and the type of income subject to the [TMT]," and said that its treatment is "highly fact-specific and must be made on a case-by-case basis." (See Calif. FTB Notice No. 2009-06 (July 20, 2009)). California has since come out with guidance stating that the TMT is not an income tax, and does not qualify for the Other States Tax Credit (OSTC) for personal income tax purposes (Calif. FTB Technical Advice Mem. No. 2016-01 (Jan. 12, 2016)). California has not yet released any specific guidance for corporate income/franchise taxes.

The states holding that the TMT is *not* an income tax emphasize the fact that the TMT did not allow for the deduction of common business expenses to arrive at net income. This emphasis is misplaced, since it is not based on the state's specific statutory definition. In most states, and indeed with the federal income tax itself, the liberality of the TMT in allowing certain deductions does not, in and of itself, means it is not a net income tax, because all income tax calculations allow certain deductions and disallow others. For example, the federal income tax is still an income tax even when deductions are limited to cost of goods sold, like the TMT (see, for example, IRC Section 280E, which prohibits drug dealers from deducting ordinary, necessary, and common business expenses, by limiting their deductions to cost of goods sold only). Arguably, the TMT is based on federal taxable income by virtue of the fact that all of the amounts used in the calculation of the TMT are drawn directly from federal forms that, as federal form 4797 illustrates, already include basis, recapture, and netting calculations necessary to arrive at federal taxable income.

Lastly, the fact that Texas calculates the margin and multiplies that margin by single sales factor apportionment is a final indication that the tax is an income tax, not a gross receipts tax. With a gross receipts tax, such as that in Hawaii, Ohio, and Washington, no apportionment is needed, because by definition, apportionment is inapplicable to a gross receipts tax. Nevertheless, many believe that because the tax must be paid whether a company is profitable or not, it is a gross receipts tax not an income tax.

In *Allcat Claims Service, L.P.*, 356 S.W.3d 455 (Tex. 2011), the Texas Supreme Court ruled that the state's margin tax was not "a tax on the net income of [a] natural person" within the state's Bullock Amendment, but that it did, like the state's prior franchise tax for which Colorado has traditionally given a credit, "constitute a tax on Allcat as an entity." The court held that debates over whether the Texas tax was an income tax or a gross receipts tax were misplaced, because Texas had adopted the entity theory of partnership taxation, and that the tax was imposed on a flow-through entity, not a natural person. As a consequence, it was irrelevant for purposes of their analysis whether the tax was defined as an income or gross receipts tax. According to the court, "because the arguments do not affect our analysis, we do not address them."

Knowledge check

4. Which is not a state that allows for a subtraction for a portion of federal income taxes paid?

    a. Alabama
    b. Iowa
    c. Louisiana
    d. South Dakota

The federal NOL

Regarding the treatment of federal NOLs, a few states simply follow the federal treatment, allowing the federal NOL in full. Most states, however, provide for a separate state NOL calculation that is often computed in the same manner as the federal. These fall into one of three categories. States using the first approach often start with line 30 of the federal form 1120. States using the second approach usually begin with line 28 of the federal form 1120. Finally, some states use a hybrid of the first two approaches, tying the state NOL to the existence of a federal NOL. Whether there is an add-back for the federal NOL is determined, in part, by whether the starting point is line 28 or line 30 of the federal 1120 form.

State variations with respect to NOLs include the years allowed for carrybacks (if any) and carryforwards, ceiling caps, and complications arising from using consolidated versus separate filing, and mergers and acquisitions. Occasionally, the states will suspend the use of NOLs altogether during times of fiscal emergency, as Illinois did from 2011 to 2014.

The IRC allows for the carryover of NOLs incurred in one year to another year. Specifically, Section 172 previously allowed for a carryback of two years, and a carryforward of 20 years. With the TCJA in general there is now no carryback and an indefinite carryforward. The JCWAA extended the carryback for 2001 and 2002 NOLs to five years. Many states have already limited their carryback and carryforward provisions, and almost half the states have eliminated their carryback entirely.

With the TCJA some states still maintain a carryback provision; we expect this to continue to be a changing facet of state tax codes.

States may limit a company's carryback and carryforward not only in number of years, but also in the amount that may be claimed in any given year. For example, Pennsylvania capped net losses at $3m, but this was found to violate the Uniformity Clause of the Pennsylvania Constitution. In November 2017, an application for reargument was filed. For years prior to January 1, 2018, Utah allows a 3-year carryback and a 15-year carryforward, but limits the carryback at $1m. For tax years subsequent to January 1, 2018, Utah disallows carryback and allows for unlimited carryforward. Given the many changes in the federal NOL rules, the number of states, and the use of NOLs as an economic fiscal tool, the variations among the states can be quite overwhelming.

Where a company in a separate filing state is filing a federal consolidated return, taxpayers generally must prepare a *pro forma* separate return as if the company had filed separate, rather than consolidated, federal returns. As a consequence, the allowable federal NOL is that which would have been allowed if the members of the consolidated return had each filed separate returns.

Generally, a company must have been subject to a state's tax in the year an NOL was incurred to avail itself of the state's NOL carryover provisions. Thus, complications exist for companies with NOLs that expand into other states, or acquire or merge with other multistate companies. For example, Rocky Mountain High (RMH) had been doing business in Colorado for the past three years. In 2011, the company suffered a loss of $12m, which it elected to carry forward. In 2012, RMH expanded its operations into Georgia. Georgia did not allow RMH to carry forward any of its 2011 loss against Georgia taxable income. (See Ga. Code Ann. Section 48-7-21(b)(3)).

The consequences to RMH in the previous example may or may not differ where RMH is merged into another company. The deciding factor in some states is whether the surviving company from the merger generated the initial losses, and was previously doing business in that state. Given the complexity of these issues, they are beyond the scope of this course.

Finally, states sometimes differ in whether their NOL is calculated pre-apportionment or post-apportionment. For example, a post-apportionment state would require that the total NOL generated be adjusted by the loss year's apportionment percentage before it is applied in the carryover year, while a pre-apportionment state would allow the total loss year's NOL be used before the carryover year's apportionment percentage is applied.

Cancellation of indebtedness income

If someone pays your debts for you, and your debts are otherwise cancelled, you generally have income to the extent of your debt relief. (See Regulation Section 1.61-12(a) and *Old Colony Trust Co. v. Commissioner,* 279 U.S. 716 (1929).) IRC Section 108 provides an exception to that rule by allowing debtors, who are either insolvent or in bankruptcy, to exclude cancellation of debt (COD) income from their tax base. Specifically, IRC Section 108(i) allows a taxpayer to defer recognition of COD income and include it ratably over a five-year period beginning in 2014. At least 24 states and the District of Columbia have decoupled from this provision. Those states include Arizona, Arkansas, California, Connecticut, Florida, Georgia, Hawaii, Indiana, Iowa, Kentucky, Maine, Maryland, Massachusetts, Minnesota, Mississippi, New Hampshire, New Jersey, North Carolina, Oklahoma, Oregon, Rhode Island, South Carolina, Virginia, and Wisconsin.

TCJA repatriation or transition income IRC Section 965

This allows certain foreign earnings and profits to be repatriated to the U.S. at a lower rate. States that require an addition for IRC Section 965 income are Alabama, Alaska, Colorado, Connecticut, Georgia, Idaho, Indiana, Louisiana, Maine, Maryland, Massachusetts, Michigan, Missouri, Montana, Nebraska, New Jersey, New Mexico, New York, North Dakota, Oklahoma, Oregon, Pennsylvania, Rhode Island, Utah, and Vermont.

Subtractions

Some of the more common subtractions from federal taxable income include the following.

Deduction for federal income tax paid

Only four states allow a subtraction for a portion of federal income taxes paid. They are Alabama, Iowa, Louisiana, and Missouri. (North Dakota used to allow such a deduction prior to 2004.)

Deduction for state income taxes paid

Most states require that deductions for other state income taxes be added back (see preceding discussion). However, several states, while requiring an add-back of their own corporate tax paid, will allow the deduction for other state taxes to stand. States denying a subtraction for their own income tax but allowing the deduction for other state taxes include Arkansas, Colorado, Illinois, Iowa, Louisiana, Rhode Island, and Tennessee. Allowable state subtractions may be limited to state tax "based upon or measured by net income." As a consequence, be careful that you do not subtract deductions for capital, net worth, or other franchise taxes twice: once in calculating federal taxable income, and a second time as a modification to the state tax base. However, there are some states that require an addback of taxes based on net income, but no addback for the various franchise/net worth taxes.

Gains and losses on asset dispositions

For those states that have decoupled from bonus depreciation or IRC Section 179 immediate expensing, there will be a difference between the federal basis and the state basis in a taxpayer's assets. In short, the state tax basis will be higher than the federal tax basis. For example, if federal bonus depreciation has been taken on a certain asset that is later sold, the gain for federal income tax purposes will be higher than the gain for state purposes in those states that have decoupled from bonus depreciation. Thus, federal taxable income will be overstated and a subtraction must be made to arrive at the proper state tax base.

Knowledge check

5. If a state has decoupled from bonus depreciation the following could be the case upon disposition of the asset?

    a. Federal taxable income would be understated so an addition must be made to arrive at the proper state tax base.
    b. Federal taxable income would be understated so a subtraction must be made to arrive at the proper state tax base.
    c. Federal taxable income would be overstated and a subtraction must be made to arrive at the proper state tax base.
    d. Federal taxable income would be overstated so an addition must be made to arrive at the proper state tax base.

Expenses related to nontaxable state and municipal interest income

(See the discussion under "Additions: State and Municipal Interest Income.")

Interest income earned on federal or U.S. obligations

Just as the federal government does not tax state or municipal bond interest, states do not tax interest earned on federal obligations. Often referred to as the intergovernmental immunity doctrine, the doctrine prohibits states from imposing a direct tax on net income from federal obligations. The doctrine was first articulated by the U.S. Supreme Court in *McCulloch v. Maryland* (1819). Contemporary application of the doctrine is codified at 31 U.S.C. Section 3124. However, the doctrine does not prohibit an indirect tax levied on federal obligations. Thus, states such as California and New York that have a franchise tax measured by net income can generally tax interest income on U.S. obligations. Therefore, federal interest income is a subtraction for those states that impose a direct tax on net income, but not for those states levying a franchise tax measured by net income.

Not all interest income earned on federal or U.S. obligations is considered exempt under the intergovernmental immunity doctrine. Income that is issued by quasipublic entities such as Ginnie Mae (Government National Mortgage Association), Sallie Mae (Student Loan Marketing Association), or Fannie Mae (Federal National Mortgage Association) can be taxed by states. Although the federal government guarantees the debt issued by these institutions, it is not debt issued directly by the federal government. Because the debt obligation by the federal government is secondary and contingent, the U.S. Supreme Court ruled that states were not prohibited from taxing the interest from that debt. (See *Rockford Life Insurance v. Illinois*, 482 U.S. 182 (1987).)

Other entities whose interest income is often taxable and thus not a subtraction from federal taxable income include the Federal Home Loan Board, the Federal Savings and Loan Insurance Corporation, the Federal Land Bank, the World Bank, and the Federal Farm Credit Bank. In addition, the U.S. Supreme Court has ruled that states can tax income from repurchase agreements (repos) and the New York

Supreme Court ruled interest income from specific loan pool certificates backed by the Small Business Administration is taxable. (See *Nebraska v. Lowenstein*, 513 U.S. 123 (1994) and *Sumitomo Trust and Banking Company v. Commissioner*, 720 N.Y.S.2d (2001).)

Refunds of state income taxes

If a state does not allow a deduction for state income taxes, it generally will not pick up as income any refunds of state income taxes, to the extent they are included in federal taxable income.

Example 2-1

JB Corporation is subject to corporate income tax only in state A. The starting point in computing state A taxable income is federal taxable income. JB's federal taxable income is $850,000, which includes a $70,000 deduction for state income taxes. During the year, JB received $40,000 interest on federal treasury bills. State A does not allow a deduction for state income tax payments. JB's taxable income for state A is

Federal taxable income	$ 850,000
Add back state income tax expense	70,000
Subtract interest income on federal obligations	(40,000)
State A taxable income	$ 880,000

Deductions disallowed by federal credits

Corporations may be entitled to a variety of federal credits on their returns for which there are no related state credits. When claiming the federal credit, the corporation is often required to reduce the expense deduction related to the credit. For example, the research activities credit allowed under IRC Section 41 provides a 20% tax credit against federal taxes. However, a taxpayer (depending upon the election chosen by the taxpayer) must reduce its expense deduction by the credit used. The expense disallowed because of the federal credit taken is a subtraction modification to arrive at state taxable income.

Most states also offer subtractions for Section 78 gross-ups and Subpart F income. Sometimes viewed as credit subtractions or dividend subtractions, both are modifications due to foreign income. When a corporation is allowed a deemed paid foreign tax credit for foreign taxes paid by a foreign subsidiary, its federal taxable income is increased to the extent of the deemed paid credit. This federal inclusion is called a "Section 78 gross-up." Because states generally do not allow for such a credit, most of them provide for a subtraction modification to back out the included income.

States also generally allow a subtraction for any Subpart F income. Subpart F income arises because of federal requirements that a U.S. shareholder in a controlled foreign corporation (CFC) include in its domestic income certain deemed pro rata shares of the CFC's income and earnings (IRC Sections 951–964).

Dividends received deduction

The purpose of the federal dividends received deduction (DRD) is to mitigate multiple taxation of corporate income. Problems arise in state taxation, because the corporations paying and or receiving the dividends may not be subject to the state's income tax. State modification will also depend upon the state's starting point for federal taxable income. If the starting point is line 28 of the federal form 1120 (federal taxable income before NOLs and DRD), the state may allow a partial or total subtraction for any DRDs depending upon the state filing method (separate, consolidated, or combined). For those states starting with line 30 (federal taxable income after NOLs and DRD), no subtraction may be necessary. Nevertheless, some adjustments may have to be made due to the different federal treatment of domestic and foreign dividends (see *Kraft General Foods, Inc. v. Iowa*, 505 U.S. 71 (1992)).

In *Kraft*, the U.S. Supreme Court ruled that Iowa's taxation of dividends violated the foreign Commerce Clause. Iowa used federal taxable income as its starting point, but provided no modifications for DRD. As a consequence, corporations were entitled to deduct domestic dividends to the same extent for Iowa as they did on their federal return. But, because there is no federal DRD for foreign dividends, the court found that Iowa discriminated against foreign dividends over domestic dividends. The court said it was indisputable that foreign dividends were treated less favorably than domestic dividends, making the Iowa statute an unconstitutional encroachment on the federal government's regulation of foreign commerce. Iowa tried to justify its approach based on administrative convenience, but the court held that Iowa could have retained its tie to federal taxable income with very little modification.

Many states since *Kraft* have amended their statutes, but the problem still arises in those states with combined reporting, who claim that the combined reporting method exempts them from the *Kraft* controversy.

Because dividends are paid out of a company's earnings and profits, it is important to verify that the dividend distributions were properly sourced, given the taxpayer's filing method (that is, separate, consolidated, or combined). (See chapter 3 for a discussion of filing methods.) For most states, earnings and profits are calculated on a separate company basis. As a consequence, a company that has apportioned income on a unitary basis may have a loss for earnings and profits on a separate company basis, a circumstance that may impact the intercompany elimination of dividends on a unitary basis. Here is an example drawn from the California audit manual:

> "Corporation P and unitary subsidiary S filed a combined report for the year in which S was formed. S's net income computed on a separate basis was $10,000; its apportioned share of the unitary business income was $50,000. S paid income taxes of $4,000. S distributed $9,000 to its parent during the taxable year. Although S's net income exceeded the amount of the distribution, S's earnings and profits were only $6,000 ($10,000 income – $4,000 taxes). Therefore, only $6,000 of the distribution is considered a dividend subject to elimination."

The preceding additions and subtractions are far from complete. States vary significantly in their modifications to federal taxable income, and a corporation must examine the available modifications not only in light of that state's specific statutes, but also with respect to the filing method (separate, consolidated, or combined) chosen for each state's specific adjustments.

California's treatment of the DRD has been particularly notorious. Briefly put, California had traditionally allowed a DRD for dividends that were paid out of income subject to California tax. If the dividends were received from a company that did not conduct business in California, and accordingly did not pay tax in California, no DRD was allowed. (The actual calculation involved deriving a percentage based on a ratio of apportioned income over the corporation's earnings and profits) The California Court of Appeals held in 2003 that California's position violated the Commerce Clause of the U.S. Constitution, because it discriminated against corporations that did not do business in California (see *Farmer Brothers v. Franchise Tax Board*, 108 Cal. App. 4th 976 (2003); rev. den. 8/27/03; cert. den. U.S.S. Ct., 2/23/04).

The Appeals Court in *Farmer Brothers* did not offer up what possible remedy there might be for California's unconstitutional DRD. The U.S. Supreme Court has provided that there are at least three possible remedies in this position: (1) a state could refund the taxes imposed on the discriminated victims; (2) the state could retroactively impose a tax on the beneficiaries of the decision to put them on an equal footing with the victims; or (3) some combination of the preceding two approaches (see *Fulton Corp. v. Faulkner*, 516 U.S. 325 (1996) and *McKesson Corporation v. Division of Alcoholic Beverages and Tobacco,* 496 U.S. 18 (1990)).

The Franchise Tax Board (FTB) decided to deny the DRD to all taxpayers, a position that was most beneficial financially for the state of California. The FTB took their position, in part, on the grounds that if any part of the law was unconstitutional, it all had to go. The FTB's position was upheld in *Abbott Laboratories v. Franchise Tax Board*, 175 Cal. App. 4th 1346 (Calif. 2009).

Although the battle may not be over, recent decisions continue to go against taxpayers. See, for example, *River Garden Retirement Home v. Franchise Tax Board*, 186 Cal. App. 4th 922 (2010), in which the taxpayer not only lost their dividends received deduction, but was subject to additional penalties for failing to take advantage of California's earlier amnesty program. Taxpayers may be wise to preserve their rights by filing protective refund claims for the taxes paid on dividend income.

TCJA: GILTI IRC Section 951A

This GILTI was created in Section 951A of the tax code by the TCJA in December 2017. This is a tax on any new foreign income that international companies earn.

States that allow a subtraction in whole or part are Colorado, Connecticut, Georgia, Illinois, Indiana, Iowa, Kentucky, Maine, Massachusetts, Michigan, Mississippi, New Hampshire, North Carolina, North Dakota, Oregon, and Virginia.

TCJA: Business interest expense IRC Section 163 (j)

This update altered the deductibility of business interest for some taxpayers. The vast majority of states currently have no adjustment to the deduction. The following states allow a subtraction when determining taxable income for the amount that exceeds the federal limit. Arizona, California, Connecticut, Georgia, Indiana, Minnesota, New Hampshire, South Carolina, Tennessee, and Wisconsin. Virginia allows a partial subtraction of 20% of the amount of interest that exceeds the federal limit.

Chapter 3

Filing Methods for Multistate Taxpayers

Learning objectives

- Distinguish among separate, consolidated, and combined filing.
- Identify the key cases defining a unitary relationship.
- Recognize the different unitary tests.
- Recognize the Multistate Tax Commission's (MTC) regulation on unitary relationships.

Introduction

If a corporation is, by itself or as a member of an affiliated group, doing business in more than one state, the tax practitioner must not only grapple with questions of nexus, but also the methodology for determining the taxpayer's tax base. In other words, for any specific state we must determine if we are filing separate company returns, a consolidated return, or a "combined" or "unitary" return.

Separate, consolidated, or combined filing

Separate filing means just that. Each company with nexus in the state must file its own separate return, regardless of whether it is part of an affiliated or consolidated group. There are a number of states that allow only separate filing, and as such, each and every company with nexus must file a separate return. It is irrelevant whether the corporation is a standalone entity or a member of a controlled, affiliated, or consolidated group. Those states requiring separate filing (some have a return for consolidated, but require each corporation to also file a return on a separate basis) include Alabama, Arkansas, Delaware, Florida, Georgia, Iowa, Louisiana, Maryland, Missouri, New Jersey, North Carolina, Oklahoma, Oregon, Pennsylvania, South Carolina, and Tennessee. Some states, such as Alabama, Arkansas, Florida, Iowa, Missouri, North Carolina, Oklahoma, Oregon, and South Carolina allow consolidated filing, but not combined. Other states, such as California, Idaho, Rhode Island, and Illinois, do not allow consolidated filing, but if applicable require combined filing. In some states a consolidated return is allowed, but it will only include those members of the affiliated group with nexus in the state. In fact, even among separate filing states, consolidated or combined filing may be required to "properly reflect income." That said, there may be a trend toward combined reporting. States have adopted combined reporting include Massachusetts, Michigan, New York, Texas, Vermont, and West Virginia. The combined reporting states now include Alaska, Arizona, California, Colorado, Connecticut, Hawaii, Idaho, Illinois, Kansas, Kentucky, Maine, Massachusetts, Michigan, Minnesota, Mississippi, Montana, Nebraska, New Hampshire, New Mexico, New York, North Dakota, Ohio, Rhode Island, Texas, Utah, Vermont, Virginia, West Virginia, Wisconsin, and the District of Columbia.

Separate filing has advantages and disadvantages. The most obvious disadvantage is that a company is prohibited from offsetting profitable subsidiaries with subsidiaries with losses. However, separate filing states offer advantages, where a multistate taxpayer can arrange its legal structure to isolate high-profit margin activities in low or no tax states, and its low-profit margin activities in states with higher tax rates. For example, isolating a company's sales and marketing functions from its manufacturing activities and conducting each in separate companies may allow shifting of income from high- to low-tax states.

Knowledge check

1. States that require separate returns for each company that is part of an affiliated or consolidated group actually

    a. Aggregate all income and loss items into the parent's return.
    b. Provide an advantage to groups that are able to isolate income and loss activities.
    c. Do not require each company with nexus to file a separate return.
    d. Can have some companies offset losses with companies that are profitable.

The majority of states, while allowing separate filing, will also permit consolidated filing if certain requirements are met. To elect consolidated filing, most states require the same stock ownership requirements (80%) as that of the federal consolidated rules (see IRC Sections 1501–1505 and accompanying regulations). In addition, a state may require that only the affiliated entities that have nexus with the state be part of the consolidated return (that is, a "nexus-consolidated" return). Consolidated filing may also be allowed or even required where separate filing does not fairly reflect a company's income or economic activities. Connecticut, Indiana, Mississippi, and Tennessee, for example, are generally separate filing states, but will permit or require consolidated and or combined filing where necessary to properly reflect income.

Combined reporting requires the members of a "unitary" group to calculate their taxable income on a "combined" or "unitary" basis. The combined or "unitary" reporting states include Alaska, Arizona, California, Colorado, Connecticut, District of Columbia, Hawaii, Idaho, Illinois, Kansas, Kentucky, Maine, Massachusetts, Michigan, Minnesota, Mississippi (elective), Montana, Nebraska, New Hampshire, New Mexico, New York, North Dakota, Ohio, Rhode Island, Texas, Utah, Vermont, West Virginia, and Wisconsin.

A combined report ignores the legal structure of a corporation or affiliated group to focus on the entities' underlying economic reality. If a group of companies are interrelated in certain specific ways, and function as one economic unit, they will be taxed as one entity, and any legal or geographic divisions or separations will be ignored. In other words, the focus is on whether there exists a single trade or business that can be viewed as a single economic enterprise. It does not matter if that single trade or business is conducted by various divisions of a single company, numerous subsidiaries of a parent company, or through a group of commonly owned or controlled corporations. Thus, even though a company may not have nexus with a particular state, its income and factors may be included in the tax base to which that state's apportionment formula is applied. If the business meets the unitary tests, the requisite connections for nexus under the Due Process and Commerce Clauses are deemed met. If there exists a single trade or business acting as a single unit, it will be required to file a combined report and taxed accordingly.

Note: The terminology can vary from state to state. For example, most states distinguish between consolidated and combined returns. However, Indiana, for example, uses the term "combined return" for what most states would call a consolidated return. It is also important to distinguish between a "combined report" and a "unitary return." Strictly speaking, there is no such thing as a "unitary return." The unitary concept, to be discussed in this chapter, is the underlying principle that requires taxpayers to file a "combined report." In addition, keep in mind that a "combined report" is not a tax return. In many states, each member of the combined group continues to file its own separate return, but does so based upon its share of income from the unitary group. For example, a company filing a separate return must still apportion its income among the states in which it does business. In short, separate filing states limit apportionment to a single legal entity, while combined reporting states apply apportionment to multiple entities in those instances where the unitary business is conducted by more than one single legal entity. So be careful with the terminology.

The following example illustrates the basic concepts of separate, consolidated, and combined filing.

An incredibly simplified example

Take three corporations: a parent and two wholly owned subsidiaries. The parent files a federal consolidated return with its subsidiaries. The parent and sub one are both doing business in, and have nexus with, State X. Sub two does not have any employees, property, or sales in State X. It is not doing business in State X, and accordingly does not have nexus with the state. Each company's income and state apportionment factors are as follows:

Corporation	Nexus in State X	Taxable Income	State X* Numerator	State X* Denominator	Apportionment Factor	Separate Filing	Consolidated Filing	Combined Filing
Parent	Y	300	40	400	10.00%	30	--	--
Sub One	Y	200	20	500	4.00%	8	--	--
Consolidated Total		500	60	900	6.67%	--	33	--
Sub Two	N	100	0	100	0.00%	--	--	--
Combined Total		600	60	1000	6.00%	--	--	36

*The numerator is the sum of the corporation's payroll, property, and sales in state X and the denominator is the corporation's payroll, property, and sales everywhere. The factors will be discussed in detail in chapter 5.

Separate filing

Parent	300 × 40/400	=	30
Sub One	200 × 20/500	=	8
Total taxable income			38

If State X allows only separate filing, the Parent and Sub One will each file a separate return, including only their own separate income and factors. Sub Two will not file a return in State X, because it is not doing business in State X, and does not have nexus with the State.

Consolidated filing

Parent and Sub One (nexus only)	500 × 60/900	=	33

If State X allows the filing of consolidated returns, but only among companies that have nexus with the State, the Parent and Sub One combine their respective income and apportionment factors to arrive at state taxable income. Again, because Sub Two does not have nexus with State X, it cannot file as part of the consolidated return.

Combined reporting

Parent and Sub One	600 × 60/1000	=	36

If State X allows or requires combined reporting, then the income and apportionment factors of all the affiliated companies are summed to calculate the state taxable income for the Parent and Sub One. There are several key points to be noted. First, the income and apportionment factors of Sub Two are included in the calculation even though Sub Two is not doing business in State X, and does not have nexus with the State. Second, combined reporting is not a return per se, but is rather a method for calculating the state taxable income of a "unitary" or "combined" group. Technically, State X is only taxing the Parent and Sub One, but they are measuring the tax base and factors of those two companies by including any other companies (Sub Two) that are deemed to be a part of the unitary group. As the Oregon Tax Court said, "[I]t is important to remember that including the income of a nontaxable member of a unitary group does not subject that income to taxation by Oregon. It merely provides the base from which the taxable corporation's share is apportioned." (*State Department of Revenue v. Penn Independent Corp.*, 15 Or. Tax 68, 74 (1999)). Combined reporting states differ in whether the Parent and Sub One will file a single return or each file separate returns, after calculating the group's combined income.

It is important to remember that a unitary worksheet or analysis, more commonly called a "combined report," is not a tax return. The point of unitary theory is to identify those segments that constitute a single economically integrated unity, whether they be individual corporations, divisions, or other entities, then combine their income and assign it to different states using a common apportionment factor. The combined report is simply a method to do that, and can be represented on a single return, separate returns for each entity, or even as an attachment to one or the other supporting the numbers on the returns themselves.

Finally, it is critical to distinguish between a federal consolidated return and a combined report. A consolidated federal return is a return made up of an "affiliated group," as that is defined in IRC Section 1504(a) consisting of a chain of corporations connected through stock ownership (more than 80% in value and voting power) with a common parent corporation. Certain corporations, such as insurance companies and foreign corporations, are not permitted to be part of a consolidated filing. A consolidated return is a method of *reporting* the taxable income of multiple corporations on a single return. A combined report is a method of *calculating* the taxable income of a unitary group. To be in a consolidated return, the entities must meet the definition of an affiliated group. However, to be in a combined report the entities must meet one of several unitary tests including the "three unities" test, the contribution and dependency test, or the tests of functional integration, economies of scale, and centralization of management (See the discussion to follow on *Butler Brothers, Edison Stores*, and *Mobil Oil*).

Combined reporting

It is important to note that the term unitary tax is a misnomer. Unitary tax is not a separate tax. In the context of state income tax, the term unitary simply refers to the principle, or tests, that define the tax base to which a state can apply its formulary apportionment. It is an accounting method for determining the taxable income base of a multistate business. Or, to put it more simply, it is a method of determining the amount to which a state can apply its apportionment formula. The approach was first used in the 19th century in property tax cases involving railroads and telegraphs. To use a simple example, the issue was how to measure the value of a railroad track crossing Kansas from Missouri to Colorado, where the whole is worth more than the sum of its parts. After all, the track's worth would be severely impaired if it ended at the Missouri/Kansas border and started up again at the Kansas/Colorado border. In 1875, the

U.S. Supreme Court held that the value of a railroad line depended upon the entire line as a unit, pointing out that each mile of track alone was worthless.

> A railroad must be regarded . . . as a unit . . . Destroy by any means a few miles of this track within [a jurisdiction and] its effect upon the value of the remainder of the road is out of all proportion to the mere local value of the part of it destroyed. . . . It may well be doubted whether any better mode of determining the value of that portion of the track within any one county has been devised than to ascertain the value of the whole road and apportion the value within the county by its relative length to the whole.

(*In re State Railroad Tax Cases*, 92 U.S. 575, 608 (1875).) For example, to calculate the appropriate property tax due from the railroad property within its boundaries, the city of Cheyenne determined the total value of the railroad line, not just the few miles within its jurisdiction. The city then computed the per mile value of the line in Cheyenne by dividing the total value of the railroad line by the total number of miles of line (*Union Pacific Railway v. Cheyenne*, 113 U.S. 516 (1884)). The unit method, as it was called in 1875, or the unitary theory, provides that the business activity in each state contributes to or enhances the activity of the whole entity, and therefore should be included in computing an assessment. In other words, forget corporate divisions, company lines, parents, and subs, and disregard geographic boundaries. The key to understanding combined reporting is two words: "economic unit." It is this existence of an economic unit, or unitary business, that determines whether a state can include income earned outside its borders in calculating the taxable income and tax to which it is entitled through apportionment. According to the U. S. Supreme Court, "the only reason for allowing a state to look beyond its borders when it taxes the property of foreign corporations is that it may get the true value of the things within it, when they are part of an organic system of wide extent, that gives them a value above what they would otherwise possess." (*Wallace v. Hines*, 253 U.S. 66, 69 (1920)).

The U. S. Supreme Court first directly acknowledged the application of the unitary method to state income taxation in *Bass, Ratcliff & Gretton, Ltd. v. State Tax Commission*, 266 U.S. 271 (1924), when it said:

> "So in the present case we are of the opinion that, as the Company carried on the unitary business of manufacturing and selling ale, in which its profits were earned by a series of transactions beginning with the manufacture in England and ending in sales in New York and other places — the process of manufacturing resulting in no profits until it ends in sales — the state was justified in attributing to New York a just proportion of the profits earned by the Company from such unitary business."

(See also, *Underwood Typewriter Co. v. Chamberlain*, 254 U.S. 113 (1920).) In addition to determining if separate accounting is appropriate, and whether the income or factors of non-nexus entities can be included in an apportionable tax base, the unitary concept has also been used to determine whether specific items, types, or categories of income such as interest income, dividend income, and capital gains, are deemed apportionable business income or allocable nonbusiness income.

> "The combined method, also known as unitary apportionment, is based on a recognition that an integrated business may operate through several separately incorporated entities. In such case,

> transactions between corporations under common control may lack economic substance; therefore, it is necessary to consider the corporate group as a whole. This method combines the income of all related business entities which are engaged in the same integrated or unitary business to arrive at net income base. A percentage of the net income base is then apportioned to the relevant taxing jurisdiction according to a formula which measures the contribution of the business activities within the taxing jurisdiction (e.g., Colorado) to the profit of the entire unitary business. This percentage of the net income base is then taxed by the state.[1]

The relationship between the unitary concept and a combined report can be confusing. A combined report is an accounting method used by a state to measure the taxable income of a single multistate corporation that is either conducting a unitary business, or is a member of a group of multistate corporations conducting a unitary business. As a consequence, the combined report may include affiliates that do not have nexus with the state. "Combined reporting is not designed to tax the income or other tax base of the nontaxable affiliates although taxpayers assert that the combined method frequently has that effect. The purpose of the combined report is to determine the income or other tax base of the in-state taxpayer by viewing the taxpayer as part of the unitary business, and applying the apportionment factors of the entire unitary business to the taxable net income of the unitary business." (J. Hellerstein & W. Hellerstein, *State Taxation,* ¶ 8.11[1] (3d ed. 2001)). The unitary concept is used to determine how divisions, operations, or parts of a single corporation do business in more than one state; or (1) to determine which commonly owned corporations are engaged in a unitary business, (2) the net income of that business, and (3) how to apportion that income.

Unfortunately, there is little agreement among the states as to what specifically constitutes a unitary group. (The MTC, in its efforts to promote state uniformity, has proposed a regulation defining a unitary business. The regulation is included at the end of this chapter.) The factors for defining what companies belong in a combined report have evolved over time and still remain unsettled. In fact, the unitary method, and its application, has traditionally not been defined by statute. It has been created by the courts, like the doctrines of economic substance and business purpose. Thus, the best approach to mastering this area is to follow the evolution of combined reporting through the landmark cases that have defined it.

[1] *Hewlett-Packard Co. v. State*, 749 P.2d 400, 401 (Colo. 1988).

The landmark cases

Let us begin with a couple of the old landmark cases. Although dated, these are still useful for understanding the history and context of the continuing disputes over the unitary method and combined reporting.

The three unities tests

Butler Brothers v. McColgan, 111 P.2d 334 (1941), aff'd, 315 U.S. 501 (1942)

Butler Brothers was an Illinois corporation selling wholesale dry goods and general merchandise. It had wholesale distributing houses in seven states, including one in San Francisco, California. "Each of its houses in the seven states maintains stocks of goods, serves a separate territory, has its own sales force, handles its own sales and all solicitation, credit and collection arrangements . . . [and] . . . keeps its own books of account." However, Butler did maintain a central buying division and allocated certain overhead expenses (executive salaries, accounting, and advertising) to each wholesale house. (Please note that these houses were controlled branches or divisions of Butler Brothers, not separate corporate entities.) The company filed its California return using separate accounting and reported a loss of $82,851 in California, while the overall company reported a profit of $1,149,677. California recomputed the company's income using a three-factor formula averaging the percentage of California payroll, sales, and property to total payroll, sales, and property. Using this formula, California figured that Butler Brothers taxable income in the state was a profit of $93,500. In the Supreme Court's first significant application of the unitary theory to an income tax case, it held two things. First, there did exist a unitary relationship among the branches based on "(1) unity of ownership; (2) unity of operation as evidenced by central purchasing, advertising, accounting and management divisions; and (3) unity of use in its centralized executive force and general system of operation." Second, the use of the three-part formula was not on its face unconstitutional; it was fairly calculated, and its assignment of income to California reasonably attributed to the business done there. The court acknowledged that the integrity of separate accounting need not be impeached, but it was up to the taxpayer to show by "clear and cogent evidence" that California's formula taxed extraterritorial values "out of all appropriate proportion to the business."

> "It is only if its business within this state is truly separate and distinct from its business without this state, so that the segregation of income may be made clearly and accurately, that the separate accounting method may property be used. Where, however, interstate operations are carried on and that portion of the corporation's business done within the state cannot be clearly segregated from that done outside the state, the unit rule of assessment is employed as a device for allocating to the state for taxation its fair share of the taxable values of the taxpayer."

Knowledge check

2. Unity of operation may be demonstrated by

    a. Central purchasing.
    b. System of operation.
    c. Preparation of affiliated group's tax return by parent.
    d. Identical address.

3. The unitary concept places importance on

    a. Legal structure.
    b. Economic structure.
    c. Control structure.
    d. Tax rates.

4. The majority of states will permit consolidated filing if the stock ownership requirements are the same as federal consolidated rules. What is this ownership requirement?

    a. 100%
    b. 90%
    c. 80%
    d. 50%

Observations

The *Butler Brothers* decision gives us our first definition of a unitary business, often called the three unities test. A business will be held to be operating a unitary business if there exists: (1) unity of ownership, (2) unity of operation, and (3) unity of use.

Unity of ownership has generally been defined as either direct or indirect ownership of more than 50% of a corporation's voting stock. A bright-line rule remains the clearest test in defining a unitary group. Generally, auditors examining unity of ownership will use not only the federal form 1120 and form 851 (affiliations schedule), but will examine for listed companies the SEC Form 10-Ks for the audit period.

Although usually the simplest of the unitary tests, even the unity of ownership test can vary from state to state. In the first example, A corporation owns 50% of B corporation and 25 percent of C corporation. B corporation owns 50% of C corporation. In many states, this would not qualify as a combined group, because the ownership percentage has to be more than 50%.

Example 3-1

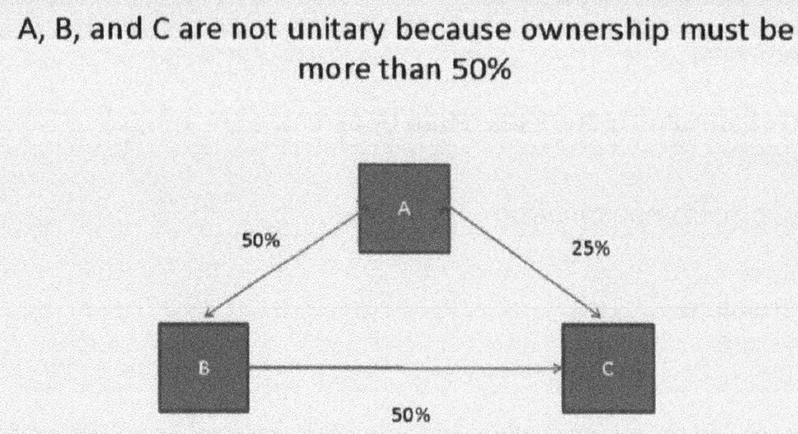

The second example, drawn from the California audit manual, is counterintuitive, but also illustrates a combined group. P provides the necessary ownership to meet the unity of ownership test, but itself is not unitary with its subsidiaries. However, that would not prevent the subsidiaries from qualifying as a unitary group.

Example 3-2

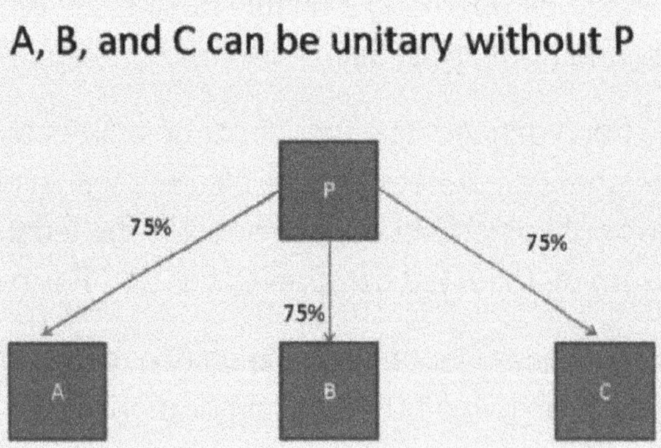

In jurisdictions that require that a unitary group be based on an affiliated group as defined in IRC Section 1504(a)(1), the following taxpayer cannot file a combined group, because it is an individual and an individual cannot be a member of an affiliated group under IRC Section 1504(a)(1). That said, in states that do not tie their definition of a unitary group to IRC Section 1504(a)(1), this arrangement might very well qualify as a combined group.

The difference between unity of operations and unity of use is not immediately apparent. A California court has described the difference this way: "Although there is not a clear demarcation between what is 'operation' and what is 'use,' in general it may be said that the acts falling within the category of 'operation' are the staff functions and those within 'use' are the line functions." (*Chase, Brass & Copper Co., Inc. v. Franchise Tax Board*, 10 Cal. App. 3d 496 (Calif. 1970), *cert denied*, 400 US 961 (1970)). Thus, the unity of operations test will be met if corporations share certain staff functions, such as purchasing, advertising, personnel, legal and accounting services, insurance, and employee benefit plans. Examples of staff functions that auditors will examine include the following:

- Centralized purchasing
  - The auditors will ask whether a centralized purchasing department exists and will probably review some purchase invoices, vendor lists, purchase contracts, and order requirements.
- Manufacture and intercompany sales of raw materials, parts, packaging, or other products
  - The auditors will review the intercompany accounts in the general ledger with some care both in volume and whether the transactions are essential to either the buyer or seller.
- Centralized or common advertising
  - The auditors will ask whether there is a centralized advertising department and whether the advertising is national or local in scope. They will also peruse the advertisements, looking for uniform trademarks or logos, and generally whether there is an emphasis in the advertising on a unitary identity.
- Equipment transfers
- Sharing of information, technology, patents, or other intangibles
- Centralized or common insurance programs, plans, or policies
- Common employee benefit and pension programs
  - The auditors will often review employee handbooks or personnel manuals to determine if there are common benefits and programs throughout the organizations.
- Centralized or common use of accounting, personnel, or legal staff.
  - Here, the auditors are looking for common accounting procedure manuals, uniform labor contracts, standardized forms, and whether there is a single legal department providing in-house counsel across companies and organizations.
- Intercompany loans, receivables, or financing
  - Intercompany financing can be used to integrate a conglomerate or to make it more diversified. As a consequence, it can be an element both for and against a unitary relationship. The auditors will look at the volume and importance of intercompany loans, the source and use of the funds, and the terms, guarantees, and collateral involved.

The staff functions must be significant. For example, a parent corporation's preparation of the affiliated group's corporate return is not an example of unity of operations. Every parent corporation probably engages in this activity. Thus, it is not a distinguishing feature of a unitary group. Centralized or common advertising is an activity that may or may not have any unitary significance. For example, the use of the same advertising agency by an affiliated group of corporations is hardly in and of itself evidence of a unitary relationship. However, if the advertising efforts are designed to create and maintain a single corporate identity or brand, then the centralized advertising is a meaningful unitary element.

Unity of use looks to whether there are shared line functions, such as a centralized management and "general system of operation." In other words, unity of use is present where there is integrated executive control exercised through the implementation of the business's major policies or direction. The development of vertical or horizontal business relationships to maximize profitability is an example of integrated executive control. An oil company that expands its operations from exploration and drilling through refining and distribution is an example of vertical integration. An oil refinery that expands by purchasing other refineries in the same market is an example of horizontal integration.

In practice, it is often difficult to distinguish between unity of operations and unity of use tests, let alone determine the quantity and quality of the activities that supposedly define the tests. It is not enough to simply list the elements of operations and use, or to apply the labels indiscriminately; there must be some substance to the tests for them to mean anything.

Nevertheless, *Butler Brothers* made it clear that a single company doing business in more than one state could not segregate its income geographically and file accordingly, where its activities were unified through use and operations.

Knowledge check

5. Under the *Butler Brothers* decision, which is a unity relationship that will establish that a business is operating a unitary business?

   a. Unity of ownership.
   b. Unity of intent.
   c. Ownership of 50% of voting stock.
   d. Unity of address.

The contribution/dependency tests

Edison California Stores v. McColgan, 176 P.2d 697, on rehearing 183 P.2d 16 (Cal. 1947)

Edison Stores took the *Butler* decision one step further. If anyone wondered after *Butler Brothers* whether the decision would have been different if the separate stores in the various states had been separate corporations, *Edison* answered that question with a resounding, "no." The *Edison Stores* decision provided that the unitary concept, applied to a single company with branches in different states, can also be applied to a group of corporations (subsidiaries) with one parent corporation. "Thus the business is unitary regardless of the fact that in the *Butler Brothers* case there was but one corporation involved, owning as parts of the unitary system seven different branches in as many states, and that in the present case there is a parent corporation owning and controlling as units of one system fifteen different branches organized as corporations in as many states. No difference in principle is discernible."

Edison also added a new test to the three unity tests of ownership, operation, and use proffered by *Butler Brothers*. The court wrote that "[i]f the operation of the portion of the business done within the state is dependent upon or contributes to the operation of the business without the state, the operations are unitary; otherwise, if there is no such dependency, the business within the state may be considered to be separate."

Observations

Edison Stores is important for illustrating that a company's legal structure will not protect it from a state's taxing powers, where the company or companies act as one economic unit. This case represents a key step because the unitary concept is applied to an affiliated group, rather than just the divisions or segments of a single corporation.

Edison Stores also added a new unitary test, the contribution or dependency test. Thus, if the operations of a business in a state are dependent upon or contribute to the business operations outside the state, the business may be taxed as a single economic unit. Examples often cited as illustrative of dependency or contribution often overlap with the three unities test, and include intercompany sales, loans, and line and staff activities. As with the three unities tests, measuring and defining what constitutes dependency and contribution in any distinguishable sense has been difficult.

It is not necessary that a company meet both the three unities test and the contribution or dependency test. The courts have confirmed that they are alternative tests, and that only one of the two must be met. (See *A.M Castle & Co. v. Franchise Tax Board*, 36 Cal. App. 4th 1794 (Calif. 1995).)

Knowledge check

6. Which is a new unitary test that was created by the *Edison Stores* case?

    a. The contribution or dependency test.
    b. The factors of profitability test.
    c. The three unities test.
    d. Single sales factor test.

Factors of profitability test

In addition to the three unities tests and the tests of contribution and dependency, the Supreme Court has offered a factors of profitability test for defining a unitary group.

Mobil Oil Corporation v. Vermont, 445 U.S. 425 (1980)

In *Mobil Oil*, Vermont included in the state's apportionable income the dividend income from Mobil's foreign subsidiaries. Vermont added the dividend income to its tax base, holding that it had a right to do so because the subsidiaries and affiliates from which the dividend income was received were unitary with Mobil Oil. In other words, the dividend income was business (apportionable) income because of the unitary relationship between the parent and the foreign subs.

Mobil naturally disagreed, arguing that the dividends were not subject to Vermont tax under either the Due Process Clause or the Commerce Clause. First, despite a unitary relationship there was no "minimum connection" as required by due process between Vermont, Mobil's management of its investments, or the business activities of the payor corporations; second, taxing the dividends "would create an unconstitutional burden of multiple taxation," because New York, as the state of domicile, could tax the entire dividend income; and finally, the foreign source of the dividend income created a risk of international multiple taxation.

The court rejected all of Mobil's arguments, stating in a now famous line, "the linchpin of apportionability in the field of state income taxation is the unitary business principle." Because there existed "factors of profitability," defined as "functional integration, centralization of management, and economies of scale," Mobil Oil was to be treated as a unitary entity, thereby making the income subject to apportionment. The fact that New York could tax the same income was irrelevant, because in fact, it did not. Additionally, the risk of international multiple taxation was also irrelevant, because that risk existed for all income, not just dividend income.

> "[T]he linchpin of apportionability in the field of state income taxation is the unitary principle . . . what appellant must show, in order to establish that its dividend income is not subject to an apportioned tax in Vermont, is that the income was earned in the course of activities unrelated to the sale of petroleum products in that State . . . appellant has made no effort to demonstrate that the foreign operations of its subsidiaries and affiliates are distinct in any business or economic sense from it petroleum sales activities in Vermont . . . Indeed, all indications in the record are to the contrary, because it appears that these foreign activities are part of appellant's integrated petroleum enterprise."

Finally, the court made it clear that its decision was not all encompassing. "Where the business activities of the dividend payor have nothing to do with the activities of the recipient in the taxing State, due process considerations might well preclude apportionability, because there would be no underlying unitary business."

Exxon Corp. v. Wisconsin, 447 U.S. 207 (1980)

Exxon, like *Mobil Oil*, involved the "state taxation of the income of a vertically integrated corporation doing business in several States." Exxon divided its operations into three categories (marketing, exploration and production, and refining), accounting for each separately. In fact, Exxon argued that the three categories represented three unitary businesses. The company's only activity in Wisconsin was marketing (which produced losses in the state), and Exxon attempted to report only those activities to Wisconsin. The company believed that its separate accounting of its three activities was sufficient to justify separate treatment for state tax purposes. "In order to exclude certain income from the apportionment formula, the company must prove that 'the income was earned in the course of activities unrelated to the sale of petroleum products in the State.' The court looks to the 'underlying economic realities of a unitary business,' and the income must derive from unrelated business activity, which constitutes a 'discrete business enterprise.'"

Exxon apparently failed to convince the court that sufficient distortion existed. The court held that Exxon's facts failed this test, stating that while "such evidence may be helpful," it is in no sense conclusive. Instead, the court found that Exxon was a "highly integrated business which benefits from an umbrella of centralized management and controlled interaction." Accordingly, "if a company is a unitary business, then a State may apply an apportionment formula to the taxpayer's total income in order to obtain a 'rough approximation' of the corporate income that is 'reasonably related to the activities conducted within the taxing State.'" In other words, instead of having three unitary businesses, the court told Exxon that what they really had were three operating functions of a single unitary business.

Taxpayer victories

After *Mobil Oil* and *Exxon*, some doubted that taxpayers could ever convince a court that a state's assertions of a unitary group or use of an apportionment method could ever be successfully challenged. Then, the *ASARCO* and *Woolworth* decisions breathed new life into the debate.

ASARCO Inc. v. Idaho, 458 U.S. 307 (1982)

At first blush, this case looks just like another *Mobil Oil* case. Again, you have a nondomiciliary state (this time Idaho, not Vermont) trying to include dividends from foreign subsidiaries in its tax base. ASARCO was a New Jersey corporation domiciled in New York. It mined, smelted, and refined nonferrous metals including gold, silver, copper, lead, and zinc. It operated a silver mine in Idaho, and the state attempted to include dividend, interest, and capital gain income derived from ASARCO's ownership in five subsidiary corporations in its apportionable (business) income.

Six other wholly owned subsidiaries were included as unitary, but were not part of the appeal. The appeal was limited to the inclusion of the dividend, interest, and capital gain income from the five subsidiaries in which ASARCO owned only a majority interest. This is an important point. When including the six wholly owned subs as unitary, Idaho pulled into the combined return their income and payroll, property, and sales factors. In the five majority owned subs, however, Idaho was pulling in only the income, and not the factors. As a consequence, Idaho's apportionable income increased without any accompanying dilution from the foreign subsidiaries' factors. Many taxpayers, then and now, have reacted to these kinds of attempts by crying "No taxation without factor representation."

Idaho tried to argue that it was unnecessary to show that the subsidiaries were unitary with their parent to satisfy due process limitations. The court rejected Idaho's attempt, stating that the facts as presented simply did not support a unitary relationship. "In this case . . . the record establishes that each of the . . . subsidiaries in question operated a 'discrete business enterprise' having 'nothing to do with the activities of [ASARCO] in the taxing state.'" In other words, *Mobil Oil* still stands and the dividend payor must be engaged in a unitary business with the dividend recipient. Further, it rejected Idaho's attempt to change the definition of a unitary business.

Idaho's proposal is that corporate purpose should define unitary business. It argues that intangible income should be considered a part of a unitary business if the intangible property (the share of stock) is "acquired, managed or disposed of for purposes relating or contributing to the taxpayer's business." Idaho asserts that "it is this integration — that is, between the business use of the intangible asset (the shares of stock) and ASARCO's mining, smelting, and refining business — which makes the income part of the unitary business."

This definition of unitary business would destroy the concept. The business of a corporation requires that it earn money to continue operations and to provide a return on its invested capital. Consequently, all of its operations, including any investment made, in some sense can be said to be "for purposes related to or contributing to the [corporation's] business." When pressed to its logical limit, this conception of the "unitary business" limitation becomes no limitation at all.

F.W. Woolworth Co. v. New Mexico, 458 U.S. 354 (1982)

This case was decided with *ASARCO* and involved the same question — Can a nondomiciliary state (New Mexico, this time) pull dividend income from foreign subsidiaries in as taxable income?

Woolworth owned retail chain stores throughout the United States. It also owned four foreign subsidiaries (three of them wholly owned) with stores in Germany, Canada, Mexico, and England. The four subsidiaries paid Woolworth approximately $40m in dividends and the question before the court was if New Mexico could tax those dividends as part of the apportionable income of the U.S. parent. The court found that the facts did not sustain a unitary relationship:

> "We conclude, on the basis of undisputed facts, that the four subsidiaries in question are not a part of a unitary business under the principles articulated in *Mobil* and *Exxon*, and today reiterated in *ASARCO*. Except for the type of occasional oversight — with respect to capital structure, major debt, and dividends — that any parent gives to an investment in a subsidiary, there is little or no integration of the business activities or centralization of the management of these five corporations."

The important point about this case is that, like *Mobil Oil*, the payors of the dividend income were in the same line of business as the parent, but the relationship between them was not unitary. Although there was certainly a potential to be unitary, potentiality is not enough. "But the *potential* to operate a company as part of a unitary business is not dispositive when, as here, the dividend income from the subsidiaries in fact is derived from unrelated business activity of the subsidiaries, each of which operates a discrete business enterprise." Instead, "the proper inquiry looks to 'the underlying unity or diversity of business enterprise' not to whether the nondomiciliary parent derives some economic benefit — as it virtually always will — from its ownership of stock in another corporation."

There was some comment in the case that the state of New Mexico just did not do a good job developing its facts. Perhaps it was easier, in *Mobil* and *Exxon* to find a unitary business because those companies were manufacturers (the first two of oil, the latter of beer), not retailers.

Finally, Justices O'Connor, Rehnquist, and Blackmun issued a strong dissent, arguing that because the dividend income constituted passive investment income, it was unnecessary for the subsidiaries to be part of a unitary business with ASARCO. For example, even ASARCO admits that Idaho can tax the interest earned on short-term investments of its working capital. Then why not income from its long-term investments? As Justice O'Connor points out, ASARCO would certainly be quick to claim apportionable interest expense on its long-term investments. To be consistent, it should also claim the income.

Flow of value test and worldwide combination

The *Container* decision discussed subsequently is important for two things. First, it gave us a fourth, and so far, final, test for measuring the existence of a unitary business, and second, it held that state efforts at requiring combined reporting did not stop at the water's edge of the United States.

Container Corporation of America V. Franchise Tax Board, 103 S.Ct. 2933 (1983)

The Supreme Court holds that the unitary concept can be extended to include foreign subsidiaries in a combined report. California recalculated Container's income tax on a combined basis pulling in its foreign subs (including their sales, property, and payroll factors). The court found that California's reliance on intercompany loans, "advice and consultation regarding manufacturing techniques," cost accounting, agency relationship in purchasing equipment, and technical service help was sufficient to support unitary treatment. "We need not decide whether any one of these factors would be sufficient as a constitutional matter to prove the existence of a unitary business. Taken in combination, at least they clearly demonstrate that the state court reached a conclusion "within the realm of permissible judgment."

Container argued that combined reporting resulted in double taxation, prohibited the federal government from speaking with one voice in international taxation, and in any event, California had an obligation in international tax to use the arm's length analysis used by the federal and other foreign governments. For example, Container pointed out that because property and labor costs in foreign countries were often lower than in the United States, the use of formulary apportionment utilizing those factors inevitably led to double taxation. The court rejected this argument, noting that "of course, even the three-factor formula is necessarily imperfect. But we have seen no evidence demonstrating that the margin of error . . . inherent in the three-factor formula is greater than the margin of error . . . inherent in the sort of separate accounting urged upon us by appellant." Thus, "it would be perverse, simply for the sake of avoiding double taxation, to require California to give up one allocation method that sometimes results in double taxation in favor of another allocation method that also sometimes results in double taxation."

Observation

There are two points of note. First, worldwide combination. Second, the court seems to back away from the factors of profitability tests set down in *Mobil*. After all, given the facts of the case and applying the standards of functional integration, centralization of management, and economies of scale, Container is arguably less unitary than *ASARCO* and *Woolworth*. In any case, the decision is not particularly helpful in clearing the ambiguity created between the *Mobil/Exxon* unitary holdings and the *ASARCO/Woolworth* nonunitary holdings. The court said that there need not be a flow of product to have a unitary relationship; a "flow of value" is sufficient. Is a flow of value the same thing as the factors of profitability? If not, what is it?

Knowledge check

7. Which of the tests for measuring the existence of a unitary business was analyzed and discussed in the *Container Corporation of America* case?

    a. The dependency or contribution test.
    b. The flow of value test.
    c. The factors of profitability test.
    d. The three unities test.

The court was to revisit worldwide combination one more time over a decade later in *Barclays Bank.*

Barclays Bank plc and Colgate-Palmolive Company v. Franchise Tax Board, 115 S.Ct. 2268 (1995)

In *Container,* the court declined to say if its application of worldwide combination applied also to corporations with foreign parents. The answer is yes. Here, the court holds that the U.S. Constitution does not prohibit worldwide combined reporting. The court noted that Congress had had 11 years to respond to its decision in *Container,* and failed to do so. Thus, if their decisions frustrated foreign policy under the Foreign Commerce Clause, it remained for Congress to correct.

Despite this decision, most states, because of political pressure from businesses and other countries, have backed away from mandatory worldwide combined reporting. Instead, most combined reporting is limited to water's edge combination. California has made worldwide combined reporting elective since 1988 as have Idaho, Montana, North Dakota, and Utah. Other states, such as Illinois and Colorado, limit combined reporting to water's edge, by prohibiting the inclusion of what is called 80/20 corporations. 80/20 corporations are defined as companies that have 80% or more of their business activities outside of the United States. The 80% measurement is usually a combination of the company's payroll and property factors. Alaska is the only state to require worldwide combined reporting, and even that is limited to the oil and gas industry.

Should the unitary business principle be abandoned?

Allied-Signal v. Director of Taxation, 112 S.Ct. 2251 (1992)

Allied-Signal was the successor-in-interest to the Bendix Corporation. During the 1970s, Bendix had acquired 20.6% of the stock of ASARCO, only to sell it back to ASARCO in 1981 for a $211.5m gain. (Yes, this is the same ASARCO as in *ASARCO v. Idaho*.) The question before the court was if New Jersey could apportion the gain. Both Allied-Signal and New Jersey stipulated that Bendix and ASARCO "were unrelated business enterprises each of whose activities had nothing to do with the other." In other words, there was no unitary relationship. Applying the factors of profitability (functional integration, centralization of management, and economies of scale), the court found that "there is no serious contention that any of the three factors upon which we focused in *Woolworth* were present. Functional integration and economies of scale could not exist because . . . the parties stipulated [they] were unrelated business enterprises." Finally, "there was no centralization of management." Thus, New Jersey could not tax the gain because (1) Bendix and ASARCO were not engaged in a unitary business and (2) the gain was from an investment function and not an operational function.

Given the stipulation that the businesses were unrelated enterprises, New Jersey advanced a new argument; that is, "that the unitary business principle must be abandoned in its entirety, arguing that a nondomiciliary State should be permitted 'to apportion all the income of a separate multistate corporate taxpayer.'" The court rejected New Jersey's suggestion, pointing out that "New Jersey's sweeping theory cannot be reconciled with the concept that the Constitution places limits on a State's power to tax value earned outside of its borders."

Perhaps responding to Justice O'Connor's dissent in *ASARCO*, the court did try to distinguish between short- (operational) and long-term investments, and the application of the unitary concept. "We agree that the payee and the payor need not be engaged in the same unitary business as a prerequisite to apportionment in all cases. *Container Corp.* says as much. What is required . . . is that the capital transaction serve an operational rather than an investment function. "The existence of a unitary relation between payee and payor is one justification for apportionment, but not the only one." The court cited short-term deposits that form a part of working capital as an example of income that may be apportioned even where no unitary relationship exists. "The existence of a unitary relation between the payor and the payee is one means of meeting the constitutional requirement . . . we did not purport, however, to establish a general requirement that there be a unitary relation between the payor and the payee to justify apportionment, nor do we do so today."

In Justice O'Connor's dissent in *Allied-Signal*, she claimed that to maintain that a unitary relationship was the only foundation for a state to include foreign income in its apportionable tax base was doctrinal foot fault. It seems evident in *Allied-Signal* that the court took notice of that criticism when it wrote that "taxation of investment income received from a nondomiciliary taxpayer's investment in another corporation requires only that the investment income be sufficiently related to the taxpayer's in-state business, not that the taxpayer's business and the corporation in which it invests be unitary." Thus, while the unitary business principle may be the linchpin of apportionability, it is not the only linchpin. So just when we thought things were becoming clearer, they are not.

Nevertheless, if we remain confused, it is not the court's fault. "If lower courts have reached divergent results in applying the unitary business principle to different factual circumstances, that is because, as we have said, any number of variations on the unitary business theme "are logically consistent with the underlying principles motivating the approach, and also because the constitutional test is quite fact-sensitive." Indeed.

Observation

Short-term out-of-state investments can be apportioned by the nondomiciliary state without a unitary relationship between the payor and payee, as long as the investments are unitary, in that they serve an operational function.

Let us sum up the unitary tests as laid out by the U.S. Supreme Court. They include the following:

- The three unities tests:
  - Unity of ownership
  - Operation
  - Use
- The dependency/contribution test
- The factors of profitability tests:
  - Functional integration
  - Centralization of management
  - Economies of scale
- The flow of value test

One commentator, Franklin C. Latcham, has observed that "the difficulty with such tests, however, is that they are so vague that they can have different meanings for different courts when applied to similar fact situations."

MeadWestvaco Corp. v. Illinois, 553 U.S. 16 (2008)

On April 15, 2008, the U.S. Supreme Court handed down its long-awaited decision on the relationship of the unitary concept and the operational function or operational purpose test. The issue before the court was whether Illinois could tax a portion of the $1bn capital gain arising from the sale of Meadwestvaco's (Mead) corporate division, Lexis/Nexis. (*Meadwestvaco Corp. v. Illinois*, 553 U.S. 16 (2008)).

Mead had purchased Lexis/Nexis (then part of Data Corporation) in 1968, and in the years since, Lexis-Nexis had been held by Mead as a separate corporate subsidiary, then a division, then a subsidiary, and then a division again when it was sold in 1994. Mead reported the sale as nonbusiness income allocable to its state of domicile, Ohio. Illinois took the position upon audit that the gain was apportionable business income, and assessed Mead roughly $4m in tax and penalties.

The Cook County Circuit Court held that while Mead and Lexis-Nexis were not unitary, the gain was nevertheless apportionable business income, not allocable nonbusiness income, because "Lexis served an operational function in Mead's business." The Illinois Appellate Court affirmed the lower court's decision citing several factors for holding that Lexis served an operational function in Mead's business. Specifically, the appellate court pointed out that, in addition to be being wholly owned, "Mead had exercised its control over Lexis in various ways, such as manipulating its corporate form, approving significant capital expenditures, and retaining tax benefits and control over Lexis' free cash." Since the court found that the operational function test was met, it did not address whether Mead and Lexis were part of a unitary business. After the Illinois Supreme Court declined to hear the case, Mead appealed to the U.S. Supreme Court who heard the case on January 16, 2008.

The Supreme Court ruled in Mead's favor, holding that "the state courts erred in considering whether Lexis served an 'operational purpose' in Mead's business after determining that Lexis and Mead were not unitary." After tracing a history of the unitary business concept, the court said that the lower court's reading of Allied-Signal had been mistaken. "Our decisions . . . did not announce a new ground for the constitutional apportionment of extra state values in the absence of a unitary business. Because the

Appellate Court of Illinois interpreted those decisions to the contrary, it erred." In fact, the court said, "Our references to 'operational function' . . . were not intended to modify the unitary business principle by adding a new ground for apportionment. The concept of operational function simply recognizes that an asset can be a part of a taxpayer's unitary business, even if what we may term a 'unitary relationship' does not exist between the 'payor and payee.'"

It seems that while the court did not simply discard the operational function test, it certainly limited its scope. "Whereas here, the asset in question is another business; we have described the 'hallmarks' of a unitary relationship as functional integration, centralized management, and economies of scale." In other words, once the courts had stipulated that a unitary relationship, based on the traditional tests, did not exist, that its stipulation was sufficient for determining whether the gain was business or nonbusiness.

The *Meadwestvaco* decision will have significant ramifications for both asset and corporate dispositions. First, many tax advisers and tax administrators, as well as the Illinois Appellate Court, believed that Allied-Signal had established a separate alternative unitary test that involved distinguishing between operational versus investment functions. The Mead Court has made it plain that that is simply not the case. In fact, that fact may be the most significant consequence of the Mead decision — that the gain on a sale of a business, whether as an asset or stock sale, is to be determined solely by the traditional unitary tests articulated in *Butler Brothers*, *Edison Stores*, *Mobil Oil*, *Woolworth*, and *Container*. To that extent, the court has added some clarity. However, since the appellate court, unlike the circuit court, did not address whether a unitary relationship existed, the Supreme Court said the appellate court "may take up that question on remand," and declined to express an opinion on whether there was indeed a unitary relationship between Mead and Lexis-Nexis. In brief, the court held that the sale of Lexis-Nexis could not be apportioned to Illinois based on the operational test; it is still an open question whether the gain could be apportioned to Illinois based on the traditional unitary tests, and the lower court was free to examine that issue upon remand.

Summarizing the cases

In *Butler Brothers,* the court found a single business activity of apportionable income, where there was one corporation with multiple stores. In *Edison Stores,* the court found a single business activity of apportionable income where there were multiple corporations. In *Exxon,* the court rejected the taxpayer's argument that they had three separate business activities housed in a single corporation. Instead, the court found that Exxon had a single unitary business activity.

The courts were then confronted with another question. Does apportionable income include intangible income such as dividends, interest, royalties, and rents? The answer, found in *Mobil Oil*, *ASARCO*, and *Woolworth,* is that if the intangible income is a part of the taxpayer's unitary business activities connected to the state, it is subject to apportionment. Where there is no unitary connection, as in *Allied-Signal*, the intangible income (capital gain) cannot be taxed. Finally, the courts were asked whether the unitary principle applied to foreign entities and operations, thereby becoming part of a state's apportionable income. Again, the answer was yes. If there exists a unitary relationship between the in-state and out-of-state business activities, the income is apportionable, regardless of whether the taxpayer is a domestic (*Container*) or foreign (*Barclays Bank*) parent with subsidiaries.

In every instance, the determining focus is not company lines, geographic boundaries, corporate divisions, or legal entities, but whether there is a link between the state and the business activity, or income, it seeks to tax. As the U.S. Supreme Court said in *Mobil Oil*, "the linchpin of apportionability in the field of state income taxation is the unitary principle."

Pulling it all together

It is not unusual at this point to be overwhelmed with the various interpretations, applications, definitions, and case law of what is, or is not, unitary.

Perhaps, it will help to focus on what it is that the various courts are trying specifically to define. In brief, it is this: A state can only tax the income connected to that state. In other words, the courts are trying to determine just what income should be apportioned among the states. What a state must show is that there is some link, some connection, between it and the business activity or income it seeks to tax. As the New Mexico Department of Revenue points out in its audit manual, "In general, a business will be considered to be unitary when the operations conducted in one state benefit and are benefited by the operations conducted in another state and if its various parts are so interdependent and of such mutual benefit that they form one integral business." In short, the key concept to keep in mind is whether there is a single, integrated, business activity (think railroad) in which the activity is so integrated and indivisible that the whole is greater than the sum of its parts — that is what all the tests are trying to determine — in measuring the income of a specific state, what we have to include to properly reflect that income.

Multistate Tax Commission

In addition to the previously mentioned cases, there is one other influential national voice addressing the unitary business concept, and that is the MTC. The MTC is an organization originally formed in 1967 by Florida, Illinois, Kansas, Nevada, New Mexico, Texas, and Washington when they adopted the Multistate Tax Compact. The MTC's function is to be an advocate on the part of its members by facilitating taxpayer convenience and compliance, performing joint audits on behalf of its members, advising legislative and administrative bodies, and promoting uniformity.

In 2004, the MTC adopted a model regulation defining a unitary business as

> a single economic enterprise that is made up either of separate parts of a single business entity or of a commonly controlled group of business entities that are sufficiently interdependent, integrated and interrelated through their activities so as to provide a synergy and mutual benefit that produces a sharing or exchange of value among them and a significant flow of value to the separate parts.

The MTC went on to indicate that just as several corporate entities could make up a single unitary group, more than one unitary group could be within a single entity.

The MTC regulation looks primarily to the U.S. Supreme Court's factors of profitability tests for determining a unitary relationship. As discussed previously, these tests include functional integration, centralization of management, and economies of scale. (See Multistate Tax Commission, Proposed Model Statute for Combined Reporting (July 29, 2011).)

Chapter 4

Apportionment and Allocation

Learning objectives

- Distinguish between apportionment and allocation.
- Identify the differences between business and nonbusiness income.
- Recognize the two tests of business and nonbusiness income.
- Identify how to handle the problem areas of rental income, gains and losses, intangible property, interest, and dividend income.

Introduction

A company doing business in more than one state really has only three alternatives for sorting out what income goes to what state. They are (1) separate accounting, (2) allocation, and (3) apportionment. As we have seen from looking at case law, separate accounting has gone the way of the horse and buggy whip. That leaves allocation and apportionment, and both methods are used in consolidated and combined filing. Allocation refers to income that is specifically assigned to a particular state. Apportionment is the sourcing of income based upon some formula, usually a combination of the company's payroll, property, and sales.

Current rules

Today's rules regarding apportionment and allocation originated in the 1950s through the efforts of state representatives. In 1957, these representatives, through the National Conference of Commissioners, drafted the Uniform Division of Income for Tax Purposes Act (UDITPA). The goal of UDITPA was to promote uniformity among the states in the allocation and apportionment of multistate corporate income. Currently, some 30 states have adopted UDITPA in whole or in part, and even in those states that have not specifically adopted UDITPA, its influence is obvious.

The scope of UDITPA is contained in Section 2, which provides that "any taxpayer having income from business activity which is taxable both within and without this state, other than activity as a financial organization or public utility or the rendering of purely personal services by an individual, shall allocate and apportion his net income as provided in this Act." Thus, all taxpayers, except for individuals, banks, and public utilities, are generally included within UDITPA's scope.

Knowledge check

1. In reference to the Uniform Division of Income for Tax Purposes Act (UDITPA), which statement is correct?

    a. Currently, all states have adopted the UDITPA.
    b. The purpose of the UDITPA was to promote uniformity among the states in the allocation and apportionment of multistate corporate income.
    c. UDITPA is mandatory for all states.
    d. Currently, 25 states have adopted the UDITPA.

Right to apportion

Before a company determines how to apportion and allocate its income, it must first determine if it indeed has the right to apportion its income. Section 3 of UDITPA provides that a taxpayer has the right to apportion if it is subject to tax in more than one state.

> For purposes of allocation and apportionment of income under this act, a taxpayer is taxable in another state if (1) in that state he is subject to a net income tax, a franchise tax measured by net income, a franchise tax for the privilege of doing business, or a corporate stock tax, or (2) that state has jurisdiction to subject this taxpayer to a net income tax regardless of whether, in fact, the state does or does not.

The key point to note here is that a taxpayer need not actually have to pay a tax to another state. It is sufficient that the state has the right to tax the taxpayer. For example, if my company is doing business in both Wyoming and Colorado, I can apportion my income between the two states, despite the fact that Wyoming has no income tax. Because I am doing business in the state, and Wyoming has the right to tax my income, it simply has decided not to do so. Do you have to file in every state to apportion income to that state? No. UDITPA only requires that a taxpayer be doing business "without this state." In other words, I need only be subject to tax in one other state in order to apportion among all the states in which I have activity.

> Griffins-R-Us is headquartered in Colorado, but does business in Kansas, Oklahoma, and Wyoming as well. Griffins need only be subject to tax in one of the three states other than Colorado to have the right to apportion income among all the states.

Must a company actually file returns in another state to allocate or apportion its income? Not necessarily. The Massachusetts Tax Board has ruled that it is only necessary that the company be "subject to tax," not that the company had actually filed. (See *Amray, Inc. v. Commissioner*, No. 119875 (Mass. App. Tax Bd., April 17, 1986).) Although it may be unconstitutional to do so, many states hold that filing in another state where it is not required to file is insufficient to establish the right to apportion, even if the filing was through neglect, ignorance, materiality, or uncertainty about filing requirements. As a practical matter, many auditors will not allow a company to apportion and allocate its income unless it can show it is filing returns in other states. (See, for example, *Technical Assistance Advisement* 95(C)1-008, Fla. Dept. of Rev., August 30, 1995.) In fact, the Multistate Tax Commission's (MTC) regulations require that a taxpayer provide proof that a tax return was filed in another state. Failure to provide that proof, such as the returns, is sufficient to disallow the taxpayer's right to apportion. (See MTC Reg. IV.3.(b).(1) and *Appeal of Olga Company*, Calif. SBE, 84-SBE-092 (June 27, 1984).) Moreover, filings with a Secretary of State, or other license fees, are often deemed insufficient. Fees are not taxes, and many auditors will not allow apportionment unless the fee is based on net income or capital, and not simply a registration or licensing payment. Query — Is the payment of a state's minimum tax sufficient? It is not clear under UDITPA whether the payment of a minimum tax would be sufficient to establish taxability. The MTC regulations attempt to distinguish between payments to a state that are revenue raisers and those that are not. If the payments raise revenue, then they qualify as a tax, thereby allowing the taxpayer to apportion income. Thus fees, which are generally regulatory, will not qualify; whereas payments that end up in the state's general fund, will probably meet the test.

Under UDITPA Section 1(h), foreign countries fall within the definition of a "state" and thus the same test, "taxable in another state," applies to both other states and other countries. It is often unclear, however, whether a state will allow apportionment when the taxpayer has a presence in another country, but the income is not taxed because of a treaty between the United States and that country.

Business versus nonbusiness income

Now that we have determined UDITPA's scope and established the right to apportion, what is it that a taxpayer can apportion? The answer is "business income," a seemingly innocuous term, which has prompted continuing battles between taxpayers and tax administrators. Here is the UDITPA definition of business income:

> "Business income" means income arising from transactions and activity in the regular course of the taxpayer's trade or business and includes income from tangible and intangible property if the acquisition, management and disposition of the property constitute integral parts of the taxpayer's regular trade or business operations.

Nonbusiness income is unhelpfully defined as all income other than business income. Furthermore, the MTC, which has incorporated the UDITPA provisions within its own compact and regulations, holds that there is a presumption that income is business income. "The income of a taxpayer is business income unless clearly classifiable as nonbusiness income."

Knowledge check

2. In reference to business-versus-nonbusiness income under the UDITPA, which statement is correct?

    a. The income of a taxpayer is nonbusiness income, unless it is clearly classifiable as business income.
    b. Business income can come from either tangible or intangible property.
    c. The nature or source of income aids in determining whether income is business or non-business.
    d. Business income can only come from tangible property.

Why is this distinction between business or nonbusiness income significant? First, because for most states, business income is subject to *apportionment* among the states while nonbusiness income is *allocable* to a specific state, usually the taxpayer's state of commercial domicile. Of course, not all states follow this distinction. Some states specifically allocate certain identified types of income, and other states apportion all income.

In July 2014, the MTC amended its definition of business income by replacing the term "business income" with "apportionable income" and "nonbusiness income" with "nonapportionable income." In addition, the MTC broadened the definition of apportionable income to include all income apportionable under the U.S. Constitution. The new definition reads as follows:

"Apportionable income" means:

1. all income that is apportionable under the Constitution of the United States and is not allocated under the laws of this state, including:
    a. income arising from transactions and activity in the regular course of the taxpayer's trade or business, and
    b. income arising from tangible and intangible property if the acquisition, management, employment, development, or disposition of the property is or was related to the operation of the taxpayer's trade or business; and
2. any income that would be allocable to this state under the Constitution of the United States, but that is apportioned rather than allocated pursuant to the laws of this state.

"Nonapportionable income" is unhelpfully defined as all income other than apportionable income.

Nevertheless, this recommended in change in definition is welcomed, if only for adding clarification and uniformity to the state's various definitions of "business income." I say "recommended" because each individual state must specifically adopt the MTC's language into its own statutes through legislative action. Thus, for our purposes here, I will continue to use the terms "business income" and "nonbusiness income."

One test or two

Read the definition of business income again. Does the definition contain just one test for business income, or are there two? The single-test advocates emphasize the phrase "activity in the regular course of a taxpayer's trade or business" and see the balance of the paragraph as an elaboration of the regular activity of the business. The two-test advocates argue that the word "and" separates a "transactional test" from a "functional test." That is, business income includes what the single-testers embrace and other income "from tangible and intangible property if the acquisition, management, and disposition of the property constitute integral parts of the taxpayer's regular trade or business operations." In brief, the transactional test refers to the routine, recurring, regular income-producing activities of the business, while the functional test looks to whether there is an integral relationship between a company's assets and its income-producing activities.

The MTC has proposed regulations that define the two tests.

Transactional test

". . . If the transaction or activity is in the regular course of the taxpayer's trade or business, part of which trade or business is conducted within [this State], the resulting income of the transaction or activity is business income for [this State]. Income may be business income even though the actual transaction or activity that gives rise to the income does not occur in [this State]."

Functional test

Business income also includes income from tangible and intangible property if the acquisition, management, and disposition of the property constitute integral parts of the taxpayer's regular trade or business operations.

Under the functional test, business income need not be derived from transactions or activities that are in the regular course of the taxpayer's own particular trade or business. It is sufficient, if the property from which the income is derived is or was an integral, functional, necessary, or operative component to the taxpayer's trade or business operations, part of which trade or business is or was conducted within this State [MTC Prop. Regs. IV(a)(3) and (4)]. Most states hold that if either of the tests are satisfied, the income will be considered business income.

An oft-quoted example illustrating the difference between the "transactional" and "functional" tests is the sale of a factory. Under the "transactional test," the sale would probably be deemed nonbusiness income. After all, selling a factory is an unusual, nonrecurring, extraordinary event not usually considered part of a company's regular daily transactions in the course of trade or business. However, under the "functional test," the gain or loss on the factory sale would probably be deemed business income because the factory had been used as an integral part of the company's regular trade or business.

The continuing disputes in this area are then first, the distinction between business and nonbusiness income; and second (a subset of the first), does the business income definition have one or two tests? Most states today have settled the second question either through litigation or legislation holding that the definition has both tests. See, for example, *Gannett Satellite Information Network Inc. v. Department of Revenue*, 201 P.3d 132 (Mont. 2009), where the state's supreme court held that Montana's statute contained both tests. That said, there are still states that adhere to the belief that the definition includes only a single transactional test. Kimberly-Clark Corporation, a multinational company that manufactures and sells paper products, sold one of its Alabama pulp mills and reported the gain as apportionable business income. The company's commercial domicile is in Alabama, and the state's Department of Revenue held that the gain was nonbusiness income under the transactional test, therefore completely allocable to Alabama. The Alabama Supreme Court agreed, holding that the gain was an extraordinary transaction unrelated to the taxpayer's ordinary and regular course of business and therefore allocable nonbusiness income (*Kimberly Clark Corp. v. Alabama*, 69 So.3d 144 (Al. 2010)). (Alabama has since enacted legislation expanding its definition of business income effectively overruling both *Kimberly Clark* and an earlier case, *Ex parte Uniroyal Tire Company*, 779 So.2d 227 (Ala. 2000).

The question of whether California has only a transactional test or a functional test was decisively answered in *Hoechst Celanese Corporation v. Franchise Tax Board*, 22 P.3d 324, (Cal. 2001), *cert denied*, 534 U.S. 1040 (2001). The court held that the definition of business income contained both a transactional and a functional test. As mentioned, the trend among most states is to move toward two tests for defining business income. In the past several years Alabama, Georgia, Kansas, Minnesota, Mississippi, New Jersey, North Carolina, Oregon, and Pennsylvania have all enacted legislation specifically broadening their definitions of business income.

The following example illustrates the importance of this seemingly ideological dispute among tax practitioners and tax administrators.

Example 4-1

Salem Company does business in both State X and State Y. It sold one of its logging mills in State X for $13m. State X believes the definition of business income contains only the transactional test and deems the sale to be nonbusiness income, and therefore allocates the entire gain to itself. After all, Salem Company is not in the business of selling its mills, and this is the first sale of a mill in over 15 years. State Y, which believes there is both a transactional and functional test in the definition of business income, holds that the sale meets the functional test. State Y accordingly apportions some of the gain to itself. As a consequence, Salem is paying tax on more than 100% of the sale of the mill. The total sale is getting taxed by State X and a portion of that same sale is being apportioned to State Y to be taxed.

Attempts to define business versus nonbusiness income

Sometimes it is easy to determine business income. For example, the sale of inventory. The problem areas are in what is often called passive income. For example, interest income from temporary investments of working capital used to purchase additional inventory would probably be business income. But interest income from long-term investments is not so easy to classify.

Several state audit manuals provide general guidelines for their auditors in distinguishing between business and nonbusiness income. Business income generally includes the following:

- Income from investments that were made in stocks, bonds, and loans for the purpose of securing a supply source or market
- Income from either short- or long-term investments of working capital
- Income from patents, copyrights, and trademarks that have been either developed or purchased by the taxpayer and used in its business
- Income traceable to reserves for the seasonal cycling or fluctuations of the taxpayer's business
- Income from investments in either horizontal or vertical business expansion, such as the creation of subsidiaries, partnerships, or joint ventures that are linked to the same line of business or industry
- Income from commonly owned and controlled corporations
- Income from the disposition of investments that produced business income while held by the taxpayer

Nonbusiness income generally includes the following:

- Income from surplus funds invested in activities or businesses unrelated to that of the taxpayer.
- Income from business activities that are unrelated to the taxpayer's core business. For example, rental income from farm land owned by a manufacturer
- Income from the disposition of investments that produced nonbusiness income while held by the taxpayer

UDITPA provides for the allocation of five types of nonbusiness income to specific states. They are rents, royalties, capital gains, interest, and dividends.

Section 4. Rents and royalties from real or tangible personal property, capital gains, interest, dividends, or patent or copyright royalties, to the extent that they constitute nonbusiness income, shall be allocated as provided . . .

The MTC has issued regulations interpreting UDITPA to read that all "income of the taxpayer is business income unless clearly classifiable as nonbusiness income." The burden of proof is put upon the taxpayer to show that the income is nonbusiness.

According to the MTC, what you may call the income is irrelevant. "The classification of income by the labels occasionally used, such as manufacturing income, compensation for services, sales income, interest, dividends, rents, royalties, gains, operating income, nonoperating income, and so on, is of no aid in determining whether income is business or nonbusiness income." Instead, MTC's proposed amendments to its regulations provide that "business income means income of any type or class, and from any activity, that meets the relationship described either [as] the 'transactional test,' or the 'functional test.'"

Problem areas

Rental income

The MTC regulations provide that if the property giving rise to the rental or royalty income is used in or incidental to the taxpayer's trade or business (included in the property factor), it is business income. The MTC regulations offer the following seven examples:

Example 1:	The taxpayer operates a multistate car rental business. The income from car rentals is business income.
Example 2:	The taxpayer is engaged in the heavy construction business in which it uses equipment such as cranes, tractors, and earth-moving vehicles. The taxpayer makes short-term leases of the equipment when particular pieces of equipment are not needed on any particular project. The rental income is business income.
Example 3:	The taxpayer operates a multistate chain of men's clothing stores. The taxpayer purchases a five-story office building for use in connection with its trade or business. It uses the street floor as one of its retail stores, and the second and third floors for its general corporate headquarters. The remaining two floors are leased to others. The rental of the two floors is incidental to the operation of the taxpayer's trade or business. The rental income is business income.
Example 4:	The taxpayer operates a multistate chain of grocery stores. It purchases as an investment an office building in another state with surplus funds and leases the entire building to others. The net rental income is not business income of the grocery store trade or business. Therefore, the net rental income is nonbusiness income.
Example 5:	The taxpayer operates a multistate chain of men's clothing stores. The taxpayer invests in a 20-story office building, uses the street floor as one of its retail stores, and the second floor for its general corporate headquarters. The remaining 18 floors are leased to others. The rental of the 18 floors is not incidental to, but rather is separate from the operation of the taxpayer trade or business. The net rental income is not business income of the clothing store trade or business. Therefore, the net rental income is nonbusiness income.
Example 6:	The taxpayer constructed a plant for use in its multistate manufacturing business and 20 years later, the plant was closed and put up for sale. The plant was rented for a temporary period from the time it was closed by the taxpayer until it was sold 18 months later. The rental income is business income and the gain on the sale of the plant is business income.
Example 7:	The taxpayer operates a multistate chain of grocery stores. It owned an office building that it occupied as its corporate headquarters. Because of inadequate space, the taxpayer acquired a new and larger building elsewhere for its corporate headquarters. The old building was rented to an investment company under a five-year lease. Upon expiration of the lease, the taxpayer sold the building at a gain (or loss). The net rental income received over the lease period is nonbusiness, and the gain (or loss) on the sale of the building is nonbusiness income.

Examples 3 and 5 illustrate the subjective nature of defining business income. In example 3, the rental of two floors is deemed incidental to the taxpayer's trade or business, and the rental income is classified as business income. However, in example 5, the rental of 18 floors is deemed not incidental and therefore classified as nonbusiness income. Query: At what point between the rental of 2 and 18 floors does the rental income transition from business to nonbusiness income? The question is not entirely facetious. It is clear that the driver in the example is materiality, but materiality is hardly sufficient as a concept that will allow a taxpayer to properly classify income as business or nonbusiness income.

Query: By definition, is passive income nonbusiness income? According to the Wisconsin Court of Appeals, passive income from equipment rentals was allocable to the equipment's location (in this case, Minnesota), and was unrelated to the taxpayer's regular printing and publishing business (*Wisconsin v. Citizens Publishing*, 520 N.W.2d 110 (1994)).

Gains and losses from real or tangible personal property dispositions

Sales of property inspire some of the most controversial arguments between taxpayers and tax administrators over business or nonbusiness income. States that adhere to the one-test interpretation of business income will not pick up a sale of property, unless the taxpayer is regularly engaged in such sales. The two-test states find the sale to meet the "functional test" and will pick it up as apportionable business income. As a consequence, the taxpayer is faced with the threat of double taxation.

The MTC states are two-test believers. "Gain or loss from the sale, exchange or other disposition of real property or of tangible or intangible personal property constitutes business income if the property while owned by the taxpayer was used in the taxpayer's trade or business."

MTC examples include the following:

Example 1:	In conducting its multistate manufacturing business, the taxpayer systematically replaces automobiles, machines, and other equipment used in the business. The gains or losses resulting from those sales constitute business income.
Example 2:	The taxpayer constructed a plant for use in its multistate manufacturing business, and 20 years later sold the property at a gain while it was in operation by the taxpayer. The gain is business income.
Example 3:	Same as example 2, except that the plant was closed and put up for sale, but was not, in fact, sold until a buyer was found 18 months later. The gain is business income.
Example 4:	Same as example 2, except the plant was rented while being held for sale. The rental income is business income, and the gain on the sale of the plant is business income.
Example 5:	The taxpayer operates a multistate chain of grocery stores. It owned an office building that it occupied as its corporate headquarters. Because of the inadequate space, taxpayer acquired a new and larger building elsewhere for its corporate headquarters. The old building was rented to an unrelated investment company under a five-year lease. Upon expiration of the lease, taxpayer sold the building at a gain (or loss). The gain (or loss) on the sale is nonbusiness income, and the rental income received over the lease period is nonbusiness income.

Please note in the previous examples, that the sale of a plant held for 18 months is business income, but the sale of a facility owned and leased for five years is nonbusiness income. The principle used to make that distinction is unclear and not addressed.

The MTC move towards full apportionment is clearly evident in some of the examples provided in their newly promulgated regulation. For example,

Example (i): Taxpayer purchases a chain of 100 retail stores for the purpose of merging those store operations with its existing business. Five of the retail stores are redundant under the taxpayer's business plan, and are sold six months after acquisition. Even though the five stores were never integrated into the taxpayer's trade or business, the income is apportionable because the property's acquisition was related to the taxpayer's trade or business.

Example (ii): Taxpayer is in the business of developing adhesives for industrial and construction uses. In the course of its business, it accidentally creates a weak but nontoxic adhesive and patents the formula, awaiting future applications. Another manufacturer uses the formula to create temporary body tattoos. Taxpayer wins a patent infringement suit against the other manufacturer. The entire damages award, including interest and punitive damages, constitutes apportionable income.

Income from asset sales has traditionally been one of the most debated areas in distinguishing business from nonbusiness income. The following are some of the more well-known decisions, and well illustrate the scope of this ongoing area of contention:

Phillips Petroleum Co. v. Iowa, 511 N.W.2d 608 (Iowa 1993).

Phillips sold a significant percentage of its assets to raise funds to purchase its own stock in an attempt to fend off a hostile takeover. None of the assets were located in Iowa. The court ruled that Iowa's definition of business income had only a transactional test. The "unprecedented" and once-in-a-lifetime nature of the sale indicated that it was clearly not transactional in nature, and thus the gain was nonbusiness income allocated outside of Iowa. The Iowa legislature immediately amended the state statute to include a functional test.

Firstar Corp. v. Commissioner of Revenue, 575 N.W.2d 835 (Minn. 1998).

A Wisconsin-based bank sold its headquarters' building and the Minnesota court ruled that all the gain is allocated to Wisconsin as nonbusiness income. Rather than running the justices out of town on a rail, the Minnesota legislature simply amended the statute to tax all the income it can constitutionally tax.

Laurel Pipeline Co. v. Commonwealth, 615 A.2d 841 (Pa. 1994).

The Pennsylvania Supreme Court found that the Pennsylvania statute contains both a transactional and functional test for determining business income. Nevertheless, the sale of a pipeline was nonbusiness income. The pipeline had been unused for three years, and the proceeds were distributed as a dividend. Because the pipeline was not an integral part of the business, the sale did not meet the functional test; and, because the company was not in the business of selling pipelines, the sale did not meet the transactional test. Thus, it was allocable nonbusiness income. Compare *Laurel Pipeline* to *Texaco-Cities Service Pipeline Co. v. McGaw*, 695 N.E.2d 481 (Ill. 1998). In *Texaco-Cities Service,* the Illinois Supreme Court ruled that because the sale proceeds from the sale of pipeline were reinvested in the business, and because the Illinois statute had both transactional and functional tests, the sale was apportionable business income. Although the gain was from a complete liquidation or termination of the business and the proceeds were distributed to the shareholders, the Illinois Supreme Court has ruled that the gains were nonbusiness income. (See *Blessing/White Inc., v. Zehnder*, 768 N.E.2d 332 (Ill. 2002) and *American States Insurance Co. v. Hamer*, 816 N.E.2d 659 (Ill. 2004).)

Patents, copyrights, and trademarks

Some states allocate intangible income from patents, copyrights, and trademarks to the taxpayer's commercial domicile; many more apportion the income. The MTC regulations offer the following three examples of how it believes this income should be treated:

Example 1:	The taxpayer is engaged in the multistate business of manufacturing and selling industrial chemicals. In connection with that business, the taxpayer obtained patents on some of its products. The taxpayer licensed the production of the chemicals in foreign countries, in return for which the taxpayer receives royalties. The royalties received by the taxpayer are business income.
Example 2:	The taxpayer is engaged in the music publishing business and holds copyrights on numerous songs. The taxpayer acquires the assets of a smaller publishing company, including music copyrights. These acquired copyrights are thereafter used by the taxpayer in its business. Any royalties received on these copyrights are business income.
Example 3:	Same as example 2, except that acquired company also held the patent on a method of producing digital audio recordings. The taxpayer does not manufacture or sell digital audio recordings. Any royalties received on the patent would be nonbusiness income.

Knowledge check

3. More states deem intangible income from patents, copyrights, and trademarks as

   a. Apportionable among the states in which the business operates.
   b. Allocable to the business's domiciliary state.
   c. Allocable among the states in which the business operates.
   d. Nontaxable income.

Interest income

UDITPA provides that interest income is business income if the underlying intangible was acquired, maintained, and disposed of as an integral part of the taxpayer's trade or business. The MTC's regulation reflects its consistently pro-apportionment stance. "Interest income is business income where the intangible with respect to which the interest received arises out of or was created in the regular course of the taxpayer's trade or business operations or where the purpose for acquiring and holding the intangible is related to or incidental to such trade or business operations."

The MTC regulations offer the following six examples:

Example 1:	The taxpayer operates a multistate chain of department stores, selling for cash and on credit. Service charges, interest, or time-price differentials and the like are received with respect to installment sales and revolving charge accounts. These amounts are business income.
Example 2:	The taxpayer conducts a multistate manufacturing business. During the year, the taxpayer receives a federal income tax refund and collects a judgment against a debtor of the business. Both the tax refund and the judgment bore interest. The interest income is business income.
Example 3:	The taxpayer is engaged in a multistate manufacturing and wholesaling business. In connection with that business, the taxpayer maintains special accounts to cover such items as workers' compensation claims, rain and storm damage, machinery replacement, and the like. The monies in those accounts are invested at interest. Similarly, the taxpayer temporarily invests funds intended for payment of federal, state, and local tax obligations. The interest income is business income.
Example 4:	The taxpayer is engaged in a multistate money order and traveler's check business. In addition to the fees received in connection with the sale of the money orders and traveler's checks, the taxpayer earns interest income by the investment of the funds, pending their redemption. The interest income is business income.
Example 5:	The taxpayer is engaged in a multistate manufacturing and selling business. The taxpayer usually has working capital and extra cash totaling $200,000, which it regularly invests in short-term interest-bearing securities. The interest income is business income.
Example 6:	In January, the taxpayer sold all the stock of a subsidiary for $20,000,000. The funds are placed in an interest-bearing account, pending a decision by management as to how the funds are to be used. The interest income is nonbusiness income.

Observation

Example 6 is an excellent example of an item that often receives contrary treatment by states. It is not unusual for one state to argue that the income is business income and apportionable, while another state, following the MTC's lead, holds that the interest income is nonbusiness income. However, this may change in light of the MTC move toward full apportionment, as is evident from the new examples from the Commission's newly proposed apportionment regulation:

Example (i): A manufacturer purchases raw materials to be incorporated into the product it offers for sale. The nature of the raw materials is such that the purchase price is subject to extreme price volatility. To protect itself from extreme price increases (or decreases), the manufacturer enters into future contracts pursuant to which the manufacturer can either purchase a set amount of the raw materials for a fixed price, within a specified time period, or resell the future contracts. Any gain on the sale of the future contracts would be considered apportionable income, regardless of whether the contracts were either made or resold in [this State].

Example (ii): A national retailer produces substantial revenue related to the operation of its trade or business. It invests a large portion of the revenue in fixed income securities that are divided into three categories; (*a*) short-term securities held pending use of the funds in the taxpayer's trade or business; (*b*) short-term securities held pending acquisition of other companies or favorable developments in the long-term money market, and (*c*) long-term securities held as an investment.

> Interest income on the short-term securities held pending use of the funds in the taxpayer's trade or business (*a*) is apportionable because the funds represent working capital necessary to the operations of the taxpayer's trade or business. Interest income derived from the other investment securities ((*b*) and (*c*)) is not apportionable as those securities were not held in furtherance of the taxpayer's trade or business.

Siegel-Robert, Inc. v. Johnson, Tenn. Ct. App., Dkt. No. M2008-02228-COA-R3-CV (10/28/2009).

The Tennessee Court of Appeals held for the taxpayer, in holding that interest income from Treasury securities was not apportionable business income, but allocable nonbusiness income taxable to Missouri, not Tennessee. The taxpayer successfully showed that the income was unrelated to its Tennessee operations and served as an investment, not an operational, function.

W.R. Grace v. Commissioner, Mass. App. Tax Bd. Dkt. No. C271787, (4/06/2009)

Keep in mind that there must be a unitary relationship, or else the income cannot be apportioned. The taxpayer was able to convince the Massachusetts Appellate Tax Board that dividend and interest income received from affiliates was not apportionable business income, because there was no unitary relationship between the taxpayer and its affiliates.

Home Interiors and Gifts, Inc. v. Illinois, 741. 2d 998 (2000), app. den. Ill. S.Ct. 2001

Home Interiors was a Texas corporation that had generated enough cash to not only cover its working capital needs, but also to invest in short-term certificates of deposit, commercial paper, and municipal bonds, while awaiting a better economic environment to expand its operations or business investments. The company had interest income of roughly $7.7 million in 1989 and $11 million in 1990 that it allocated to Texas as nonbusiness income. Illinois auditors believed that the interest income was business income, and apportioned some of it to that state, arguing that the funds were available for business investment, and were not separately segregated from the Company's operational funds. The Illinois Appellate Court ruled in favor of Home Interiors, holding that the mere availability of the funds, as opposed to their use, was insufficient to render the interest business income rather than nonbusiness income. The company had treated the funds as investment funds, not operational funds, and reported them as such on its financial statements. In addition, the company had paid tax to Texas on all of its interest income from the investments.

Appeal of Consolidated Freightways, 2000-SBE-001 (September 14, 2000)

Consolidated Freightways received $281 million from the sale of a subsidiary that it invested in short- and long-term securities while awaiting the opportunity to use the funds to expand its transportation business. Although it was seven years before it used the funds to acquire another transportation company, the fact that the company engaged in an active and ongoing effort to acquire another transportation company, and that the funds were "earmarked" for acquisition of a specific business purchase convinced the California State Board of Equalization that the interest income from the funds was business income. See also *Appeal of Cullinet Software, Inc.*, 95-SBE-002 (May 4, 1995).

Income from stock sales

Income from the sale of stock continues to be one of the most litigated areas in the business or nonbusiness income arena. Of course, the landmark case in this area is *Allied Signal* (discussed in the previous chapter), in which the U.S. Supreme Court held that New Jersey could not tax the gain on a sale of stock, because there was no unitary relationship between the entities and the gain was not from business operations, but from nonbusiness investments. The following three decisions reflect some of the ongoing differences in this area of contention:

In re Chief Indus., Inc., 875 P.2d 278 (Kan. 1994).

The Kansas Supreme Court ruled that the Kansas statute contains only a transactional test, not a functional test. Thus, the gain on the sale of a subsidiary's stock was nonbusiness income and allocable outside of Kansas. The Kansas legislature very quickly amended the state statute to include a functional test.

Ex Parte Uniroyal Tire Co., 779 So.2d 227 (Ala. 2000)

The Alabama Supreme Court ruled that the sale of a partnership interest was not business income because the state statute had only a transactional test. The court found that the transactional test does not apply to the complete termination or liquidation of a business. The fact that the underlying assets were used to generate business income was deemed irrelevant. The Alabama legislature overruled the decision in 2002 by changing the state statute.

Appeal of Crane Co, SBE, Dkt. No. 357027 (11/02/2009)

The California State Board of Equalization held that because the income from a stock sale served an operational rather than an investment function, the gain was business income subject to apportionment. (Is this consistent with the Supreme Court's position in the Meadwestvaco decision discussed at the end of the prior chapter?)

Dividend income

Dividend income has presented a conundrum ever since *Mobil Oil and Asarco* (see discussion in previous chapter). In *Mobil Oil,* dividend income, because Mobil's operations were held to be unitary, was held to be business income apportionable to Vermont. In *Asarco,* the Court held that dividend income could not be apportionable business income in the absence of a unitary relationship. The MTC regulations predictably provide that dividends are business income "where the stock with respect to which the dividends are received arises out of or was acquired in the regular course of the taxpayer's trade or business operations or where the purpose for acquiring and holding the stock is related to or incidental to such trade or business operations."

The MTC provides the following six examples:

Example 1:	The taxpayer operates a multistate chain of stock brokerage houses. During the year, the taxpayer receives dividends on stock it owns. The dividends are business income.
Example 2:	The taxpayer is engaged in a multistate manufacturing and wholesaling business. In connection with that business, the taxpayer maintains special accounts to cover such items as workers' compensation claims, and the like. A portion of the monies in those accounts is invested in interest-bearing bonds. The remainder is invested in various common stocks listed on national stock exchanges. Both the interest income and any dividends are business income.
Example 3:	The taxpayer and several unrelated corporations own all of the stock of a corporation whose business operations consist solely of acquiring and processing materials for delivery to the corporate owners. The taxpayer acquired the stock to obtain a source of supply of materials used in its manufacturing business. The dividends are business income.
Example 4:	The taxpayer is engaged in a multistate heavy construction business. Much of its construction work is performed for agencies of the federal government and various state governments. Under state and federal laws applicable to contracts for these agencies, a contractor must have adequate bonding capacity, as measured by the ratio of its current assets (cash and marketable securities) to current liabilities. To maintain an adequate bonding capacity, the taxpayer holds various stocks and interest-bearing securities. Both the interest income and any dividends received are business income.
Example 5:	The taxpayer receives dividends from the stock of its subsidiary or affiliate, which acts as a marketing agency for products manufactured by the taxpayer. The dividends are business income.
Example 6:	The taxpayer is engaged in a multistate glass manufacturing business. It also holds a portfolio of stock and interest-bearing securities, the acquisition and holding of which are unrelated to the manufacturing business. The dividends and interest income received are nonbusiness income.

Arizona Hearing Officer Decision, Case No. 201100309 (Az. Bd. Tax App. 10/29/2012)

Dividend and interest income generated by an investment account that was not used in the taxpayer's regular course of business was allocable nonbusiness income.

In re Appeal of 20th Century-Fox Film Corporation, No. 83A-860-MW, 1989 Cal. Tax LEXIS 7 (1989).

A stock dividend received from a subsidiary engaged in bottling soft drinks was nonbusiness income, because the subsidiary was not managed as an integral part of the company's regular trade or business. See also *In re Appeal of Willamette Industries, Inc.* No. 83A-291-MW, 1989 Cal. Tax LEXIS 8 (1989), where dividend income earned by subsidiaries, before they became unitary with the parent, was deemed nonbusiness income. Where the subsidiary is unitary with the parent, dividend income is business income. See *In the Matter of the Appeal of Rio Doce Limited*, No. 402204 (Calif. SBE 11/17/2010).

Liquidations

It is difficult to see at first how going out of business can be business income, but the functional test in the definition of business income includes "the acquisition, management, and disposition of the property [that] constitute integral parts of the taxpayer's regular trade or business operations." The language seems to refer only to partial liquidations, or the disposal of parts of a business's operations, rather than a complete liquidation. Several state decisions have indicated that complete liquidations where the funds are not reinvested, but distributed to the shareholders, will be treated as nonbusiness income. Nevertheless, California has treated complete liquidations as business income, arguing that the taxpayer has wrongly focused on the nature of the transaction, rather than on the fact that the assets were an integral part of the business operations, thereby meeting the functional test of business income.

Jim Beam Brands Co. v. California, 133 Cal. App. 4th 514, 34 Cal. Rptr. 2d 874 (1st Dist. 2005)

Jim Beam acquired, managed, and later disposed of the stock of a subsidiary, Taylor Foods, and distributed the proceeds from the disposition, rather than use them in its other operations. Beam reported the income as nonbusiness income. The California court rejected Beam's treatment, arguing that under the functional test, if an asset generated business income prior to its disposition, it should also generate business income upon its disposition.

For other cases adopting a business liquidation exception to the functional test, for Illinois see *Blessing/White Inc., v. Zehnder*, 768 N.E.2d 332 (Ill. 2002); *American States Insurance Co. v. Hamer*, 816 N.E.2d 659 (Ill. 2004); and *National Holdings, Inc. v. Zehnder*, 369 3d 977 (Ill. App. Ct., 2007); for Ohio, see *Kemppel v. Zaino*, 746 N.E.2d 1073 (2001); and for North Carolina, see the following discussion of *Lenox v. Tolson*.

Lenox v. Tolson, 548 S.E. 2nd 513 (2001)

Lenox, a New Jersey company that manufactured various consumer products, sold its fine jewelry division and distributed the proceeds to its sole shareholder, the parent company. Because the jewelry division was segregated both functionally and financially from the rest of the company's operations, and because the sale represented the cessation of the company's involvement with jewelry, Lenox treated the sale as nonbusiness income. The North Carolina Department of Revenue disagreed with this treatment, and argued instead that the proceeds were apportionable business income under the functional test in the definition of business income. Both the North Carolina Court of Appeals and the Supreme Court held for the taxpayer, emphasizing that in addition to the transaction and functional tests, one had to look at the "totality of the circumstances," and that doing so dictated that Lenox was correct in treating the proceeds as nonbusiness income.

For states that have rejected a business liquidation exception, for Oregon see *Crystal Communications, Inc. v. Department of Revenue,* 297 P.3d 1256 (Ore. 2013); for Arizona, see *Harris Corp. v. Arizona*, 312 P3d 1143 (Az. Ct. App. 2013); and for Pennsylvania, see *Glatfelter Pulpwood Company v. Pennsylvania*, 19 A.3d 572 (Pa. Commw. Ct. 2011) *aff'd by* 61 A.3d 993 (Pa. 2013).

Other income

Companies often receive income or receipts from other than sales, interest, dividends, rent, or royalties. The following well-known cases illustrate yet again the widely divergent views and approaches to business or nonbusiness income issues.

Polaroid Corp. v. Offerman, 507 S.E. 2d 284 (NC 1998), *cert. denied*, 526 US 1098 (1999).

Polaroid received millions of dollars in damages in a successful patent infringement suit. Was it business income? "Yes," at least according to the North Carolina Supreme Court. The court held that North Carolina law contains both transactional and functional tests and that "once a corporation's assets are found to constitute integral parts of the corporation's regular trade or business, income resulting from the acquisition, management, and/or disposition of those assets constitutes business income regardless of how that income is received." As a consequence, the damage award was treated as apportionable business income. (Note that this decision seems to conflict with the court's later holding in Lenox.)

Union Carbide Corp. v. Offerman, 526 S.E. 2d 167 (NC 2000).

The North Carolina Supreme Court found that pension plan reversion income does not meet the functional test of the state's two tests for business income. The pension was not an integral or essential functional part of the company, because Union Carbide held only a contingent property right to the income in the event of termination. In addition, the assets of the fund were not used in any transactional sense, so they were not used to generate sales, used as working capital, used for purchases, used in research and development, or used as collateral. The question of how to treat pension reversion income was also addressed in *Hoechst Celanese Corporation v. Franchise Tax Board*, 22 P.3d 324 (Cal. 2001), *cert. denied*, 534 U.S. 1040 (2001).

Pennzoil Co. v. Department of Revenue, 33 P.3d 314 (Ore. 2001), *cert. denied*, 535 US 927 (2002).

Texaco paid Pennzoil $3bn in settlement for Texaco's wrongful interference with Pennzoil's attempt to acquire Getty Oil Company. The Oregon Supreme Court held that the income was business income under the transactional test because Pennzoil's contract negotiations with Getty were part of its regular business and served an "operational function."

Section 338(H)(10)

Taxpayers and tax advisors all too often focus on the federal advantages of a particular transaction, and fail to pay proper attention to its state income tax consequences. Making an IRC Section 338(h)(10) election is often one of those circumstances. IRC Section 338 provides that parties to a corporate acquisition may elect to treat a qualified stock purchase "as if" it was an asset purchase, providing for the step-up in the basis of the assets of the acquired corporation. Although Section 338 provides for two ways to achieve this purpose, the most popular is probably a Section 338(h)(10) election. If the election requirements are met, the stock sale is disregarded for federal income tax purposes, and the purchaser gets a stepped-up basis in the deemed asset sale. Because most states that piggyback off federal taxable income generally conform to the 338 rules, the key question at the state level is whether the gain from the deemed asset sale is apportionable business or allocable nonbusiness income.

States holding that the 338(h)(10) gain is allocable nonbusiness income include Illinois, Minnesota, Missouri, New Jersey, Pennsylvania, and Utah. (See *Nicor Corp. v. Dep't of Revenue*, Nos. 1-07-1359 & 1-09-1591 (Ill. App. Ct. Dec. 5, 2008) and *Am. States Ins. Co. v. Hamer*, 816 N.E.2d 659 (Ill. App. Ct. 2004); *Nadler v. Commissioner of Revenue*, No. 7736R (Minn. Tax Ct. Apr. 21, 2006); *ABB C-E Nuclear Power, Inc. v. Dir. of Revenue*, 215 S.W.3d 85 (Mo. 2007); *McKesson Water Products Co. v. Div. of Tax.*, 974 A.2d 443 (N.J. Super. Ct. App. Div. 2009); *Canteen Corp. v. Commonwealth*, 854 A.2d 440 (Pa. 2004); *Commonwealth v. Osram Sylvania, Inc.*, 863 A.2d 1140 (Pa. 2004); and *Chambers v. State Tax Comm'n*, No. 050402915 (D. Utah Jan. 25, 2007), *vacated by joint motion*, No. 2007-467-SC (UT 2008).)

States holding that the 338(h)(10) gain is apportionable business income include Arizona, California, Oregon, and Tennessee. (See *First Data Corporation v. Arizona*, 313 P.3d 548 (Ariz. App. 2013); *Appeal of Imperial, Inc.*, SBE, Case Nos. 472648 and 477927 (July 13, 2010); *CenturyTel, Inc. v. Department of Revenue,* No. TC 4826 (Or. T.C. Aug. 9, 2010); and *Newell Window Furnishing, Inc. v. Johnson*, 311 S.W.3d 441 (Tenn. Ct. of App. 2008).)

As these decisions indicate, state auditors generally take the position that Section 338 gains are business income (unless, of course, nonbusiness income treatment means it will all be allocated to the auditor's state). Other than factual matters, the key elements in the decisions include (1) whether the state statute defining business income has both a transactional and functional test; and (2) the scope of the functional test (for example, does it include dispositions, liquidations, or dissolutions). Given this controversy, tax practitioners entertaining a Section 338(h)(10) election will do well to consider carefully the impact of such an election on the taxpayer's state taxes.

The MTC recommends in its newly promulgated regulation that the gain in a 338(h)(10) transaction should be treated as apportionable business income. Here is the example from the MTC regulation:

> *Example (iv)*: A manufacturer decides to sell one of its redundant factories to a real estate developer and transfers the ownership of the factory to a special purpose subsidiary SaleCo (Taxpayer), immediately prior to its sale to the real estate developer. The parties elect to treat the sale as a disposition of assets under IRC 338(h)(10), resulting in Taxpayer recognizing a capital gain on the sale. The capital gain is apportionable income. Note: although the gain is apportionable, application of the standard apportionment formula in Section 17 may not fairly reflect the taxpayer's business presence in any state, necessitating resort to equitable apportionment pursuant to Section 18.

Partnership interests: Business or nonbusiness income?

Partnership taxation is difficult, in part because of the tension between two competing theories of a partnership's nature. The aggregate theory of partnerships sees the partnership as an aggregation of its owners, each of which is a direct owner of the partnership's assets. As a consequence, if the partnership is doing business in a particular state, then all the partners are deemed to be doing business there as well; such as, they each have nexus with the state, and consequently, a filing obligation in the state.

The entity theory of partnerships, adopted by the Revised Uniform Partnership Act (RUPA), places more emphasis on the partnership as an entity separate from its partners. Thus, the partnership is treated more like a corporation with shareholders. Just as an investment in a corporation does not create nexus for its shareholders in whatever state the corporation is doing business, the ownership of a partnership interest, in and of itself, should not trigger nexus in those states that have adopted RUPA. That is the theory of course, but the reality is that states, for state tax purposes at least, ignore the distinctions between the Uniform and Revised Uniform Partnership Acts.

The problem is even more pronounced with respect to limited liability companies (LLCs), because many state LLC statutes specifically embrace the entity theory. For example, New York's statute explicitly states that a member does not have an ownership interest in the LLC's property, and that "all property of the limited liability company is property of the limited liability company itself." (NY Ltd. Liab. Law Section 601.) Nevertheless, whether a state leans more towards an aggregate or entity approach, many states have adopted specific rules with regard to limited partners or members of limited liability companies, thus requiring practitioners to inquire into each state's specific treatment.

In addition to specific treatment of limited partners, states vary in whether the business or nonbusiness income distinction is made at the partnership level or at the partner level. California, for example, makes the distinction at the partnership level.

Because the business or nonbusiness income distinction is often driven by if a unitary relationship exists, the latter will often determine the treatment of the partner's share of the partnership income. For example, if there is a unitary relationship, many jurisdictions will simply roll up the partner's share of income and factors into the rest of the partner's business income and factors. If there is no unitary relationship, then the income and its factors are treated as a separate trade of business. (See the example and a copy of the California regulation at the end of chapter 5.)

The Hercules cases

There is no better example of the inconsistency of treatment with respect to business income, the unitary principle, and the difference between an operational and investment function than the *Hercules* cases in Illinois, Kansas, Maryland, Minnesota, Utah, and Wisconsin.

Hercules was a manufacturer of polypropylene incorporated in Delaware, domiciled in New York, but doing business in many states. In 1983, Hercules and an unrelated Italian company, Montedison, each contributed their polypropylene manufacturing activities to a newly created entity, Himont. Hercules and Montedison each owned 50% of Himont. In 1987 Hercules sold its share of Himont to Montedison at a capital gain of more than $1.3bn. Hercules treated the sale as nonbusiness income and accordingly, allocated the entire gain to New York, its state of domicile.

The revenue departments of Illinois, Kansas, Maryland, Minnesota, Utah, and Wisconsin all believed that they too should share in taxing the $1.3 billion capital gain, and accordingly treated the sale as business income apportionable to their states. Hercules's sale received different treatment depending upon the court.

Illinois

The Illinois appellate court held that contrary to the revenue department's findings and the decision of the lower level circuit court, there was no unitary relationship, and thus the capital gain was properly allocated to New York as nonbusiness income. The court also rejected the department's argument that the Himont investment served an operational function (as in *Allied-Signal*) and should be apportionable income on that basis (*Hercules, Inc. v. Department of Revenue*, 324 Ill. App. 3d 329, 753 N.E. 2d 418 (1st Dist. 2001), *appeal denied*, 197 Ill. 2d 560, 763 N.E. 2d 770 (2001)).

Kansas

The Kansas Board of Tax Appeals determined that because the Himont sale did not meet the "transaction" test, it was not business income and thus not apportionable to Kansas (*Appeal of Hercules Inc.*, No. 1998-1666-DT, (Kan. 2000)).

Maryland

The Maryland Court of Appeals, in overturning a lower court decision, found there was no evidence of either a unitary relationship or that the investment served an operational function (*Hercules Inc. v. Comptroller*, 351 Md. 101, 716 A.2d 276, (1998)).

Minnesota

The Minnesota Supreme Court, in reversing the state's tax court, found there was "scant evidence of a unitary relationship between Hercules and Himont." In addition, there was no evidence that the ownership of Himont served an operational rather than an investment function. Thus, the capital gain was not apportionable to Minnesota but properly allocated to New York (*Hercules Inc. v. Commissioner*, 575 N.W. 2d 111 (Minn. 1998)).

Utah

The Utah State Tax Commission ruled that the capital gain was business income apportionable to the state because it found both a unitary and operational relationship between Hercules and Himont (*Hercules, Inc. v. Utah State Tax Commission*, 974 P.2d 286 (Utah 1999)).

Wisconsin

The Wisconsin Tax Appeals Commission ruled that the capital gain was business income apportionable to the state because it found both a unitary and operational relationship between Hercules and Himont (*Hercules Inc. v. Wisconsin Department of Revenue*, No. 94-I-1494, Wisconsin Tax Appeals Commission (Feb. 26, 1997)).

In summary, given the exact same transaction, Kansas, and then upon appeal, Illinois, Maryland, and Minnesota, agreed with Hercules' allocation of the capital gain to New York, while Utah and Wisconsin apportioned part of that gain to themselves.

Having your cake and eating it too

Given the states' differing interpretations of business or nonbusiness income, is it appropriate for a taxpayer to take conflicting positions on the same transaction in different states? In fact, given the states' inconsistent positions, taxpayers routinely take inconsistent positions where required by state law and or court findings. However, where the state guidance is arguably ambiguous, is it appropriate for a taxpayer to treat a transaction inconsistently between states? That question was addressed by the Oregon Tax Court in *Oracle v. Dept. of Rev.*, Or. Tax Ct., Magis. Div., TC-MD 070762C, (02/11/2010).

Oracle treated certain gains from the sale of stock and other assets as *business income* on its California return, and *nonbusiness income* not allocable to Oregon on its Oregon return. The filing position benefited Oracle who is headquartered in California. Oregon challenged Oracle's filing position, claiming that it "thwart(s) the goal of uniformity if they take inconsistent positions as to identical items of income in the same tax year." In addition, the Department of Revenue (DOR) in Oregon held that the taxpayer had a duty of consistency that required that it disclose inconsistent positions taken on returns. The court declined to adopt Oregon's position, pointing out that "a favorable ruling for Defendant would require the court to become an expert in the laws of 49 other states as they pertain to the definition of business and nonbusiness income, not only as set forth in the various states' statutes, but as those statutes are refined and clarified by years of judicial opinions." The court went on to ask, if it did adopt the DOR's position, which state's treatment would prevail?

> For example, suppose a taxpayer reports an item of income as nonbusiness income in one state and business income in another, and that one of those states is Oregon. Which state's reporting would govern in determining how the income should be characterized for purposes of Oregon's tax? This case is a prime example. Plaintiffs reported certain income as business income in California and nonbusiness income in Oregon. Why should plaintiffs' characterization of the income on its California return dictate how the income should be reported in Oregon?
>
> If the court were to rule favorably on defendant's motion, the result would be a ruling mandating that plaintiffs' characterization of the income in another state (California) controls how that income is reported in Oregon for purposes of this state's tax. An obvious question raised by that outcome is whether Oregon will accept in all cases a taxpayer's characterization of an item of income in another state as controlling in Oregon, including situations where the department felt that a "correct" application of the law dictated a contrary result.

The Supreme Court: Once again

The landmark U.S. Supreme Court cases summarized in chapter 3 in the discussion of the unitary concept are equally useful in thinking about the distinctions between business and nonbusiness income. Given the interrelationship between the unitary concept, combined filing, and business or nonbusiness income, it is common to confuse them. As a rule of thumb, the unitary concept generally refers to the *relationship* between entities, while the business or nonbusiness income principle more often refers to the role a particular property, asset, or stream of income plays in the hands of its owner. In *MeadWestvaco,* the Supreme Court distinguished between "enterprise" unity and the operational or investment function test. The tests of functional integration, centralized management, and economies of scale are the "hallmarks" for determining whether a unitary relationship exists between enterprises. For example, in *Mobil Oil*, *Exxon*, *ASARCO*, and *Woolworth,* the Supreme Court focused on the *relationship* between the parents and subsidiaries. Once the relationship was determined to be unitary, the income was deemed business or apportionable income. Nevertheless, one can have business income absent a unitary relationship between businesses or enterprises. The unitary relationship is a sufficient but not necessary condition. As a logician might say, "A is a sufficient, but not necessary condition for B."

In short, *MeadWestvaco* says that even if there is not a unitary relationship between two separate businesses, individual assets of a business can be treated as apportionable income if they serve an operational rather than investment function. You just cannot use the operational or investment function test as a test for determining a unitary relationship between two separate enterprises. Or to put it more simply, the court is simply saying that the unitary principle can be applied, not just between two legal entities, but also between an entity and an asset or stream of income. "[t]he concept of operational function simply recognizes that an asset can be a part of a taxpayer's unitary business even if what we may term a 'unitary relationship' does not exist between the 'payor and payee.'" For example, apportionable income includes "interest earned on short-term deposits in a bank located in another State, if that income forms part of the working capital of the corporation's unitary business, notwithstanding the absence of a unitary relationship between the corporation and the bank."

It was only with *Allied Signal* that the court arguably began to apply unitary principles to a stream of income. The change in focus prompted questions more in the order of: "Why does this company own this property and for what purpose?" Successfully or not, the court tried to answer that question by distinguishing an *operational* from an *investment* function, such as a business purpose from a nonbusiness purpose. The former may be apportionable income; the latter, perhaps not.

The key point is that the unitary concept is applied to two things in multistate corporate income tax. First, it is used in determining what legal entities rightfully belong together in defining the economic unit to which the tax is applied (remember the railroad example and *Butler Brothers*). Second, it is also used in determining just what income should be attributed to that economic unit: that is, what is apportionable business income and what is allocable nonbusiness income. Keeping in mind those two uses of the unitary concept will help you not only steer through the confusing case law on the topic, but will help you guide your clients or your company in properly applying the concept.

In contrast to the U.S. Supreme Court's decision in *MeadWestvaco*, the *Tate & Lyle* decision in Alabama is a model of clarity (*Tate & Lyle Ingredients Americas, Inc. v. Alabama*, Adm. Law Div., Dkt. No. CORP. 07-162, January 15, 2008). In *Tate & Lyle*, the taxpayer realized a $345m gain upon the sale of its one-third stock interest in a foreign corporation based in Belgium. The key issues were (1) whether Alabama could even constitutionally tax the gain; and (2) if the state could tax the gain, determining whether the gain was apportionable business or allocable nonbusiness income. In short, there was a unitary question, and a business or nonbusiness income question. Because both companies were in the business of selling cereal sweeteners and owned by the same holding company, the state of Alabama held that the gain was apportionable business income taxable to the state.

The judge found that despite the common ownership by a holding company, there was no unitary relationship between the two corporations.

The companies have no common directors. They separately purchase their own raw materials, and have no shared facilities, employees, or officers. They also have separate accounting, payroll, legal, and tax departments, and different customer and technical service employees. They have separate management teams, and independently manufacture, price, market, and sell their respective products. They sell to some of the same customers, but the sales are in different geographical locations, for separately negotiated prices, and with different terms and conditions.

In fact, "the taxpayer uses corn to manufacture its products and sells to customers in North America, whereas [the foreign company] uses wheat and sells to customers in Europe."

The court went on to examine whether the stock gain was business income "under the transactional, functional, or operationally related tests," and determined that "the income was nonbusiness income and not apportionable to Alabama."

The *Tate & Lyle* decision is a particularly helpful one for the tax practitioner. The judge provides a clear and useful history of the unitary principle, its application, and its relationship with the business or nonbusiness income tests.

Chapter 5

Apportionment Formulas and Factors

Learning objectives

- Recognize the calculation of the traditional "Massachusetts formula."
- Recognize the elements of the payroll factor.
- Identify the computation problems of the property factor.
- Recognize the boundaries of the sales factor.

Introduction

Once we have established the right to apportion, we must turn our attention to the apportionment formula and the factors within that formula. The U.S. Supreme Court has declined to favor one apportionment method over another. For example, the Court upheld Iowa's use of a single factor (sales) in apportioning income in *Moorman Mfg. Co. v. Bair*, 437 U. S. 267 (1978). With *Moorman* the court has let it be known that, absent clearly flagrant distortion (*Hans Rees' Sons, Inc. v. North Carolina*, 283 U.S. 123 (1931), perhaps), it is not going to be in the business of judging the validity of various state apportionment methods.

Although there is increasing variation in state formulas, most states initially adopted some form of the "Massachusetts formula." (Supposedly, the drafters of the Uniform Division of Income for Tax Purposes Act or UDITPA used Massachusetts as an example in their drafting.) Historically, the "Massachusetts formula" was derived by determining the average of three separate factors: payroll, property, and sales.

Payroll, property, and sales factors

Put simply, the payroll factor is determined by comparing *in-state payroll* to *payroll everywhere.* The property factor is determined by comparing the *average value of in-state property to the average value of property everywhere.* The sales factor is determined by comparing *in-state sales* to *sales everywhere*. This three-factor approach is the basis of both the UDITPA provisions and Multistate Tax Commission (MTC) regulations (with some modifications).

Each of the three factors is used in an attempt to represent fairly a business's activity in a state. The payroll factor is used, because it both represents the contribution of labor towards the creation of wealth, and is a measure of the taxpayer's physical presence in the state. The payroll factor includes all compensation paid to individuals, including wages and other taxable fringe benefits, like meals and lodging.

The property factor, like the payroll factor, represents both the contribution of property toward the creation of wealth, and the measure of business presence in the state. Both rented and owned properties are included in the property factor. According to UDITPA and MTC regulations, owned property is measured at original cost, and rented property at eight times its annual rent. Intangible property is not included in the property factor.

Knowledge check

1. In applying the property factor, UDITPA and the MTC say rented property is measured at

    a. Four times annual rent.
    b. Three times annual rent.
    c. Eight times annual rent.
    d. Five times annual rent.

The sales — or gross receipts — factor provides for the contribution of the market states in the creation of wealth. Its use balances the effect of the payroll and property factors, which favor the states in which a company's headquarters and manufacturing are located. Sales of TPP, with two exceptions, are apportioned to where the product is shipped. The two exceptions include (1) purchases by the United States; and (2) sales into states where the taxpayer is not taxable. In both these instances, the sales are typically thrown back into the state of origin. Unlike the property factor, which does not include intangible property, the sales factor includes receipts from intangible property sales.

Knowledge check

2. Compensation for the payroll factor is usually assigned to the state in which

    a. Unemployment compensation is reported.
    b. The most employees are situated.
    c. The home office is located.
    d. The CEO of the company is located.

Finally, there are specific provisions in most states for the apportionment factors of certain industries in transportation (air, rail, ship, and truck), entertainment, and finance (banks, credit companies, insurance companies, and savings and loans).

Because each state has its own formula and interpretations thereof, generalization is difficult. In addition, change is continual. For example, there has been a trend lately to increase the role of the sales factor by doubling it, because it generally lessens the tax burden of in-state businesses at the expense of out-of-state businesses (probably the dream of local politicians everywhere). Twenty-four states: Arizona (optional); California; Colorado; Connecticut (effective 2016 except for manufacturers), Washington, DC; Georgia; Illinois; Indiana; Iowa; Kentucky; Louisiana; Maine; Michigan; Minnesota; Mississippi (for retailers and those providing services); Missouri (optional); Nebraska; New Jersey; New York; North Carolina; North Dakota (optional); Oregon; Pennsylvania; Rhode Island; South Carolina; Texas; and Wisconsin use a single factor (sales) in apportioning income. There are a number of states that use the traditional three-factor formula, but double weight the sales factor. They include Alabama, Arkansas, Arizona (optional), Florida, Idaho, Massachusetts, New Hampshire, Vermont, Virginia, and West Virginia. Other multiples of the sales factor can be found. Currently Delaware and Tennessee are using triple sales. Starting in 2019, Maryland is three factor with quadruple sales. This is phasing to sales only in 2022. For 2020 and 2021, it will have a three-factor formula with quintuple and sextuple sales factors, respectively. Utah is also phasing towards a sales-only apportionment factor (optional) for years after 2020. In 2019, they use three factor with quadruple sales, 2020 will use a three factor with octupled sales. The states with a traditional equally weighted three-factor apportionment include Alaska, Hawaii, Kansas, Missouri (optional), Montana, New Mexico, North Dakota (optional), and Utah (optional).

Several states have gradually moved to a single sales factor. For example, Minnesota shifted to a single sales factor for tax years beginning on or after January 1, 2014. For 2013, its factors were weighted at 96-2-2 (sales, property, payroll). Pennsylvania's formula was weighted at 90-5-5 (sales, property, payroll), but effective January 1, 2013, the state adopted single sales factor apportionment. As of 2013, California shifted from a double-weighted sales factor with property and payroll to a single sales factor for apportionment. As mentioned already, Maryland and Utah are currently in transition.

Some states provide specific industries special weighting of the factors. For example, Mississippi provides a single sales factor for retailers, wholesalers, and service companies. Manufacturers who sell at wholesale must use an evenly weighted three-factor formula, whereas manufacturers who sell at retail use a three-factor formula with double-weighted sales.

Despite all the variances among state apportionment formulas, most still base their application and take their interpretative guidance from the UDITPA and MTC rules and regulations. Accordingly, we make them our focus.

Example 5-1

Before we begin a detailed examination of the individual factors, let us look at a simple example illustrating the previous discussion.

ABC Corporation does business in two states and has collected the following data with respect to their sales, property, and payroll. The company's federal taxable income after state modifications was $1,000,000.

	State X	State Y	Total
Sales	12,000,000	4,000,000	16,000,000
Property	3,000,000	2,000,000	5,000,000
Payroll	1,200,000	800,000	2,000,000

If both states use an equally balanced three-factor apportionment, ABC's taxable income is apportioned in the following manner:

State X	
Sales (12,000,000/16,000,000)	75%
Property (3,000,000/5,000,000)	60%
Payroll (1,200,000/2,000,000)	60%
Total of factors	195%
Divided by three (195/3)	65%
Times taxable income	× 1,000,000
State X taxable income	$650,000
State Y	
Sales (4,000,000/16,000,000)	25%
Property (2,000,000/5,000,000)	40%
Payroll (800,000/2,000,000)	40%
Total of factors	105%
Divided by three (105/3)	35%
Times taxable income	× 1,000,000
State Y taxable income	$350,000

In reality, companies rarely pay tax on exactly 100% of their income. Because many states differ in how they weight their factors and the composition of the factors, it is highly likely that a company may pay tax on more (or less) than 100% of its taxable income. For example, what if State X used only a single sales factor? Its factor would then be 75%, and State Y's would still be 35%, meaning that ABC Corporation would be paying tax on 110% of its income.

Is the MTC's three-factor apportionment a mandatory option?

It is not an understatement to say that the most significant development in apportionment in 2012 and 2013, or perhaps in the last decade, is the decision by the California Court of Appeals that California, as a member of the MTC, must offer the MTC's three-factor equally weighted apportionment formula as an option to the state's three-factor double-weighted sales factor (see *Gillette Company v. Franchise Tax Board*, 209 Cal.App.4th 938, 147 Cal.Rptr.3d 603 (Calif. Ct. App. Oct. 10, 2012)).

California joined the MTC in 1974. One of the provisions of the MTC Compact is that its members must offer multistate taxpayers the option of using either the state's apportionment formula or the MTC's equally weighted three-factor formula. Because California was already using the equally weighted three-factor formula in 1974, the adoption of the MTC Compact had no effect on apportionment. However, in 1993 California changed its apportionment formula by requiring all taxpayers not subject to special apportionment rules, to double-weight the sales factor.

Gillette filed a refund claim arguing that the company should be able to use the MTC formula instead of California's statutory formula. Gillette argued that because California was still a member of the MTC, it was required to offer the MTC formula as an alternative apportionment methodology. In short, Gillette argued that the MTC was a binding, enforceable contract between the states and California could not eliminate the MTC formula option unless it withdrew from the MTC Compact. Because it had not withdrawn from the MTC Compact, the MTC formula remained a filing option. The Court of Appeals agreed, holding that California could not unilaterally repeal provisions of the MTC Compact. The California Supreme Court reversed this, holding that the MTC was more of an advisory body than a binding compact to which the state had to adhere (*The Gillette Company, et. al. v. California Franchise Tax Board*, 209 Case No. S206587 (Cal 2015)).

The consequences of Gillette are significant and far reaching. First, given the protective refund claims already filed pursuant to the decision, there are millions of dollars at stake. Second, the decision has implications for the roughly 20 other states that are members of the MTC, but like California, require other apportionment formulas. The MTC Compact members include Alabama, Alaska, Arkansas, Colorado, Hawaii, Idaho, Kansas, Missouri, Montana, New Mexico, North Dakota, Oregon, Texas, Utah, Washington, and the District of Columbia. Of those states, only Alaska, Hawaii, Kansas, Missouri, Montana, North Dakota, and Utah use equally weighted three-factor apportionment.

Courts in Oregon and Texas have already addressed the issue and held, in contrast with the California Court of Appeals, that the MTC Compact is not binding on the state's apportionment methodology (see *Health Net Inc. v. Department of Revenue*, No. 120649D, Oregon Tax Ct. (July 2, 2012); and *Graphic Packaging Corp. v. Hegar*, No. 15-0669, 2017 WL 6544951 (Tex. Dec 22, 2017)). Interestingly enough, we have split court decisions coming out of Michigan. In 2012, the Michigan Court of Appeals held for the state, arguing that the MTC Compact was not a binding contract, and that the passage of the Michigan Business Tax (MBT) "repealed by implication" the apportionment election provided by the MTC Compact (*International Business Machines Corp. v. Department of Revenue*, S. Ct. No. 146440, No. 306618, Mich. Ct. App. (Nov. 26, 2012)). However, in 2013, the Michigan Court of Claims held that the MTC Compact was binding, and was not repealed by the adoption of Michigan's MBT (see *Anheuser-Busch, Inc. v. Michigan*, Michigan Court of

Claims, No. 11-85-MT (June 6, 2013)). That case is now on appeal to the same Michigan Court of Appeals that held against IBM. In any event, the Michigan Supreme Court ruled on July 14, 2014, that IBM was entitled to use the MTC's equally weighted three-factor apportionment formula (*International Business Machines Corp. v. Department of Treasury*, Dkt. No. 146440 (July 14, 2014)).

A third consequence of Gillette is that states may withdraw from the MTC Compact and thereby threaten its continued existence. In fact, California did just that by passing S.B. 1015 on June 27, 2012 during the litigation with Gillette. Not only does the bill withdraw California from the MTC, it also clarifies that the MTC election had not been available since 1993. Finally, the bill provides that any election affecting apportionment of tax must have been made on an original timely filed return, and so in effect, negated any refund claims.

Not to be outdone, the Michigan legislature passed a bill retroactively repealing the state's membership in the MTC, effective January 1, 2008. The state Attorney General Bill Schuette then asserted that the new law is applicable to the Supreme Court's decision in *IBM,* and now overrides that decision. This action raises so many questions, that it is difficult to know where to begin. There are constitutional issues at both the state and federal levels involving due process, the MTC compact, separation of powers, and of course, the simple question of whether a state can change a statute retroactively six years after the fact (for a recent decision by the U.S. Supreme Court on retroactive legislation, see *United States v. Carlton*, 512 U.S. 26 (1994)).

It is difficult to say what will happen next. On December 31, 2015, the California Supreme Court issued its decision in *Gillette,* reversing the California Court of Appeals, and holding that the MTC Compact was not a binding compact among its member states (*Gillette Co. v. Franchise Tax Board*, No. S206587 (Calif. Sup. Ct., Dec. 31, 2015)). On October 11, 2016, the Supreme Court denied cert, foreclosing the possibility of using three-factor apportionment for the time being.

Courts in several states have now rejected the argument that the Compact is binding. Will this turn the momentum? Or will appeal to the U.S. Supreme Court keep the issue alive? The taxpayers do intend to appeal. *Gillette* has already been appealed, and cert was denied. Most of the other states are still working their way through their respective supreme courts. In any case, what impact might this decision have on other nontax state compacts? What impact may there be on the MTC itself? California, South Dakota, and Utah have all left the compact as a result of the apportionment cases. If any state sees success with the Supreme Court, it is likely that more states will leave as well. There is also the question of whether S.B. 1015 was properly passed. Any legislative tax increase in California must be passed by the legislature with a two-thirds vote. S.B. 1015 only passed with a simple majority, and therefore may be an unconstitutional increase in taxes. In any case, taxpayers should evaluate whether filing a protective refund claim is beneficial in the affected states, and act accordingly. That said, it may be quite a while yet before all this is sorted out, thus prudent taxpayers will file appropriate protective refund claims.

The payroll factor

Let us begin with the simplest of factors — payroll. UDITPA Section 13 defines the payroll factor as "a fraction, the numerator of which is the total amount paid in this state during the tax period by the taxpayer for compensation, and the denominator of which is the total compensation paid everywhere during the tax period."

MTC regulations provide that in determining the amount of compensation to be included in that payroll factor, the business's accounting methods (cash or accrual) are to be followed. However, if a state requires the cash method to be used for unemployment taxes, then the business may use the cash method, even if it otherwise uses the accrual method. Consequently, many states accept the federal Form 940 and state unemployment returns to apportion payroll. In fact, as a practical matter, compensation for the payroll factor is usually assigned to the state where the unemployment compensation is reported, and it is not uncommon for many auditors to give the payroll factor only a cursory examination.

Nevertheless, there can be some traps for the unwary. For example, payroll that is capitalized as part of a self-constructed asset is included in the payroll factor (MTC Reg. IV.13.(a)(2)). But, don't forget that only payroll that generates business income should be included in the factor. Thus, it is not always clear if payroll that is being capitalized as part of the incomplete construction of a new plant should be included in the payroll factor. The MTC regulations provide that capitalized payroll is not excluded from the payroll factor, while at the same time, they provide that payroll that doesn't generate business income should be excluded. Arguably, if a taxpayer excludes incomplete property from the property factor, it should also exclude any capitalized payroll associated with that property.

Example 5-2

A manufacturing company owns an apartment building it acquired through the death 20 years ago of one of the company's founders. The company has one employee whose only duties are to manage the property for the company. The employee's salary should not be included in the company's payroll factor nor the property in the property factory, because the rental income is not business income.

Throwbacks, usually associated with the sales factor, can exist with the payroll factor. Technically speaking, the throwback payroll rule provides that even though an employee is neither a resident of the state nor performing services in the state, the payroll will be thrown back if (*a*) the employee is directed or controlled from an office in the state to which he/she periodically returns; and (*b*) the employer does not have nexus with the state of the employee's residency. For example, a Selma, Alabama, company doing business only in Alabama has a sales employee who lives in Cheyenne, Wyoming, soliciting sales. (This activity creates nexus for sales tax purposes, but not income tax purposes.) The employee rarely stops in at the Selma office. Alabama will throw back that employee's compensation into the Alabama payroll factor.

States with payroll throwbacks include Missouri, North Dakota, and the District of Columbia. Payroll throwbacks are necessary, say such states, because if payroll is assigned to a state where the employer does not have nexus, it does not show up in any state numerator, and results in the creation of "nowhere income."

Generally, the payroll factor, unlike the sales and property factors, is simple to administer. Two controversial areas are the treatment of executive salaries and leased employees. Some states want to carve out executives' salaries for specific allocation rather than apportionment, arguing that the payroll factor is otherwise distorted. Other states exclude officer comp as an incentive for companies to locate their headquarters in the state. For example, North Carolina excludes "All compensation paid to general executive officers and all compensation paid in connection with nonapportionable income shall be excluded in computing the payroll factor. General executive officers shall include the chairman of the board, president, vice-presidents, secretary, treasurer, comptroller and any other officer serving in similar capacities." (N.C. Section 105-130.4(k)). Oklahoma excludes officer compensation, and New York used to exclude officer comp before it adopted single sales factor apportionment.

The dilemma with leased employees is which company should include them in their factor — the lessor, the lessee, or both? The employees should be included in the lessor's (leasing company) payroll factor because, as a matter of fact, that is who is paying for their services. On the other hand, the employees should be included in the lessee's payroll factor because, as a matter of fact, the lessee is the common law employer. As a consequence, many auditors will include them in both, arguing that both parties are using them in the state as a source of income. This is the same rationale for including leased property in both the lessor and lessee's property factors.

According to surveys performed by CCH, states that include the employees in the lessor's factor include Alabama, Arkansas, Delaware, Florida, Kansas, Kentucky, Louisiana, Montana, New Jersey, New Mexico, Tennessee, Utah, and West Virginia. States including the employee in the lessee's factor include Alabama, Alaska, Arizona, California, Florida, Hawaii, Idaho, Kansas, Mississippi, Missouri, Montana, New Hampshire, North Carolina, North Dakota, Oklahoma, Rhode Island, Vermont, Virginia, and the District of Columbia. Please note some of these states include the factor for both the lessee and lessor.

For a discussion of the different rationales resulting in conflicting decisions, see *UPS Worldwide Forwarding, Inc. v. Pennsylvania*, Nos. 62-65 F.R. 2001 (Commonwealth Court of Pennsylvania (2004), *aff'd UPS Worldwide Forwarding, Inc. v. Pennsylvania*, No. 1-4 MAP (Supreme Court of Pennsylvania 2005) (individuals paid by a third party other than the taxpayer were not employees because the taxpayer stipulated that it had no control over the employees and did not, in fact, have any employees); *Plantation Pipe Line Co. v. Alabama*, Corp. 05-948 (Ala. Admin. Law Div., May 23, 2006); and *C & D Chemical Products, Inc. v. Alabama*, No. 00-288 (Ala. Admin. Law Div., Feb. 9, 2001). According to an Illinois letter ruling, the employee-leasing company is no more than an intermediary, and thus the loaned employees should be included in the payroll factor of the company for whom they performed services. "The Department considers that the compensation of the loaned employees should be included in the payroll factor of the client company rather than the leasing company. The client company is the one which ultimately paid the compensation. Furthermore, the services of these loaned employees were actually performed for the business of the client company, rather than the leasing company which was only an intermediary." (Private Letter Ruling IT 91-17-PLR (January 23, 1991)).

It is no surprise that states have come to conflicting opinions on this matter. A Missouri company that paid salaries for one of its subsidiaries did not include the payroll in its factor, despite reporting the compensation for unemployment purposes and being reimbursed by the subsidiary. The Missouri Supreme Court held that because the parent, not the subsidiary, issued the checks, made the payroll deductions and supplied the W-2 forms, that it had to include the payroll in its payroll factor (*Phillip Morris, Inc. v. Missouri*, 760 S.W.2d 888 (Mo. 1988)).

The Kentucky Court of Appeals came to a different decision than that of the Missouri Supreme Court. A parent and several subsidiaries pooled their employees such that employees of one subsidiary might work for other subsidiaries or the parent. The company receiving the services reimbursed the company for whom the employees worked. The taxpayer argued that the compensation should be included in the payroll factor of the company who received the services.

The Court of Appeals agreed because

- the state defined compensation as wages and other forms of remuneration paid to employees for personal services;
- the subsidiary receiving the services reimbursed the other companies; and
- neither the parent nor any of the subs profited from loaning its employees to others.

The court held that the subsidiary receiving the services should include the cost of those services, or payroll, in its payroll factor (*Cincinnati, New Orleans, & Texas Pacific Railway Co., v. Kentucky*, 684 S.W.2d 303 (Ky. Ct. App. 1984)).

For employees who work in more than one state, UDITPA offers the following guidelines:

- "Compensation is paid in this state if
  - the individual's service is performed entirely within the state; or
  - the individual's service is performed both within and without the state, but the service performed without the state is incidental to the individual's service within the state; or
  - some of the service is performed in the state and (*a*) the base of operations or, if there is no base of operations, the place from which the service is directed or controlled is in the state; or (*b*) the base of operations or the place from which the service is directed or controlled is not in any state in which some part of the service is performed, but the individual's residence is in this state."

The preceding rules are drawn from the federal Model Unemployment Compensation Act, which helps explain why so many auditors look to a taxpayer's unemployment reports for testing the payroll factor.

Please note that the rules result in an employee's payroll being sourced to a single state. Although this is certainly easy from an administrative point of view, it certainly does not reflect today's employment patterns, where, for example, software consultants may work from home, or move from job to job in different states.

Example 5-3

ABC Corporation employs a pharmaceutical salesman whose region covers the west Rocky Mountains, including the states of Arizona, Nevada, Idaho, Montana, Wyoming, Colorado, and New Mexico. The salesman works out of his home in Colorado, but receives his directions from the company's headquarters in California. The salesman's payroll will likely be sourced to Colorado. Why? The company cannot use California as a base of operations, because the salesman never works in California, and the salesman's activities are spread across seven states.

Knowledge check

3. *Employee*, while not specifically defined in UDITPA, is usually defined as anyone subject to the Federal Insurance Contribution Act rules. This approach implicitly excludes independent contractors. The Administrative Law Division of ________ held that if no difference exists between the generation of income by an employee or a nonemployee, then the nonemployee should be included in the payroll factor.

    a. Colorado.
    b. California.
    c. Alabama.
    d. New York.

The property factor

The property factor is more difficult to interpret and apply. The difficulties arise from problems of definition (what is property?), problems of value (what cost is applied to the property?), computational problems (the use of averages and moveable property), and finally, problems related to unusual and nonrecurring transactions.

Property included in the factor

UDITPA provides that "the property factor is a fraction, the numerator of which is the average value of the taxpayer's real and tangible personal property owned or rented and used in this state during the tax period and the denominator of which is the average value of all the taxpayer's real and tangible personal property owned or rented and used during the tax period."

The MTC regulations define "real and tangible personal property" as land, buildings, machinery, stock of goods, equipment, and other tangible property excluding cash used in the regular course of the taxpayer's trade or business.

Intangible property is excluded from the property factor. Intangible property generally includes cash, shares of stock, notes, accounts receivables, credits, franchises, goodwill, or any other evidence of debt. Property giving rise to nonbusiness income is generally excluded from the factor.

MTC Reg. Section 10(b) provides that property is included in the property factor if it is actually used, or is available for or capable of being used in the regular course of the taxpayer's trade or business. Thus, property held in reserve or standby is included in the factor. Many states treat property that is "available for use" or "capable of being used" as used, and include the same in the property factor. But what does it mean to use a property? For example, the Indiana Tax Court held that the lessor of automobiles did not have to include their value in its property factor, because the taxpayer did not actually physically use them (*Enterprise Leasing Co. v. Indiana*, 779 N.E.2d 1284 (Ind. Tax Ct. 2002)). On the other hand, the Oregon Tax Court held that cars leased on behalf of independent salespeople were included in the company's property factor, despite not being used by the company (*Mary Kay, Inc. v. Department of Revenue*, Dkt. No. 4552 (Ore. Tax Ct. 5/15/2003)). The Ohio Supreme Court seemed to take inconsistent positions until a 2003 change in the statute settled the matter by including the property in the lessor's factor (see *Illinois Tool Works, Inc. v. Lindley*, 436 N.E.2d 220 (Ohio 1982) and *Columbia Properties, Inc. v. Limbach*, 537 N.E.2d 210 (Ohio 1989), and Ohio Rev. Stat. Section 5733-05(B)(2)(a) (June 26, 2003)). A temporarily idle plant and raw material reserves are examples of property held in reserve or standby.

Property or equipment qualifying as construction-in-progress during the tax period is excluded. Thus, a plant under construction is excluded, while an idled plant is included. But see *Commissioner of Revenue v. New England Power Co.*, 411 Mass. 418 (1991), which included the property factor of an electric power company property under construction. The property was included because it contributed to the company's revenue by being a factor in setting the utilities' rate base.

Once in the factor, the property stays there until it is disposed. The MTC regulations provide that "property used in the regular course of the trade or business of the taxpayer shall remain in the property factor until its permanent withdrawal is established by an identifiable event such as its conversion to the production of nonbusiness income, its sale, or the lapse of an extended period of time (normally, five years) during which the property is held for sale."

Section 11 of UDITPA requires that the property factor include rental property, by multiplying the annual rentals by eight. Part year rent is not annualized. If a taxpayer pays only nominal or no rent for the use of government property, then a fair market value for the rent must be computed and included in the property factor.

MTC Reg. IV.10.(b) summarizes what is included in the property factor:

"Property shall be included in the property factor if it is actually used or is available for or capable of being used during the tax period in the regular course of the trade or business of the taxpayer. Property held as reserves or standby facilities or property held as a reserve source of materials shall be included in the factor. For example, a plant temporarily idle or raw material reserves not currently being processed are includable in the factor. Property or equipment under construction during the tax period (except inventoriable goods in process) shall be excluded from the factor until such property is actually used in the regular course of the trade or business of the taxpayer. If the property is partially used in the regular course of the trade or business of the taxpayer while under construction, the value of the property to the extent used shall be included in the property factor."

The regulation also provides the following examples:

Example 1:	Taxpayer closed its manufacturing plant in State X and held the property for sale. The property remained vacant until its sale one year later. The value of the manufacturing plant is included in the property factor until the plant is sold.
Example 2:	Same as example 1, except that the property was rented until the plant was sold. The plant is included in the property factor until the plant is sold.
Example 3:	Taxpayer closed its manufacturing plant and leased the building under a five-year lease. The plant is included in the property factor until the commencement of the lease.
Example 4:	The taxpayer operates a chain of retail grocery stores. Taxpayer closed Store A, which was then remodeled into three small retail stores such as a dress shop, dry cleaning, and barber shop, which were leased to unrelated parties. The property is removed from the property factor on the date on which the remodeling of Store A commenced.

MTC Reg. Section 11(b)(3) defines annual rent as "the actual sum of money or other consideration payable, directly or indirectly, by the taxpayer for its own benefit for the use of the property." Indirect consideration paid includes real estate taxes and insurance, but not service charges for utilities, cleaning, or security. See *Nelson's Office Supply Stores v. Commissioner of Revenue*, 508 N.W.2d 776 (1993), where the court held that the taxpayer includes its pro rata share of property taxes and utilities in its property factor.

The MTC regulations offer the following examples:

Example 1:	A taxpayer, pursuant to the terms of a lease, pays a lessor $1,000 per month as a base rental, and at the end of the year pays the lessor 1% of the gross sales of $400,000. The annual rent is $16,000 ($12,000 plus 1% of $400,000 or $4,000).
Example 2:	A taxpayer, pursuant to the terms of a lease, pays the lessor $12,000 a year, plus taxes in the amount of $2,000, and interest on a mortgage in the amount of $1,000. The annual rent is $15,000.
Example 3:	A taxpayer stores part of its inventory in a warehouse. The total charge for the year was $1,000, of which $700 was for the use of storage space, and $300 for inventory insurance, handling and shipping charges, and C.O.D. collections. The annual rent is $700.

Leasehold improvements are generally included in the lessee's property factor at original cost, regardless of if the property can be removed by the taxpayer at the end of the lease.

There is little consistency among the states in treating mobile property such as trucks, planes, and automobiles used in more than one state. Usually some apportionment method based upon miles or time is appropriate. But, see *Cooper Tire & Rubber Co. v. Tax Commissioner*, 639 N.E.2d 27 (1994). There, the court rejects the percentage of use method, and requires all leased trucks and aircraft to be included in the Ohio property factor.

Rent paid for tangible personal property used in the construction of an asset should be capitalized and excluded from the property factor. For example, if a taxpayer constructed its own building and rented forms and scaffolding during the construction, the rent paid for the forms and scaffolding should be capitalized. Because the incomplete building is not included in the property factor until it is available for use, it follows that the rent paid for the forms and scaffolding used during the construction should not be included in the property factor, because like the property, it is not in use (that is, it is not generating business income).

Other areas of dispute over the property factor include sourcing satellites, off-shore drilling platforms and equipment, and work-in-process inventory (see, for example, *Communications Satellite Corp. v. Franchise Tax Bd.*, 156 Cal. App.3d 726 (Cal. Ct. App. 1984) (satellites located in outer space were used in California because the ground station was located in California), and TV Guide, Inc. v. Illinois, Dkt. No. 00 l50616 (Ill. Cir. Ct. 2002) (transponders located on satellites could be included in the denominator of the taxpayer's property factor without being in any state's numerator. In other words, the creation of "nowhere income."))

Be careful that your payroll factor does not get counted twice — once in the payroll factor, and again in the property factor in manufactured equipment or construction.

Property's value

UDITPA defines a property's value as its cost. "Property owned by the taxpayer is valued at its original cost. Property rented by the taxpayer is valued at eight times the net annual rental rate. Net annual rental rate is the annual rental rate received by the taxpayer from sub-rentals."

Both UDITPA and the MTC provide that the property be valued at historical cost. Examples from the MTC regulations include:

Example 1:	The taxpayer acquired a factory building in this state at a cost of $500,000, and 18 months later expended $100,000 for major remodeling of the building. Taxpayer files its return for the current taxable year on the calendar-year basis. Depreciation deductions in the amount of $22,000 were claimed on the building for its return for the current taxable year. The value of the building includable in the numerator and denominator of the property factor is $600,000, as the depreciation deduction is not taken into account in determining the value of the building for purposes of the factor.

In the case of tax-free reorganizations, the transferor's basis is usually carried over to the transferee, and included in the transferee's property factor at its carryover basis plus any gain or boot recognized on the transaction.

Example 2:	During the current taxable year, X Corporation merges into Y Corporation in a tax-free reorganization under the Internal Revenue Code. At the time of the merger, X Corporation owns a factory that X built five years earlier at a cost of $1,000,000. X has been depreciating the factory at the rate of two percent per year, and its basis in X's hands at the time of the merger is $900,000. Because the property is acquired by Y in a transaction in which, under the IRC, its basis in Y's hands is the same as its basis in X's, Y includes the property in Y's property factor at X's original cost, without adjustment for depreciation, (in other words, $1,000,000).

Knowledge check

4. UDITPA defines a property's value as its

    a. Fair market value.
    b. Cost.
    c. Net book value.
    d. Replacement value.

5. Which is not usually found in the property factor?

    a. Construction in progress.
    b. Buildings.
    c. Machinery.
    d. Inventory.

Example 3:	Corporation Y acquires the assets of Corporation X in a liquidation by which Y is entitled to use its stock cost as the basis of the X assets under Section 334(b)(2) of the 1954 IRC (that is, stock possessing 80% control is purchased and liquidated within two years). Under these circumstances, Y's cost of the assets is the purchase price of the X stock, prorated over the X assets.

One of the consequences of valuing property at historical cost is the distortion between legacy property purchased years ago and newly purchased property. For example, one taxpayer unsuccessfully argued that historical film masters should be valued at their fair market value, rather than their historical cost (see *In the Matter of Disney Enterprises, Inc. v. New York*, 830 N.Y.S. 2d 614 (New York Supreme Court, App. Div. 40 AD 3D 49, March 1, 2007) and *In the Matter of Disney Enterprises, Inc. v. New York*, (New York Tax App. Trib. October 13, 2005)).

Inventory is to be valued as it is for federal income tax purposes, including any uniform capitalization rules applicable. If the property's original cost is unknown, then the taxpayer is to use the property's fair market value at the time it was acquired.

Assets subject to depletion are included in the property factor at original cost. No reduction is made for depletion. As for intangible drilling costs, they are generally included in the property factor, if they are capitalized.

Computational problems

Finally, "the average value of property shall be determined by averaging the values at the beginning and ending of the tax period but the tax administrator may require the averaging of monthly values during the tax period if reasonably required to reflect properly the average value of the taxpayer's property."

Example 5-4

The monthly value of Geppetto's property was as follows:

January	$ 3,000	July	$ 3,000
February	1,000	August	17,000
March	1,000	September	20,000
April	15,500	October	20,000
May	23,000	November	4,000
June	10,000	December	2,500
Total			$120,000

The average value of the taxpayer's property to be included in the property factor is $10,000 ($120,000/12).

Intangible property is not included in the factor, but see *Crocker Equipment Leasing, Inc. v. Department of Revenue*, 838 P2d 552 (Ore. 1992); a bank is allowed to include intangible property (in other words, loans and leases in its property factor), because the intangibles were responsible for roughly 98% of the bank's income. A New York administrative judge held that payments for the right to use spaces at New York City's Port Authority terminal were not rental payments for purposes of the company's property factor (*In the Matter of Peter Pan Bus Lines, Inc.* DTA Nos. 819131 and 819132 (N.Y. Tax App. Trib. 7/28/2003)). Another New York court held that amounts paid for license agreements for television programming were payments for the rental of tangible personal property, despite the fact that the programming was no longer delivered by videotape, but by satellite transmission. The state had always treated the payments as rents, and the court saw no rational distinction between programming delivered by videotape and programming delivered by satellite (*In the Matter of the Petition of Meredith Corporation*, 102 A.D.3d 156 (N.Y. App. Div. 2012)).

Some states treat inventory or property in transit at the end of the tax period as in the property factor of the state of destination. Some states simply delete the in-transit inventory from both the numerator and denominator. The general rule is that property in transit between a buyer and seller, and which is included by a taxpayer in the denominator, must be included in the numerator of the state of destination (*Montgomery Ward and Co., Inc. v. Franchise Tax Board*, 6 Cal. App. 3d 149, *appeal dismissed* 400 U.S. 913 (1970)). Nevertheless, many states' provisions are silent on the matter. In *Mercedes Benz of North America, Inc. v. Comptroller of the Treasury*, Md. Tax Ct., Oct. 7, 1988, Dkt. No. Income Tax 2813, the taxpayer included cars in-transit from Germany to Maryland in the Maryland denominator, but not the numerator. The court held that the cars must be either in both the numerator and denominator, or neither.

See *Cooper Tire & Rubber Co. v. Tax Commissioner*, 639 N.E.2d 27 (1994) for problems associated with computing the inclusion of mobile property.

The sales factor

As with everything in tax law, we must begin by defining our terms. The term "sales factor" may cause more confusion than the other two factors. It is more helpful to think of the sales factor in terms of gross receipts, because it will include not only sales from inventory, but interest, dividend, rental, and royalty income as well. Keep in mind that the term is generally applied to include only "receipts," which generate apportionable business income.

Definitions

The UDITPA rules provide that "the sales factor is a fraction, the numerator of which is the total sales of the taxpayer in this state during the tax period, and the denominator of which is the total sales of the taxpayer everywhere during this period."

The MTC regulations add to that definition by including interest income, service and carrying charges, and federal and state (including sales) excise taxes. The MTC excludes from the sales factor receipts from an incidental or occasional sale of a fixed asset used in the regular course of business, insubstantial amounts of gross receipts arising from incidental or occasional transactions or activities, and business income from intangible property, if the income cannot readily be attributable to any particular income-producing activity of the taxpayer. An example of the latter includes dividends and interest that result from the mere holding of the intangible property.

The California Supreme Court recently addressed one of the more controversial questions involving the sales factor. The question was simply this — when the statute says that gross receipts should be included in the sales factor, does it really mean "gross" receipts?

In one year, Microsoft's treasury department generated $5.7bn in gross receipts on short-term investments such as repurchase agreements (repos). However, the income from those investments only amounted to $10.7m. Microsoft included the gross receipts in the denominator of its sales factor for California, which cut the company's California income tax almost in half. The California Franchise Tax Board (FTB) disallowed the portion of the proceeds that represented return of capital. The question before the California Supreme Court then was whether the sales factor should include the gross proceeds from short-term securities investments, or only the net return.

The FTB argued that including the gross proceeds from such investments distorted the sales factor and proposed an alternative formula that excluded the return of principal from the sales factor. Microsoft pointed out that whether it was distortive or not, the plain language of the statute clearly said that gross receipts were to be included in the sales factor.

The California Supreme determined that both parties were right. Gross receipts did mean gross receipts. However, the FTB was successful in arguing that, at least in this case, the numbers were distortive. Under California law (Section 25137), if the standard apportionment formula fails to "fairly represent the extent of the taxpayer's business activity in this state," the taxpayer may petition, or the FTB may require, an alternative method of calculation. (See the discussion in the Relief Provision section that follows.) (See *Microsoft Corp. v. Franchise Tax Board*, 139 P.3d 1169 (Calif. 2006) and its companion case, *General Motors Corp. v. Franchise Tax Board*, 139 P.3d 1183 (Calif. 2006).)

Given the court's ruling, how is a taxpayer to file? Because distortion is, at least to some extent, in the eye of the beholder, it is clear that this controversy is not over. An alternative calculation case involves General Mills, who failed in their attempt to argue that futures transactions were gross receipts to be included in the sales factor. The San Francisco Superior Court ruled that while the sales may have been gross receipts, the inclusion distorted the sales factor and justified the use of an alternative formula (*General Mills, Inc., Inc. et al. v. Franchise Tax Board*, Super. Ct. (San Francisco Cty.), Case No. CGC05–439929, (November 1, 2010)). For example, the court noted that in 1992 and 1996, the futures trading generated no income, but did generate 8% and 30% of the company's sales respectively. Critics of the court point out that tying income to the sales factor is mixing apples with oranges. The first addresses the tax base while the second addresses the apportionment of that tax base. If income is to be a measure in apportionment, then any company with losses has sales factor issues. As a result of this case and other litigation, California promulgated a regulation on this issue. Both the regulation and this case were largely obsoleted by a Cal Rev and TC 25120(f), which enacted a throwout rule effective in 2011.

The MTC responded to the question posed in *Microsoft* as early as 2001 by proposing that the definition of "gross receipts" exclude proceeds from the repayment of principal on the sales of intangibles such as bonds, loans, or investments in mutual funds. The MTC resolution amended MTC Reg. IV.2(a), and was clearly an attempt to resolve whether net profits or gross receipts should be included in the sales factor. In any case, as a practical matter the term "sales factor" is really a misnomer; it is better to think of it as a gross receipts factor.

What kinds of sales: Property and services

One approach to addressing the sales factor is to begin by distinguishing between sales of tangible personal property and sales of services. UDITPA does this, but actually divides sales into tangible personal property sales and sales of everything else.

The UDITPA rules provide that

- Sales of tangible personal property are in this state if
  - the property is delivered or shipped to a purchaser within this state, other than the United States government, regardless of the f.o.b. point or other conditions of the sales; or
  - the property is shipped from an office, store, warehouse, factory, or other place of storage in this state; and (*a*) the purchaser is the United States government, or (*b*) the taxpayer is not taxable in the state of the purchaser.
- Sales, other than sales of tangible personal property, are in this state if
  - the income-producing activity is performed in this state; or
  - the income-producing activity is performed both in and outside this state, and a greater proportion of the income-producing activity is performed in this state than in any other state, based on the costs of performance

Sales of tangible personal property

The problem areas for tangible personal property sales usually lie with sourcing the sale (into which state's numerator should it go), and its related problems of dock sales and throwbacks.

Destination sales

Some 40 states follow the UDITPA rule that receipts from the sale of tangible personal property are sourced to the state of destination. The MTC regulations add that items such as FOB point, risk of loss, and passage of title are not to be considered in sourcing a sale.

Under UDITPA Section 16(a), tangible personal property sales are to be sourced to the state in which the property is "delivered or shipped to a purchaser . . . within this state." The question created by UDITPA is whether the phrase "within this state" modifies the word "purchaser" or the word "delivered." In other words, should the sale be sourced to the state of ultimate destination, or the place-of-delivery? For example, if a Colorado seller ships goods to a distributor's dock in Denver for pickup by a Kansas purchaser, should the sale be sourced to Colorado, the place of delivery? Or should it be sourced to Kansas, the purchaser's domicile and place of ultimate destination?

Most state courts have held that because the purpose of the sales factor is to measure the contribution of the market state, the sale should be sourced to the place of ultimate destination. The *McDonnell Douglas* case is most instructive. McDonnell Douglas, a Maryland corporation, manufactured and sold aircraft worldwide. Some of these aircraft were delivered to customers in California for transportation to the aircraft's ultimate destination. The California FTB held that the sales were California sales, and should be accordingly included in the California numerator. The State Board of Equalization, however disagreed, and overturning the FTB, held that because the purpose of the sales factor is to measure the contribution of the market state, then the sale should be sourced to the customer's ultimate destination. In other words, if a purchaser's receipt of goods in California is for the sole purpose of immediate transportation to another state, then that sale is not included in the California numerator, because the purchaser is not deemed as being within the state. That said, if the purchaser takes possession for any other purposes such as adding accessories, repackaging, or storage, then the sale is a California sale for purposes of the sales factor. (See *McDonnell Douglas Corp. v. Franchise Tax Board*, 33 Cal. Rptr. 2d 129 (Calif. Ct. of App. 1994); *Olympia Brewing Co. v. Commissioner of Revenue*, 326 N.W. 2d 642 (Minn. 1982); *Pabst Brewing Co., v. Wisconsin Department of Revenue* (1984); *Pennsylvania v. Gilmour Manufacturing Co.,* 822 A.2d 676 (Penn. 2003); and *Paccar, Inc. v. Alabama*, Adm. Law. Div., No. Corp. 04-715 (Jan. 11, 2006). *Department of Revenue v. Parker Banana Co.*, 391 So.2d 762 (Fla. Dist. Ct. App. 1980); But see also *Rohm and Haas Kentucky, Inc.*, 929 S.W.2d 741, (Ky. App. 1996).)

Throwback sales

"Throwback sales" are an exception to the destination test. The throwback rules provide that if the seller is not taxable in the destination state, then any sales to that state are thrown back into the sales numerator of the state of origin. Throwback sales apply to (*a*) sales to the U.S. Government; and (*b*) sales into states where the seller is not taxable. For example, a Colorado computer retailer makes only mail-order sales into Nebraska. The retailer does not have nexus with Nebraska, and is not subject to tax there. Consequently, those Nebraska destination sales are thrown back into the Colorado sales numerator.

The purpose of this rule, adopted by both UDITPA and MTC, is to avoid the creation of "nowhere sales" (that is, sales that do not show up in any state's numerator). The throwback rules try to ensure that the sales factor accounts for 100% of a company's sales. Naturally, some states have a "do not throw it back" rule. Examples include Arizona, Delaware, Florida, Georgia, Indiana, Iowa, Kentucky (unless to U.S. Government), Maryland, Michigan, Minnesota, Nebraska, New Jersey, New York, North Carolina, Ohio, Pennsylvania, South Carolina, Tennessee (unless to U.S. Government), Texas, and Virginia. For an exception to the rule that sales to the U.S. government are thrown back, see *Jim Beam Brands Co.* (KBTA Order No. K-14942, 7/23/93).

Other states have adopted a double throwback rule to make certain that drop shipments are accounted for in the sales factor. The classic drop shipment scenario goes like this. Say, for example, that you have ordered some boots from L.L. Bean. The boots are manufactured at a company in Kansas. Instead of L.L. Bean having the boots sent to their store in Maine and then reshipped to Colorado, they simply have the boots drop-shipped directly to Colorado. The double throwback provides that if L.L. Bean is not taxable in Colorado (it is not), the sale is thrown back into Kansas. If the company is not taxable in Kansas, the sale is thrown back again into Maine. Again, the function of the rule is to avoid the creation of nowhere sales.

Because the throwback rule (aside from government sales) only comes into play when a seller is not taxable in the destination state, the question naturally arises — how is taxability in the other state defined? Following UDITPA, most state statutes read that a taxpayer is deemed to be taxable in another state, if in that state the taxpayer is subject to a net income tax, a franchise tax measured by net income, a franchise tax for the privilege of doing business, or a corporate stock tax.

The Indiana Tax Court held that Michigan's Single Business Tax (SBT) met the definition of a franchise tax, thereby deeming the taxpayer to be subject to tax in Michigan. The Indiana Department of Revenue argued that although the SBT was certainly a tax on the privilege of doing business, it was not a franchise tax on the privilege of doing business. The court rejected the revenue department's argument holding that the SBT is indeed a franchise tax on the privilege of doing business in Michigan. Therefore, the taxpayer did not have to throw back its Michigan sales into the Indiana numerator (*Welch Packaging Group, Inc. v. Indiana*, Ind. Tax Ct. No. 49T10-0503-TA-21 (Nov. 13, 2007)). Given the move of several states to a gross receipts tax, such as Ohio's Commercial Activity Tax and the Texas Margin Tax, we will be sure to see more cases of this nature.

Michigan courts have held in a series of cases that sales need not be thrown back into Michigan. The courts held that the test was not if the business is subject to tax in the delivery state, but if the taxpayer demonstrated more than a "slightest presence" in the delivery state (see *Guardian Industries Corp. v. Department of Treasury*, 499 N.W.2d 349 (Mich. 1993); *Howmet Corp. v. Michigan*, No. 87-11161-CM, Mich. Ct. Claims (Jan. 1, 1989); and *Magnetek Controls, Inc. v. Revenue Division*, 566 N.W.2d 219 (Mich. 1997)).

A variation of the throwback rule is the throwout rule. Under this rule, if the business is not taxable in the state of destination, the sales are thrown out of both the numerator and denominator of the sales factor. For a multistate business, the interplay between two states, one using throwbacks and the other using throwouts, can result in the business paying tax on more than 100% of its income. Illinois, Maine, California, and West Virginia use a throwout rule. New Jersey enacted a throwout rule in its 2002

Business Tax Reform Act. Pfizer, Inc. challenged New Jersey's throwout rule and lost in 2008 (see *Pfizer v. Director*, 24 NJ Tax 116 (5/29/2008)). Pfizer appealed, and its appeal was consolidated with Whirlpool Properties. See also *Whirlpool Properties, Inc. v. Director, Division of Taxation*, 25 NJ Tax 519 (July 12, 2010). The taxpayers lost on appeal, but in the meantime the New Jersey legislature has repealed its throwout rule for tax years beginning on or after July 1, 2010 (*Whirlpool Properties, Inc. v. Director*, Division of Taxation, 26 A.3d 446 (N.J. 2011)). This case involved a very unusual throwout rule that only applied to the denominator of the sales factor (not the numerator and denominator).

Joyce versus Finnigan

The throwback rule is further complicated by its interaction with the reporting requirements of combined filing unitary states. The confusion is created by differences in the definition of the phrase "taxable in another state" as used in defining "throwback" sales in UDITPA's Section 3. "For purposes of allocation and apportionment of income under this Act, a taxpayer is taxable in another state if . . . " Does the term "taxpayer" mean an individual corporation, or does it mean a unitary group?

In brief, the question is this: When determining whether you must throw back sales into your state numerator, do you look to each individual corporation, or do you look to the unitary group as a whole? If a state follows *Joyce*, it counts throwbacks on a separate company basis. If a state follows *Finnigan*, it counts throwbacks on a combined reporting or unitary method. Joyce and Finnigan come from two court cases in California, Appeal of Joyce, Inc., Cal. State Bd. of Equalization, Nov. 23, 1966, Dkt. No. 66-SBE-070 and Appeal of Finnigan, Cal. State Bd. of Equalization, Aug. 25, 1988, Dkt. No. 88-SBE-022, on reh'g, Jan. 24, 1990.

California initially followed the *Joyce* rule, then later switched to the *Finnigan* rule, then back to *Joyce*, and effective January 1, 2011, back to *Finnigan*.

Example 5-5

Flintstone Corporation does business in California, Illinois, and Nebraska. The corporation has two subsidiaries: Fred, Inc. and Wilma, Inc.

Fred Company only has nexus with California, and Wilma Company only has nexus with Colorado. Neither Fred nor Wilma have nexus or do business in any other state. However, Fred, Inc. does have catalog and online sales in Colorado.

If California is following *Joyce*, then because Fred does not have nexus with Colorado, its Colorado sales will be thrown back into the California numerator. However, if California is following *Finnigan*, then because Wilma has nexus in Colorado and is filing a combined report with Flintstone in California, the sales are not thrown back into Fred's California numerator.

States with throwbacks are split on whether to apply the *Joyce* or the *Finnigan* rule. According to the Multistate Corporate Tax Guide,[1] *Finnigan* states include Arizona, California (effective January 1, 2011),

[1] Healy, John C. and Michael S. Schadewald, Multistate Corporate Tax Guide 2010 (New York: Aspen Publishing, 2014), Vol. 1, p. 680.

Indiana, Kansas, Maine, Massachusetts, Michigan, Utah, and Wisconsin. *Joyce* states include Arkansas, Colorado, Hawaii, Idaho, Illinois, Montana, New Hampshire, New Mexico, North Dakota, Oregon, and Vermont. Despite not having a throwback rule, a New York appellate court recently ruled that the state could include in the numerator of a company's sales factor the sales of a subsidiary that did not have nexus with the state (see *In the Matter of Disney Enterprises, Inc. v. Tax Appeals Tribunal*, 40 A.D.3d 49 (New York 2007)). The court's holding is not clear, and because the court did not mention either *Joyce* or *Finnigan* in its decision, it could be that the court was confusing unitary theory with an apportionment problem. Richard Pomp, a University of Connecticut law school professor who testified for Disney, said that unitary theory "does not justify taking a sale made by one corporation and treating it as if it were made by another. The difficulty of measuring income when there are flows of value, which is the rationale for a combined report, has nothing to do with the difficulty of measuring the sales made by each corporation included in the combined report." Nevertheless, the New York Court of Appeals upheld the lower court's decision (see *In the Matter of Disney Enterprises, Inc. v. New York*, 888 N.E.2d 1029 (New York 2008)).

Example 5-6

The ABC combined group is made up of three separate corporations, A, B, and C. A and B have nexus in both Colorado and Utah, but C only has nexus in Colorado. However, C makes sales into Utah. Here are the companies' respective sales:

	Colorado	Utah	
A	$ 6,000	$ 1,000	
B	$ 6,000	$ 8,000	
C	$ 6,000	$ 3,000	
Totals	$ 18,000	$12,000	$ 30,000

Colorado is a *Joyce* state and its factor is 70% because the $3,000 in Utah sales are thrown back into the Colorado numerator.

A	$ 6,000	
B	$ 6,000	
C	$ 9,000	
Total	$ 21,000	$21,000 divided by 30,000 = 70%

Because Utah is a *Finnigan* state, its factor is 40% because C's Utah sales of $3,000 are not thrown back into the Colorado numerator, but stay in the Utah numerator, because C is part of a combined group in which A and B have nexus with Utah.

A	$ 1,000	
B	$ 8,000	
C	$ 3,000	
Total	$ 12,000	$12,000 divided by 30,000 = 40%

Notice that in the previous example, more than 100% of the sales of the combined group of ABC have been apportioned. In short, ABC is paying tax on more than 100% of their sales. Thus, sales from a *Joyce* state with throwbacks into a *Finnigan* state will result in the sale being in both state's numerators, and you will be paying tax on more than 100% of your income. State tax administrators do not seem to be bothered by this as much as taxpayers. However, sales from a *Finnigan* state into a *Joyce* state with throwbacks will result in the sale being excluded from both state's numerators, and you will be paying tax on less than 100% of your income. Taxpayers do not seem to be bothered by this as much as state tax administrators.

Sales of services

Receipts from sales of services, unlike sales of tangible personal property, are not sourced under the destination test. Instead, sales, other than sales of tangible personal property, are sourced by looking at the income-producing activity, and measuring that activity by its cost of performance. Specifically, UDITPA provides that service sales are in-state sales if (*a*) the income-producing activity is performed in the state; or (*b*) "the income-producing activity is performed both in and outside this state and a greater proportion of the income-producing activity is performed in this state than in any other state, based on costs of performance." Simply put, Section 17 of UDITPA allocates sales of services to where the bulk of the income-producing activity takes place as measured by cost of performance.

UDITPA and MTC are not always consistent. For example, the MTC regulation for personal services provides that

> "Gross receipts for the performance of personal services are attributable to this state to the extent that such services are performed in this state. If services relating to a single item of income are performed partly within and partly without this state, the gross receipts from the performance of such services shall be attributable to this state only if the greater proportion of such services was performed in the state, based on costs of performance. Usually, where services are performed partly within and partly without this state, the services performed in each state will constitute a separate income producing activity; in such case the gross receipts from the performance of services attributable to this state shall be measured by the ratio which the time spent in performing the services in this state bears to the total time spent in performing the services everywhere."

Not surprisingly, there are at least two areas in which taxpayers and tax administrators differ. The first is in defining the "income-producing activity," and the other is in defining "cost of performance." For example, what is a travel agency's "income-producing activity?" Is it the individual sale of travel packages, or is it the operation of bundling the packages together? The difference is important, because the costs of performance between the two vary. The costs of a European travel package may include airfare, hotel accommodations, and ground transportation, only some of which are incurred in the United States. But, the costs of simply bundling the packages together may very well be done in offices in the United States. It is probably not too difficult to guess where Massachusetts thought those costs and the accompanying, income-producing activity occurred. See *Interface Group v. Commissioner of Revenue*, 918 NE2d 97

(Mass. App. Ct., 2009), *aff'g* Mass. App. Tax Bd., Nos. C266670-76, C266680, and C266677-79, 10/17/08, 2008 WL 4642961, *rev. den.* Mass. S.Ct., (March 31, 2010). Massachusetts has also tackled the question of whether the "income-producing activity" of a hockey team was the playing of individual games or the operation of the franchise as a whole. The Department of Revenue naturally argued that it was the latter, because the cost of performance of each individual game would have sourced more income away from Massachusetts. The court upheld the department's position. See *Boston Professional Hockey Ass'n*, 820 NE2d 792 (2005).

In *Bellsouth Advertising & Publishing Corp. v. Chumley*, 308 SW3d 350 (Tenn. Ct. App. 2009) app. den., Tenn. Sup. Ct, (March 1, 2010), the Tennessee Commissioner held that, despite the fact that the bulk of the cost of performance occurred outside the state, the result was distortive, because all the advertising itself (delivery of the telephone directories) occurred inside Tennessee. For a similar decision, see *Ameritech Publishing, Inc., v. Wisconsin*, 788 NW2d 383, Wisc. Ct. App. (June 24, 2010).

The key dispute reflected in these cases is whether a transactional or operational approach should be taken in defining the income producing activity and its cost of performance. For example, Massachusetts took an operational approach in *Boston Professional Hockey,* arguing that the income producing activity was the overall operation of a sports franchise and not the playing of individual games. The state also took the operational approach in *Interface,* holding that the income producing activity was not each individual sale of a travel package to each customer, but the operation of assembling and marketing vacation packages.

The differences between a transactional and operational approach are most striking in two cases involving AT&T. The Oregon Tax Court held that the income producing activity was each telecommunications transaction, and thus the direct costs were those primarily associated with each transaction. However, the Massachusetts court held that transactional approach was inappropriate, given that AT&T's income producing activity was the operation of a nationwide telecommunications network. The cost of performance test was the integrated operation of the overall network, rather than each separate call or transmission. In other words — same company, same facts, same cost of performance rules — but opposite conclusions. (Compare *AT&T Corp. v. Dep't of Rev.*, TC 4814 (Ore. Tax Ct. 2012) and *AT&T Corp. v. Comm'r of Revenue*, No. 11-P-1462, aff'g Ma. App. Tax Bd. C293831 (Mass. App. Ct. 2012).)

Under UDITPA, the cost of performance (COP) is an all-or-nothing approach. If 75% of the COP is in State A and 25% in State B, the entire sale is sourced to State A. However, the states vary from UDITPA rules by sometimes applying preponderance, or greater proportion test, or a pro rata approach. For example, in a preponderance state, if the cost of performance is apportioned among three states where 40% of the COP was in one state and 30% each in the other two states, the sale would be sourced entirely to the 40% state. A pro rata state would pro-rate the sale proportionately, so each state would receive its applicable share. The risk, of course, is that in our example, the 40% state might put the entire sale in its numerator, while one of the 30% states, being a pro rata state, would put 30% of the sale in its numerator. As a consequence, the taxpayer ends up paying tax on more than 100% of its income. As you can see, the inconsistency between the two methods presents tax traps for the unwary and opportunities for others. Some pro rata states include Louisiana, Mississippi, North Carolina, Rhode Island, and South Carolina.

The problem is compounded by the vague definition of cost of performance. In short, cost of performance is measured by direct costs determined in a manner consistent with generally accepted accounting principles (GAAP), and in accordance with accepted industry practices.

Direct costs generally include such things as salaries and wages, taxes, interest, and depreciation. Indirect costs are usually defined as all costs that are not direct costs — not much help there.

As mentioned previously, personal services often are singled out for specific measurement. The MTC rule quoted previously is often referred to as the "time-spread" method and in such cases, the income from the performance of the services is usually measured by the ratio of time spent in the state performing the services divided by the total time spent performing the services everywhere.

In 2005, California issued Legal Ruling 2005-01, holding that the term "personal services" for purposes of the sales factor included the performance of any service, where capital was not a material income-producing factor. In personal service contracts, where capital is not a material income-producing factor, the special time-spread rule will be used to determine the corporation's costs of performance. Most importantly, the time each employee spends in each state will constitute a separate income-producing activity for purposes of determining the numerator of the sales factor. Finally, where capital is a material income-producing factor, the special time-spread rule does not apply. Instead, the standard cost of performance rule would assign the receipts to the state with the greatest cost of performance.

To market, to market

Several states are abandoning cost of performance and are moving toward a market/destination-based approach to service sales. They include Alabama, California, Connecticut, the District of Columbia, Georgia, Illinois, Iowa, Kentucky, Louisiana, Maine, Maryland, Massachusetts, Michigan, Minnesota, Montana, Nebraska, New Jersey, New York, Ohio, Oklahoma, Oregon, Pennsylvania, Rhode Island, Tennessee, Utah, and Wisconsin. Basically, the move is an effort to source sales of services in the same fashion as sales of goods — by destination. The belief is that this approach is more consistent with the rationale for a sales factor; that is, it represents the contribution of the market states. After all, cost of performance, particularly for services, often looks just like the payroll factor. Finally, one shouldn't forget the political appeal. Market-based sourcing generally shifts the tax burden to out-of-state sellers over their in-state counterparts, an appeal that is irresistible to most politicians.

Certain industries have always taken a market approach. In *The New Yorker Magazine, Inc. v. Department of Revenue of State of Illinois*, (Illinois Circuit Court, Cook County, 1/12/88), advertising revenue was deemed included in the sales factor to the same extent as circulation revenue. See also *McGraw-Hill, Inc.*, TAT (H)93-64(GC), 12/30/93, where it was determined that advertising revenues are sourced based on the location of subscribers.

The move toward market-based sourcing of service sales has prompted a host of questions and problems. For example, when sourcing based on the market, does that mean where the service is performed or where the benefit is received? Louisiana looks to where the service is performed, and

Maryland to where it is received. Thus, a software developer writing code in Louisiana for a client in Maryland may very well end up having to include the sales in the numerators of the sales factor calculations of both states. Because sourcing service sales by market may mean where the service is performed (so it looks like cost of performance), where the benefit is received, or where the customer is located, such sourcing may be just as problematic as the traditional cost of performance test.

One of the problems often overlooked is simply the variety of services provided and the difficulty of applying market-based sourcing to services as varied as: financial institutions, telecommunication companies, advertisers, detective, analytical, and investigatory services, healthcare providers, software consultants, online learning and research organizations, and accounting and law firms.

The growth in cloud computing, including application service providers, software as a service (SaaS), infrastructure as a service (IaaS), and platform as a service (PaaS), has added yet another layer of complexity to sales factor sourcing. Although the debate over how to source these activities for sales tax has caught the attention of many, equally important is how to source the same activities in a taxpayer's sales factor. There are several options that states have taken. For example, SaaS could simply be treated as the sale of tangible personal property and sourced by destination. As one auditor noted to the author, "you are basically getting constructive receipt of the software and so it's a rental or lease of tangible personal property." SaaS might also be treated as an information service and sourced based upon either cost of performance or market. Finally, SaaS might even be treated as the sale or lease of an intangible, and apportioned in the same way patents and trademarks are treated.

States have and are using all of these approaches and not consistently. Unfortunately, until recently formal guidance was meager, and largely limited to state surveys by tax publications that are not always consistent with each other. However, this has started to change.

In July 2014, the MTC replaced its COP rules for services and adopted market-based sourcing for the sales of services and other intangibles as follows:

a. Receipts, other than receipts described in Section 16, are in this state if the taxpayer's market for the sales is in this state. The taxpayer's market for sales is in this state:
   i. in the case of sale, rental, lease, or license of real property, if and to the extent the property is located in this state;
   ii. in the case of rental, lease, or license of tangible personal property, if and to the extent the property is located in this state;
   iii. in the case of sale of a service, if and to the extent the service is delivered to a location in this state; and
   iv. in the case of intangible property,
      (1) that is rented, leased, or licensed, if and to the extent the property is used in this state, provided that intangible property used in marketing a good or service to a consumer is "used in this state" if that good or service is purchased by a consumer who is in this state; and
      (2) that is sold, if and to the extent the property is used in this state, provided that:
         (a) a contract right, government license, or similar intangible property that authorizes the holder to conduct a business activity in a specific geographic area is "used in this state" if the geographic area includes all or part of this state;

(b) receipts from intangible property sales that are contingent on the productivity, use, or disposition of the intangible property shall be treated as receipts from the rental, lease or licensing of such intangible property under subsection (a)(4)(i); and
(c) all other receipts from a sale of intangible property shall be excluded from the numerator and denominator of the sales factor.

b. If the state or states of assignment under subsection (a) cannot be determined, the state or states of assignment shall be reasonably approximated.

c. If the taxpayer is not taxable in a state to which a sale is assigned under subsection (a) or (b), or if the state of assignment cannot be determined under subsection (a) or reasonably approximated under subsection (b), such sale shall be excluded from the denominator of the sales factor.

d. (The tax administrator may prescribe regulations as necessary or appropriate to carry out the purposes of this section.)

Several states have already issued guidance on their market-based sourcing, and their pronouncements illustrate some of the difficulties in applying the new standards.

California — For tax years beginning on or after January 1, 2013, sales of other than tangible personal property are to be sourced in the following fashion:

1. Sales of services are in California to the extent the purchaser receives the benefit of the services in the state.
2. Sales from intangibles are sourced to California to the extent the intangible property is used in the state (California Code of Regulations (CCR) 25136-2).

The benefit of the service received is generally defined as the location where the customer receives the value from the delivery of that service. For individuals, the location is presumed to be the customer's billing address (CCR 25136-2(c)(1)(A)). However for businesses, the location is presumed to first be the location identified in the taxpayer's books and records (that is, contract). If not identifiable from the books and records, the taxpayer is to make a reasonable approximation, and if that is not possible, the taxpayer should look to where the customer placed the order. If that information isn't available, then the fallback is to the customer's billing address (CCR 25136-2(c)(2)).

New York — For tax years beginning on or after January 1, 2015, sales of services are attributed to New York "if the location of the customer is within the state." In defining location, the taxpayer applies a cascade of steps beginning with where the benefit is received, delivered, and apportioned in either the past or current year (New York Tax Law Section 210(-A)(-10)).

Pennsylvania — For tax years beginning on or after January 1, 2014, sales of services are sourced to the state if the "service is delivered to a location in this State." Although the statute does not define either "delivered" or "location," state guidance provides that it is where the benefit of the service is received. If unknown, the location for individuals is presumed to be the billing address, and for businesses it is presumed to be the ordering location first and the billing address second (Pennsylvania Informational Notice Corporation Income Tax 2014-01 (12/12/2014)).

Unfortunately, state statutory language regarding sourcing sales of services varies, as seen from the following:

Alabama — "service is delivered to a location in this state" (Ala. Admin. Code 810-27-1-4-.17.01(2)).

Arizona — "purchaser received the benefit of the service in this state" (Ariz. Rev. Stat. Section 43-1147(E)(4)).

Georgia — "are derived from customers within this state" (Ga. Code Section 48-7-31(d)(2)(A)(i)).

Illinois — "the services are received in this State" (Ill. Stat. Section 5/304(a)(3)(C-5)(iv)).

Iowa — "recipient of the service receives the benefit of the service in this state" (Iowa Admin. Rule 701-54.6(422)).

Maine — "where the services are received" (Me. Rev. Stat. Section 5211(16-A)(A)).

Maryland — "receipts are derived from customers within this State" (Md. Code Regs. Section 03.04.03.08(C)(3)(c)).

Massachusetts — "service is delivered to a location in the commonwealth" (Mass. Gen. Laws, Section 38(f)(3)).

Michigan — "recipient ... receives ... benefit of the services in this state" (Mich. Laws Section 206.665(2)(a)).

Minnesota — "state where the services are received" (Minn. Rev. Stat. Section 290.191; Subd.5(j)).

Nebraska — "sales are derived from a buyer within this state" (Neb. Rev. Stat. 77-2734.14(3)(a)).

Oklahoma — "derived from customers within this state" (Okla. Admin. Code Section 710:50-17-71(1)(A)(ii)).

Utah — "receives a greater benefit of the service in this state than in any other state" (Utah Code Section 59-7-319(3)(a)).

Wisconsin — "received the benefit of the service in this state" (Wis. Stat. Section 71.25(9)(dh)).

The state of Washington has been in the forefront on these issues, passing legislation in 2009 that specifically addressed the taxation of digital products, goods, and services. Nebraska recently enacted legislation that provides that SaaS, IaaS, and PaaS be sourced to the state, if the purchaser is an individual with a billing address in the state, or a business using the service in the state (See L.B. 872, enacted April 10, 2012).

Finally, it is important not to assume that the way a state treats cloud computing for sales tax is going to be reflective of how it will be treated for sales factor apportionment or vice versa. There is no necessary connection between transaction taxes like sales tax and taxes on income.

Outsourcing and independent contractors

In 2007, the MTC added an amendment to its uniform regulations to include in the definition of an income-producing activity "transactions and activities performed on behalf of a taxpayer, such as those conducted on its behalf by an independent contractor." The amendment also includes "payments to an agent or independent contractor for the performance of personal services which give rise to the particular item of income." The change by the MTC is recognition of the growing importance of outsourcing in both manufacturing and services.

California addressed the application of a similar rule in the context of a combined report in Legal Ruling 2006-02. In the ruling, the FTB clarified the application of the "on behalf of" rule, when a member of a combined reporting group has a sale of other than tangible personal property and that member pays another member of the combined reporting group to perform activities related to that sale.

Specifically, the ruling excludes from a taxpayer's income-producing activity any acts performed on its behalf by an independent contractor, unless the independent contractor is a member of the same unitary group. Payments made by one member of a combined reporting group to another member (that is, subcontractor) are only counted as costs of performance for the member, if the payment reflects an arm's-length price for the performance of the service. The payment will be considered a direct cost, and will be used to measure the member's and not the subcontractor's costs of performance. If the member does not pay at an arm's-length price, the actual costs incurred by the subcontractor may be imputed to the member to measure the member's costs of performance.

Specialized industries

Most states have special rules for specific industries such as airlines, railroads, financial organizations, construction companies, television and radio, publishing, and trucking companies. The MTC has issued final or proposed regulations on construction contractors, railroads, airlines, radio and television broadcasting, and trucking. These rules vary from industry to industry and are beyond the scope of this course, but a couple of examples are in order. In 1986, the MTC adopted a special apportionment formula for the trucking industry (see MTC Regulation IV.18(g)). In brief, the regulation modifies the traditional three-factor apportionment formula by multiplying the numerators of the factors by a ratio of the in-state miles of the mobile property to total miles everywhere. Applied to the property factor, for example, the numerator would include all owned and leased property in the state, multiplied by the ratio of in-state miles to total miles, while the denominator would include all owned and leased property everywhere.

On November 17, 1994, the MTC adopted model special apportionment rules for financial institutions. The formula apportions all business income under the three-factor approach. Only interest, dividends, net gains, and other business income from investment assets and activities (including trading) are included in the receipts factor. Investment assets and activities include, but are not limited to, investment securities, federal funds, repurchase agreements (repos), swaps, futures contracts, equities, forward contracts, and foreign currency transactions. The MTC recommended adoption for tax years beginning after January 1, 1996. The definition of what is a financial institution is left up to the states.

The relief provision

Section 18 of UDITPA is commonly referred to as the "Relief Provision," because it provides for modification of the formula.

If the allocation and apportionment provisions of the act do not fairly represent the extent of the taxpayer's business activity in this state, the taxpayer may petition for, or the tax administrator may require, in respect to all or any part of the taxpayer's business activity, if reasonable,

- separate accounting;
- the exclusion of any one or more of the factors;
- the inclusion of one or more additional factors that will fairly represent the taxpayer's business activity in this state; or
- the employment of any other method to effectuate an equitable allocation and apportionment of the taxpayer's income.

The taxpayer may petition for relief under Section 18, or the tax administrator may require "with respect to all or any part of the taxpayer's business activity, use of separate accounting, exclusion of any one or more of the factors, inclusion of one or more additional factors, or employment of any other method that will result in an equitable allocation and apportionment of the taxpayer's income." Because most courts provide a presumption of correctness on the part of the state, it is not surprising that tax administrators have been more successful invoking Section 18 relief than have taxpayers. See, for example, *Hans Rees' Sons, Inc. v. North Carolina,* 283 U.S. 123 (1931); *Container Corp. of America v. Franchise Tax Board,* 463 U.S. 159 (1983); and *Crocker Equipment Leasing v. Department of Revenue*, Supreme Court of Oregon, SC S38059 (August 20, 1992). Given the long history, as illustrated by the previous cases, of taxpayers failing in their efforts to receive Section 18 relief, it was surprising to see a taxpayer not only win relief, but win relief based on combined filing in a separate-filing state.

South Carolina has traditionally been a separate-filing state, and has rebuffed past attempts by taxpayers to file a combined report there. See *NCR Corp. v. South Carolina*, 402 SE2d 666 (1991) and *NCR Corp. v. South Carolina*, 439 SE2d 254 (1993), often known as NCR I and NCR II. However, since the NCR decisions, the state had enacted into South Carolina law an identical version of Section 18 relief at S.C. Code Section 12-6-2320(A). Because the statute now provided for "the employment of any other method to effectuate an equitable allocation and apportionment" of income, Media General Communications petitioned, pursuant to an audit, for the use of combined reporting. Although the Department of Revenue agreed with the taxpayer that separate filing did not fairly reflect the taxpayer's income and that combined reporting did do so, the department declined to allow the taxpayer to use the latter method, on the grounds that as a separate-filing state, it did not have the authority to permit combined filing. The South Carolina Supreme Court ruled in favor of Media General, stating that because the statute provided for "any other method," the plain language of the law provided for combined filing. In addition to the language of the statute, the court pointed out that both parties had stipulated that combined filing more fairly reflected income than separate filing, that the state had not offered any other filing methodology, and that the U.S. Supreme Court had recognized combined filing apportionment as an acceptable methodology for apportioning a company's income. See *Media General v. South Carolina*, 694 SE2d 525 (2010).

The most controversial decision of late regarding alternative apportionment comes out of Mississippi. Equifax is engaged in the credit reporting business. It has customers in Mississippi but little physical presence, because its services are largely provided electronically. Equifax applied Mississippi's regulation regarding services and cost of performance, and determined that none of its income-producing activity or COP occurred in the state. Nevertheless, the Mississippi Department of Revenue determined that the state's statutory apportionment formula did not accurately reflect Equifax's activity in the state. Invoking the state's version of UDITPA Section 18, the department recalculated the company's income using market based sourcing and slapped on penalties and interest, despite the fact that Equifax had properly computed its income according to the department's regulations (see *Equifax, Inc. v. Mississippi*, No. 2010-SCT-01857 (Miss. 2013)). Several state practitioners were outraged, calling it "hunting season on apportionment." Historically, Section 18 relief has been usually restricted to occasional, nonrecurring transactions that are arguably clearly distortive, and so the Equifax case raises the specter that both tax administrators and taxpayers may ignore state statutory provisions and invoke Section 18 alternative apportionment whenever it suits their fancy. The U.S. Supreme Court denied cert, but the state has since amended its statutes to narrow the provisions of its Section 18 equivalent, and to eliminate penalties for its imposition.

How much distortion is enough?

Is there even enough distortion to overcome a state's apportionment methodology? That was the question facing the U.S. Supreme Court in *Hans Rees*. *Hans Rees* was a victory for the taxpayer. Admittedly, there have not been many. In this case, North Carolina used a single factor, property, to apportion the income of a company with a manufacturing plant in North Carolina and its corporate offices in New York. Using its single formula, the state determined that 85% of the company's income was taxable in North Carolina. Hans Rees was able to show that only 20% of its income came from its manufacturing activities in North Carolina. Apparently, the gulf between 20% and 85% was such that the court held for Hans Rees, stating that apportionment formulas cannot be intrinsically arbitrary, unreasonable, or tax extraterritorial income. "The difficulty of making an exact apportionment is apparent and hence, when the State has adopted a method not intrinsically arbitrary, it will be sustained until proof is offered of an unreasonable and arbitrary application in particular cases."

The treatment of factors in partnerships

The key question for partnerships is whether the apportionment and allocation take place at the partnership or partner level. Most states require apportionment and allocation at the partner level. For example, if a corporation owns 30% of a partnership (and they have a unitary relationship), it simply picks up its share of the partnership's income and adds its 30% share of the partnerships' factors (sales, property, and payroll) to its own.

Example 5-7

Corporation A had $3,000,000 in taxable income last year and does business in states X and Y. Its factors are as follows:

	State X	State Y	Total
Sales	10,000,000	15,000,000	25,000,000
Property	3,000,000	4,000,000	7,000,000
Payroll	500,000	700,000	1,200,000

Corporation A owned 30% of Partnership B. Partnership B had $900,000 of taxable income and did business in states Y and Z. Its factors are as follows:

	State Y	State Z	Total
Sales	3,000,000	1,000,000	4,000,000
Property	600,000	900,000	1,500,000
Payroll	300,000	150,000	450,000

After adding its 30% share of Partnership B to its own activities, Corporation A will have $3,270,000 in taxable income, and its apportionment factors will look like this.

	State X	State Y	State Z	Total
Sales	10,000,000	15,900,000	300,000	26,200,000
Property	3,000,000	4,180,000	270,000	7,450,000
Payroll	500,000	790,000	45,000	1,335,000

The income for State Z, which uses an equally-weighted three-factor formula, would be $88,617, calculated as follows:

	State Z	Total	Appt %
Sales	300,000	26,200,000	01.14
Property	270,000	7,450,000	03.62
Payroll	45,000	1,335,000	03.37
Total			08.13
Divided by 3 equals			2.71%

$3,270,000 × 2.71% = $88,617

Example 5-8

If the allocation and apportionment is done at the partnership level, the corporate partner simply adds the partnerships' resulting state income to the corporation's income for that state.

Because Corporation A is not doing business of its own in State Z, it has no taxable income for State Z.

Calculation of Partnership B's State Z income:

	State Z	Total	Appt %
Sales	1,000,000	4,000,000	25.00
Property	900,000	1,500,000	60.00
Payroll	150,000	450,000	33.33
Total			118.33
Divided by 3 equals			39.44%

$900,000 × 39.44% = $354.960 × 30% (Corp. A's interest) = $106,488

Corporation A's Total Taxable Income for State Z is $106,488

The preceding example assumed that the corporation and partnership were not unitary, nor were there any intercompany sales between the corporation and the partnership. Naturally, things become more complicated if there is a unitary relationship or intercompany sales. The majority of states simply do not address such issues either in their statutes, regulations, rulings, or policies. These states often follow the lead of larger states, such as California, that do address these issues. The following is a portion of California Reg. 25137-1, and contains several helpful examples of how to calculate the appropriate corporate income of a partnership interest.

25137-1. Apportionment and allocation of partnership income

(a) In general.

When a taxpayer has an interest in a partnership as defined in Section 17008, Revenue and Taxation Code, the division of its distributive share of partnership items shall be determined in accordance with chapter 10 of part 10 of Division 2 of the Revenue and Taxation Code. The determination of the portion of such distributive share (constituting business and nonbusiness income), which has its source in this state or which is includable in the taxpayer's business income subject to apportionment, shall be made in accordance with these regulations provided that the taxpayer, or the partnership, or both, have income from sources within and without this state. The taxpayer in computing net income for its income year shall include its distributive share of partnership items referred to previously for any partnership year ending within or with the taxpayer's income year.

The first step is to determine which portion of the taxpayer's income and its distributive share of the partnership items constitute "business income" and "nonbusiness income" under Section 25120, Revenue and Taxation Code, and the regulations thereunder. The various items of nonbusiness income are then directly allocated to specific states pursuant to the provisions of Section 25124 to 25127, Revenue and Taxation Code. The taxpayer's distributive share of partnership business income is apportioned by the formula set forth in subsections (f) or (g), whichever is applicable. The sum of

1. the items of nonbusiness income directly allocated to this state; plus
2. the amount of business income attributed to this state is the portion of the taxpayer's entire net income, which is subject to tax.

   Income arising from transactions and activity in the regular course of the partnership's trade or business constitutes business income. Thus, a corporate partner's distributive share of partnership business income constitutes business income to the corporate partner, but the determination of whether the partnership's activities and the activities of the corporate partner constitutes a single trade or business or more than one trade or business turns on the facts in each case. If the partnership's activities and the taxpayer's activities constitute a unitary business under established standards, disregarding ownership requirements, the taxpayer's share of the partnership's trade or business shall be combined with the taxpayer's trade or business as constituting a single trade or business.

   Example 1: Corporation A's distributive share of income in partnership P is 20%. Corporation A manufactures toys that are sold in the seven western states by partnership P. Corporation A's business income for the year was $1,000,000 and partnership P's business income for the same year was $800,000. The business income of Corporation A is $1,160,000 ($1,000,000 plus 20 percent of $800,000).

   Example 2: Corporation A's distributive share of income in partnership P is 90%. Partnership P manufactures toys of which approximately 30% are sold by Corporation A in the seven western states. The remainder is sold to outsiders by partnership P. In addition, Corporation A also sells other lines of toys not manufactured by partnership P. Corporation A handles all financing, management, accounting, advertising, and purchasing functions for partnership P as well as for itself. Corporation A incurred a loss of $500,000 for the year but partnership P's income was $1,000,000. The business income of Corporation A is $400,000 (90% of $1,000 = $900,000 less the loss of $500,000).

   When the activities of the partnership and the taxpayer do not constitute a unitary business under established standards, disregarding ownership requirements, the taxpayer's share of the partnership's trade or business shall be treated as a separate trade or business of the taxpayer. In such a case the taxpayer is engaged in two trades or businesses.

   Corporation A's distributive share of income in partnership P is 20%. Corporation A manufactures and sells toys in the seven western states. Partnership P operates farms within and without this state. Corporation A's income for the year is $1,000,000 and partnership P's income is $800,000 for the same year. Corporation A is engaged in two trades or businesses, and will be required to apportion its income of $1,000,000 from its own operations to this state on the basis of a three-factor apportionment formula. Partnership P would attribute part of its business income of $800,000 to this state on the basis of its own three-factor apportionment formula. Accordingly, Corporation A would report 20% of the partnership income apportioned to this state plus a portion of its income from its toy manufacturing business.

* * * *

(f) Apportionment of business income — single trade or business

If the partnership's activities and the taxpayer's activities constitute a unitary business under established standards, disregarding ownership requirements, the business income or such single trade or business attributable to this state shall be determined by a three-factor formula consisting of property, payroll and sales of the taxpayer and its share of the partnership's factors for any partnership year ending within or with the taxpayer's income year as follows:

(1) Property factor

In general the numerator and denominator of the property factor shall be determined as set forth in Regulations 25129 to 25131, inclusive, and 25137(b). However, the following special rules shall apply:

(i)

(A) A portion of the partnership's real and tangible personal property, both owned or rented and used during the income year in the regular course of such trade or business, to the extent of the taxpayer's interest in the partnership, shall be included in the denominator of the taxpayer's property factor. The value of such property located in this state shall also be included in the numerator of the property factor.

(B) The value of property that is rented or leased by the taxpayer to the partnership or vice versa shall, with respect to the taxpayer, be excluded from the property factor of the partnership or eliminated to the extent of the taxpayer's interest in the partnership, whatever the case may be, to avoid duplication.

Example 1: Corporation A's interest in partnership P is 20%. Corporation A's distributive share of partnership P's income is included in business income of Corporation A to be apportioned by formula. Corporation A owns a building (original cost of $100,000), which is rented to partnership P for $12,000 per year. Corporation A must include the original cost of $100,000 for the building in its property factor. Therefore, no portion of the value of the rented property will be reflected in the property factor of Corporation A.

Example 2: Same facts as in example 1 except partnership P owns the building and rents it to Corporation A. Corporation A will include $20,000 (20% of $100,000) in its property factor because of its interest in partnership P. In addition, Corporation A will take into account $9,600 ($12,000 less 20% thereof) of rental expense into its property factor to give weight in the property factor to the rented building used in Corporation A's operation. Thus, the value of the building to be used in the property factor of Corporation A is $96,800 ($20,000 plus 8 × $9,600).

(2) Payroll factor

In general, the numerator and denominator of the payroll factor shall be determined as set forth in Regulations 25132 and 25133. However, the following special rules shall apply:

The partnership's payroll used to produce business income, shall be included in the denominator of the taxpayer's payroll factor to the extent of the taxpayer's interest in the partnership. The amount of any such payroll applicable to this state shall also be included in the numerator of the taxpayer's payroll factor.

Example: Corporation A's interest in partnership P is 20% and its distributive share of partnership P's income is included in business income of Corporation A to be apportioned by formula. Corporation A's own payroll is $1,000,000 and the payroll of partnership P is $800,000. Corporation A's total payroll for purposes of the payroll factor is $1,160,000 ($1,000,000 plus 20% of $800,000).

(3) Sales factor

In general, the numerator and denominator of the sales factor shall be determined as set forth in Regulations 25134 to 25136, inclusive, and 25137(c). However, the following special rules shall apply:

(*A*) The partnership's sales which give rise to business income, shall be included in the denominator of the taxpayer's sales factor to the extent of the taxpayer's interest in the partnership. The amount of such sales attributable to this state shall also be included in the numerator of the taxpayer's sales factor. Intercompany sales between the partnership and the taxpayer shall be eliminated from the denominator and numerator of the taxpayer's sales factor as follows:
- (i) Sales by the taxpayer to the partnership to the extent of the taxpayer's interest in the partnership
- (ii) Sales by the partnership to the taxpayer not to exceed the taxpayer's interest in all partnership sales

(*B*) Notwithstanding any intercompany eliminations described in subparagraph (*A*), sales made to nonpartners shall be included in the denominator of the taxpayer's sales factor in an amount equal to such taxpayer's interest in the partnership.

(*C*) Application of the preceding rules is illustrated by the following examples:

Example 1: Corporation A's interest in partnership P is 20%, and its distributive share of partnership P's income is included in business income of Corporation A to be apportioned by formula. Corporation A's sales were $20,000,000 for the year, $5,000,000 of which were made to partnership P. Partnership P made sales of $10,000,000 during the same year, none of which were to Corporation A or the other partner(s). The denominator of Corporation A's sales factor is $21,000,000 determined as follows:

Sales by Corporation A	$20,000,000
Add: Corporation A's interest (20%) in Partnership P's sales	2,000,000
Less: Corporation A's interest (20%) in Corporation A's sales to Partnership P	(1,000,000)
Denominator of sales factor	$ 21,000,000

Example 2: The following facts are applicable to examples 2(a) to (c), inclusive. Corporation A's interest in partnership P is 20% and Corporation B's interest is 80%. The distributive share of partnership income is included in business income of Corporation A and Corporation B, respectively.

(*a*) The sales made by Corporation A, Corporation B, and Partnership P are as follows:

Corporation A		$20,000,000
Corporation B		60,000,000
Partnership P:		
To Corporation A	$2,000,000	
To Corporation B	8,000,000	
		$ 10,000,000

The denominator of Corporation A's sales factor is $20,000,000 determined as follows:

Sales by Corporation A	$20,000,000
Add: Corporation A's interest (20%) in Partnership P's sales	2,000,000
Less: Partnership P's Sales to Corporation A	(2,000,000)
Denominator of Corporation A's sales factor	$ 20,000,000

The denominator of Corporation B's sales factor is $60,000,000 determined as follows:

Sales by Corporation B	$60,000,000
Add: Corporation B's interest (80%) in Partnership P's sales	8,000,000
Less: Partnership P's sales to Corporation B	(8,000,000)
	$ 60,000,000

(*b*) The sales made by Corporation A, Corporation B, and Partnership P are as follows:

Corporation A		$20,000,000
Corporation B		60,000,000
Partnership P:		
To Corporation A	$1,000,000	
To Corporation B	9,000,000	
		$10,000,000

The denominator of Corporation A's sales factor is $21,000,000 determined as follows:

Sales by Corporation A	$20,000,000
Add: Corporation A's interest (20%) in Partnership P's sales	2,000,000
Less: Partnership P's sales to Corporation A	(1,000,000)
Denominator of Corporation A's sales factor	$21,000,000

The denominator of Corporation B's sales factor is $60,000,000 determined as follows:

Sales by Corporation B	$60,000,000
Add: Corporation B's interest (80%) in Partnership P's sales	8,000,000
Less: Intercompany sales between Partnership P and Corporation B*	(8,000,000)
Denominator of Corporation B's sales factor	$ 60,000,000

(*c*) The sales made by Corporation A, Corporation B, and Partnership P are as follows:

Corporation A	$20,000,000
Corporation B	80,000,000
Partnership P:	
To Corporation A	$3,000,000
To Corporation B	6,000,000
To Corporation X	1,000,000
	$ 10,000,000

The denominator of Corporation A's sales factor is $20,200,000 determined as follows:

Sales by Corporation A	$20,000,000
Add: Corporation A's interest in Partnership P's sales to Nonpartner X Corporation (20% × $1,000,000)	200,000
Corporation A's interest in Partnership P's sales to Partners (20% × $9,000,000)	1,800,000
Less: Intercompany sales from Partnership P to Corporation A*	(1,800,000)
Denominator of Corporation A's sales factor	$ 20,200,000

The denominator of Corporation B's sales factor is $81,800,000 determined as follows:

Sales by Corporation B	$80,000,000
Add: Corporation B's interest in Partnership P's sales to Nonpartner X Corporation (80% × $1,000,000)	800,000
Corporation B's interest in Partnership P's sales to Partners (80% × $9,000,000)	7,200,000
Less: Intercompany sales from Partnership P to Corporation B	(6,000,000)
Denominator of Corporation B's sales factor	$ 82,000,000
* Not to exceed taxpayer's interest in Partnership P's sales.	

* * * *

(4) Common accounting period

If a partnership and a corporation are engaged in a unitary business and their accounting periods are different, if necessary, to avoid distortion, the income and factors of the partnership will be determined on the basis of the corporate partner's accounting period.

(g) Apportionment of business income — two or more trades or businesses

When the activities of the partnership and the taxpayer do not constitute a unitary business under established standards, disregarding ownership requirements, the taxpayer's share of the partnership's trade or business shall be treated as another trade or business of the taxpayer. The determination of the amount of the partnership's business income and the taxpayer's distributive share of that income attributable to sources within this state shall be as follows:

(1) If the partnership derives business income from sources within and without this state, the amount of business income derived from sources within this state shall be determined on the basis of a three-factor formula of property, payroll, and sales. The factors shall be determined in accordance with the provisions of Section 25129 to 25137, inclusive, Revenue and Taxation Code, and the regulations thereunder. After determining the amount of business income attributable to this state by the three-factor formula, the taxpayer's distributive share of such business income shall be reported as business income from a separate business by the taxpayer. That income when added to the taxpayer's other business income apportioned to this state and nonbusiness income allocable to this state is the taxpayer's measure of tax for its income year.

Corporation A's distributive share of income in partnership P is 20%. Partnership P derives income from sources within and without this state but its business is unrelated to the business of Corporation A. Partnership P has business income of $500,000 for the year of which 40% is apportioned to this state by its three-factor formula of property, payroll and sales. Corporation A shall include in its measure of tax its income received from partnership P $40,000 ($500,000 × 40% × 20).

(2) If the partnership derives business income from sources entirely within this state, or entirely without this state, such income shall not be subject to formula apportionment. The taxpayer's distributive share of such business income attributable to this state (if any) shall be added to the taxpayer's other business income apportioned to this state plus nonbusiness income, if any, allocable to this state, the total of which is the taxpayer's measure of tax for its income year.

Example 1: Corporation A's distributive share of income in partnership P is 20%. The distributive share of P's business income is not an integral part of A's trade or business so as to be considered one business. Corporation A derives business income from sources within and without this state. Partnership P is engaged in business wholly within this state. Corporation A's business income for the year is $5,000,000 of which 50% is apportioned to this state. Partnership P has a loss on its operations for the same year of $500,000. Corporation A's measure of tax is $2,400,000 ($5,000,000 × 50% = $2,500,000 - $100,000 ($500,000 × 20%)).

Example 2: Same facts as in example 1, except partnership P operates its business wholly outside this state. Corporation A's measure of tax is $2,500,000 ($5,000,000 × 50%) as no portion of partnership P's loss is attributable to this state.

AICPA® & CIMA®

Appendix A

Basic Ideas of Multistate Income Tax Planning

This chapter is not part of the required reading for self-study participants.

Introduction

State and local taxes have, for many companies, become a much larger expense than federal taxes. In addition, the state and local field has become a growth industry with no end to the growth in sight. As a consequence, increased attention has been focused in the past few years on reducing state tax liabilities.

We engage in this effort, keeping in mind the oft-quoted words of Judge Learned Hand that "any one may so arrange his affairs that his taxes shall be as low as possible; he is not bound to choose that pattern which will best pay the Treasury; there is not even a patriotic duty to increase one's taxes." (*Helvering v. Gregory*, 69 F.2d 809, (1934)).

Finally, any tax planning strategy must be considered in light of overall company objectives, implementation costs, administrative complexity, practical realities, economic substance, and business purpose. In our enthusiasm to save taxes, we often forget that businesses do not exist to minimize taxes. Reducing a company's tax burden is only one of many tools used by management to achieve a company's larger objectives.

Identifying goals and methodologies

General planning goal

Our general planning goal is to shift income from states with high taxes to those with low tax rates by either moving income away from those states, decreasing the apportionment factors in those high rate states, or capitalizing on the inconsistencies among the states in their treatment of the unitary concept, business or nonbusiness income, state modifications, payroll, property, and sales factors, and filing elections. If state laws define the company and its subsidiaries or affiliates as a unitary group, then shifting income from domestic to foreign may be ineffective.

Specific tactics

Review your factors

Examine the makeup and application of your apportionment factors. Can you isolate payroll, property, or sales that generate nonbusiness income from business income? Once separated, identify the allocation rules of the states in which you are doing business. Sometimes simple identification and separation will result in savings.

Compare, for example, the interaction of your specific sales factor with your state's treatment of such items as drop shipments, dock sales throwbacks, throwouts, and cost-of-performance related to service sales. Savings are sometimes possible by changing the method or location of shipment and delivery. Identify property that is obsolete and remove it from your property factor. Check to see if leasing employees in your state will lower your payroll factor, or whether certain employees can be replaced with independent contractors. The latter are not included in the payroll factor. Double-check to make sure that property or payroll that is generating nonbusiness income is not included in your apportionment factors for business income.

The overall goal in reviewing your factors is to move either operations, or highly profitable activities, into low-tax states and operations, or activities that generate losses or low-profit margins, into high-tax states. Computer spreadsheet models are particularly helpful in performing various "if-this-then-that" analyses. The following simple examples illustrate the benefits of shifting a company's factors.

Example A-1

High-Value, Inc. does business in two states, A and B. State A has a 10% income tax rate and state B has a 5% income tax rate. Both states use a traditional three-factor formula that equally weights sales, property, and payroll. High-Value manufactures, stores, and distributes its products in state A. The operations in state B are largely limited to sales, repair, and maintenance activities. The company's taxable income is $10,000,000 and its activities within the two states are as follows:

	State A	State B	Total
Sales	$ 70,000,000	$ 20,000,000	$ 90,000,000
Property	5,000,000	1,500,000	6,500,000
Payroll	3,000,000	1,000,000	4,000,000

High-Value's tax liability for both states currently totals $882,850.

	State A	State B
Sales factor	77.78%	22.22%
State A ($70,000,000/$90,000,000)		
State B ($20,000,000/$90,000,000)		
Property factor	76.92%	23.08%
State A ($5,000,000/$6,500,000)		
State B ($1,500,000/$6,500,000)		
Payroll factor	75.00%	25.00%
State A ($3,000,000/$4,000,000)		
State B ($1,000,000/$4,000,000)		
Sum of apportionment factors	229.7%	70.3%
Divided by 3	÷3	÷3
Equals state apportionment percentage	76.57%	23.43%
Times business income	$ 10,000,000	$ 10,000,000
Equals state taxable income	$ 7,657,000	$ 2,343,000
Times state tax rate	10%	5%
State income tax	$ 765,700	$ 117,150

Example A-2

If High-Value were to move its inventory and distribution center, and research and development operations representing $2,000,000 in property and $800,000 in payroll from state A to state B, its factors and apportionment would change as follows:

	State A	State B	Total
Sales	$ 70,000,000	$ 20,000,000	$ 90,000,000
Property	3,000,000	3,500,000	6,500,000
Payroll	2,200,000	1,800,000	4,000,000

	State A	State B
Sales factor	77.78%	22.22%
State A ($70,000,000/$90,000,000)		
State B ($20,000,000/$90,000,000)		
Property factor	46.15%	53.85%
State A ($3,000,000/$6,500,000)		
State B ($3,500,000/$6,500,000)		
Payroll factor	55.00%	45.00%
State A ($2,200,000/$4,000,000)		
State B ($1,800,000/$4,000,000)		
Sum of apportionment factors	178.93%	121.07%
Divided by 3	÷3	÷3
Equals state apportionment percentage	59.64%	40.36%
Times business income	$ 10,000,000	$ 10,000,000
Equals state taxable income	$ 5,964,000	$ 4,036,000
Times state tax rate	10%	5%
State Income Tax	$ 596,400	$ 201,800

High-Value's tax liability for both states is now $798,200; a savings of $84,650 ($882,850 –$798,200).

Given that fewer states still use equally weighted factors in their apportionment formulas, it is more critical than ever to analyze a company's operations in light of their impact on its apportionment factors. The following examples illustrate the dramatic distortion that can occur doing business in states that double-weight (or more) the sales factor, or use just sales as a single-factor.

Example A-3

High-Value, Inc. does business in two states, A and B. State A has a 10% income tax rate and State B has a 5% income tax rate. State A uses single-factor sales, and state B uses a traditional three-factor formula that equally weights sales, property, and payroll. High-Value manufactures, stores, and distributes its products in state A. The operations in state B are largely limited to sales, repair, and maintenance activities. The company's taxable income is $10,000,000 and its activities within the two states are as follows:

	State A	State B	Total
Sales	$ 70,000,000	$ 20,000,000	$ 90,000,000
Property	5,000,000	1,500,000	6,500,000
Payroll	3,000,000	1,000,000	4,000,000

High-Value's tax liability for both states currently totals $894,950.

	State A	State B
Sales factor	77.78%	22.22%
State A ($70,000,000/$90,000,000)		
State B ($20,000,000/$90,000,000)		
Property factor	N/A	23.08%
State A N/A		
State B ($1,500,000/$6,500,000)		
Payroll factor	N/A	25.00%
State A N/A		
State B ($1,000,000/$4,000,000)		
Sum of apportionment factors	77.78%	70.3%
Divided by 3	N/A	÷3
Equals state apportionment percentage	77.78%	23.43%
Times business income	$ 10,000,000	$ 10,000,000
Equals state taxable income	$ 7,778,000	$ 2,343,000
Times state tax rate	10%	5%
State income tax	$ 777,800	$ 117,150

Reversing the percentages in the previous example illustrates the dramatic impact these factors have on a company's tax liability.

Example A-4

High-Value's tax liability for both states currently totals $623,200.

	State A	State B
Sales factor	22.22%	77.78%
Property factor	23.08%	N/A
Payroll factor	25.00%	N/A
Sum of apportionment factors	70.3%	77.78%
Divided by 3	÷3	N/A
Equals state apportionment percentage	23.43%	77.78%
Times business income	$ 10,000,000	$ 10,000,000
Equals state taxable income	$ 2,343,000	$ 7,778,000
Times state tax rate	10%	5%
State income tax	$ 234,300	$ 388,900

Review where you are doing business

Nexus usually has bad connotations. We generally think of it as something you do not want to create. But that is not necessarily true. By creating nexus in a lower tax rate or no tax state, you can decrease your total state and local tax liability. For example, if your Colorado company makes online sales into Wyoming, send an employee up there and deliberately create nexus. Doing so will allow you to apportion your income between Colorado and Wyoming (which, of course, has no income tax).

On the other hand, if you have a state in which you have limited sales activities, perhaps a single sales person or small office, you may be able to break nexus with that state by closing the office and having the sales personnel operate out of their homes. The obvious rule here is to avoid nexus in high-tax states and create nexus in low-tax states.

Examine your state's cost-of-performance rules for service sales. Can you reduce your income by shifting costs between Uniform Division of Income for Tax Purposes Act (UDITPA; all-or-nothing test) and states that have adopted the Multistate Tax Commission (MTC) proportional allocation method? For example, if based on cost of performance, service income is apportioned 30% to State A, 30% to State B, and 40% to State C, then, under the UDITPA rules, all income is sourced to State C. However, there may be non-UDITPA states that simply allocate the service income to the state where more than 50% of the cost of performance occurs. In this case, the sale would not be allocated to any state because no state has more than 50% of the cost of performance. Other states may source the service income to the state of the recipient. Finally, if the three states have adopted the MTC rules (MTC Regulation IV.17(B)), then the service income is divided among the states based upon their apportioned percentage. As a consequence, depending upon the states and the cost of performance measurement, some service sales may be counted in more than one state.

Have you checked your state's rules on executive compensation or payroll throwbacks?

Note: Be sure to check with your legal department before you go around creating nexus. There may be other business reasons, known only to your staff attorneys, for avoiding nexus in particular states.

Move income from separate filing states into combined reporting states

Here are three examples. First, if your company is operating in a separate filing state and it owns a subsidiary operating in a combined filing state, sell property to the subsidiary and then lease it back. Your income in the combined reporting state will, of course, not change because the rental income of the subsidiary is offset by the rental expense of the parent. Your income, however, in the separate filing state will be reduced by the lease expense and decreased property factor. Second, if your company is considering selling an asset with a large capital gain, drop the asset down into an existing subsidiary in a low or no tax state. When the subsidiary sells the asset, deem the capital gain to be allocable nonbusiness income to the low or no tax state. Or, break some of the ties between the parent and subsidiary and deem the latter to be nonunitary. Finally, create a unitary relationship with those subsidiaries that have losses or net operating losses.

Review the tax credits available in the states in which you are doing business

It sounds simple. It is. And, it is often overlooked because the time invested doesn't seem to justify the benefits, or more likely, a company's tax department is understaffed. Keep in mind that there are firms that make a living just off finding underused tax credits and incentives. Why pay them if you can do it yourself?

Review your state's filing elections

Besides trying to match up for-profit divisions with loss operations, be sure to review your state's filing methods. Check to see if filing consolidated or combined reports will decrease your total tax bill. Again, a simple step to take, but one often missed in the rush to file on time.

AICPA® & CIMA®

Appendix B

AUDIT DEFENSE STRATEGIES[1]

[1] This section is based on an article published in the May 1999 issue of the *Journal of Multistate Taxation and Incentives*, and is used here with their permission. Copyright 1999 RIA.

Introduction

Going through an audit is, under the best of circumstances, always an adversarial process, and not for the squeamish or weak of heart. The topics discussed here are not pretty. Nevertheless, taxpayers and their advisors will find it useful to learn how audits get chosen, what auditors look for before they arrive, what they want to see once they do show up, and what, if anything, can be done about it.

Audit selection

Several things may prompt state or city taxing authorities to select a particular business for audit. First, and probably most frequent, is some sort of statistical modeling (kind of like winning a lottery, but not nearly as much fun). At the federal level, the IRS has its infamous statistical program, the computerized discriminant function (DIF) technique. IRS selects returns for examination based on, for example, discrepancy with information returns, a history of deficiencies, random sampling, and the "questionable refund" program. Using DIF scores, IRS ranks and selects returns having the greatest audit potential. With the IRS approach as a guide, many states and cities have fashioned their own models.

Formulas and statistics

The process begins when taxpayers file their first sales tax or income tax return, and the data is entered, evaluated, and graded. Using formulas that everyone learned in college, but now generally have forgotten, the state or city tries to calculate which returns would likely produce the greatest yield on audit. Naturally, the formulas and analyses vary in sophistication, depending on the political jurisdiction involved. Although few people know exactly how these formulas are composed and applied, some uses are so common as to be evident to anyone. For example, if a company is experiencing extremely rapid growth in sales or assets, an audit should not be a surprise. Face it, if a business is growing that quickly, mistakes are being made. Taxpayers know it, MBA students know it, and the government knows it.

Another example of statistical modeling is "trend analysis." By aggregating returns by industry, state revenue departments often can use trend analysis to spot specific taxpayer anomalies and assign audits accordingly. The technique is particularly helpful in cash-intensive businesses such as restaurants and bars, where trend analysis can highlight irregular relationships between sales, inventory, and cost of goods sold.

Prior audits, data from outside sources

Aside from the prosaic world of number crunching, several other situations may prompt a state to audit a particular company. Probably the most obvious is a previous audit. If the government found lots of mistakes, it will be back again and again until the taxpayer gets it right. Also consider for example, a taxpayer's failure to charge a customer sales tax, or the failure to issue 1099 forms. One generally would call those mistakes. An auditor examining the customer and finding the erroneous invoice or information omission, however, would call it an audit lead.

Audits also may be prompted by routine information exchanges between government entities. For example, the Federal Aviation Administration regularly reports on registration of aircraft, and a state's parks and recreation department may accumulate data on new boat registrations. (Was sales tax paid on those purchases?) Applicable regulatory agencies report information on licensed professionals such as CPAs, attorneys, doctors, and dentists. (One state found, for example, an unusually high number of income tax nonfilers among both attorneys and those people who order vanity plates for their cars.) Also, departments of labor exchange wage and unemployment information, and secretaries of state provide data on bankruptcy filings. Counties and cities may report on the issuance of building permits. And last but not least, states maintain information exchange programs with the IRS. Although all this exchange of information may sound scary, one may take some comfort in the fact that most large marketing and credit reporting agencies have more such information than the taxing authorities. Nevertheless, many state governments, like all good direct marketers, are beginning to buy that information.

And, do not forget the proverbial "snitch." To avoid problems, happily married taxpayers should try to stay that way. Also, workers may be happy as long as they are employed. If any irregularities exist in a business, however, the next round of downsizing just may get that information to the local revenue department.

In any event, there is little that one can do to prevent an audit, other than following the common-sense rules of filing returns accurately and promptly. Prevention planning must begin long before a business is selected for audit, with accurate and complete recordkeeping, good internal control, and a competent and knowledgeable accounting staff.

The pre-audit

A taxpayer's initial contact with an auditor may be by telephone or letter. At that time, the taxpayer must take certain critical steps.

Who to contact

Get the auditor's name and phone number. This action may seem obvious, but it is amazing how often taxpayers fail to get this most basic information (people in shock are often like that).

Type of tax; audit period

Find out precisely what taxes are under examination and for what period. For example, is it sales tax or use tax, income tax, or franchise tax? Some states' revenue departments encourage the examination of all state taxes (sales, use, withholding, and income being the most common) during one audit, thinking that this approach is more efficient (like, for example, removing all four wisdom teeth on one visit to the dentist).

Required documentation

Ask the auditor to specify exactly what records should be made available for examination. The answer may include every scrap of paper the business has. Nevertheless, any attempts to limit the scope of the audit should begin here.

Time and place of audit

Finally, settle on a mutually agreeable audit date and location. Generally, auditors schedule their examinations weeks, even months, in advance. Taxpayers also should allow plenty of time to prepare for the audit and to check staff scheduling and contact the company's outside tax professionals. Auditors do not need to examine a taxpayer's records with only a day or two of notice. Out-of-state auditors commonly bring "filler audits" with them when they travel. For example, a hard-working auditor from California on assignment in Colorado may finish one examination sooner than expected and call another local taxpayer to try and fit in another audit at the last minute. The taxpayer should be kind, but should decline the auditor's invitation and suggest another later date. Hard-working, conscientious auditors from out of state are to be admired, but perhaps should be encouraged to take a little time to view the local scenery, rather than show up on short notice to conduct the audit.

Once the audit is assigned and an appointment date established, the auditor will perform several pre-audit tasks, including the following:

- Reviewing any prior audits or department correspondence with the taxpayer
- Pulling a sampling of prior returns for review
- Determining all of the company's locations and taxing jurisdictions
- Learning exactly what the company's business is and how and where it is carried on

The revenue agent should not be the only one doing pre-audit work. The taxpayer and its advisors should be preparing as well, performing the following tasks:

- Review internal controls and the flow of records.
- For an income tax audit, review your returns in light of that state's specific rules regarding state modifications, apportionment and allocation, business/non-business income, throwback sales, and the specific makeup of the state's apportionment factors (sales, property, and payroll).
- Take some time to review the state's current legislative activity and any recent state tax cases, not just for possible exposure, but also for potential refunds.
- Be sure to scan the state's various income tax credit provisions. Surprisingly, income tax credits are often overlooked in the hurry to get the return filed on time.
- If the state has a "taxpayer bill of rights," become familiar with the taxpayer's audit responsibilities and protections.
- Identify the company's exposure (for example, gray areas of the law or weaknesses in the company's accounting system).
- Ascertain the statute of limitations for the items and the taxes under audit.
- Finally, identify the company's contact or liaison person to work with the auditor.

Initial meeting and audit work

At the initial meeting with the auditor, review the scope of the audit and establish the company's liaisons. It is absolutely critical to know what tax will be audited and for what period. Strategies to pursue during the audit should include the following:

- Controlling the flow of information
- Avoiding commitments
- Setting limits (time and distance)
- Being personable and professional

Controlling the flow of information

Just what can auditors look at? Probably just about anything they please. But, the fact of the matter is that auditors always ask for more than they want or ever intend to examine. So, help them out; give them limits. Specifically, a document request form of some fashion should be mandatory. With such a form, the taxpayer can keep track of exactly what the auditor has and has not seen. This may help in understanding a position the auditor is taking. In addition, it may keep the auditor from requesting additional documentation for items that have already been substantially supported.

Finally, it is not a good idea to turn the company into a local photocopy center. If the auditor wants something copied, the item should be given to an appropriate, close-lipped clerk who will make two copies, one for the auditor and another for the taxpayer's file.

Avoiding commitments

Taxpayers should be very careful of entering into commitments. The key questions that usually arise in this regard are whether to (1) fill out nexus questionnaires, (2) agree to particular statistical sampling methodologies, and (3) sign statute of limitation waivers. The general rule is never sign anything unless absolutely necessary.

Nexus

States use nexus questionnaires to determine whether a company is doing business in their taxing jurisdiction. Taxpayers receiving such a questionnaire should not automatically fill it out. If a response is called for, do so by letter instead.

Nexus questionnaires usually are just a list of yes-and-no questions, generally worded in such a way that the taxpayer cannot win (such as, "Have you stopped beating your dog?"). Given the complexity of the issues surrounding nexus, it is much easier to deal with them in an independently composed letter rather than by filling out the taxing authority's standardized form.

Sampling

Where possible, taxpayers should consider cooperating with a statistical sampling approach, rather than specifically committing to it. For example, an auditor may propose a survey strategy for sampling the sales factor or accounts payables and ask the taxpayer to approve it. The taxpayer might be better off inviting the auditor to proceed with that plan, and then reviewing the results to see whether the sample really was valid. That way, if some items or issues seem distortive, the taxpayer still has some leverage in getting the auditor to change the sample. Once a taxpayer signs off on the sampling methodology, however, the taxpayer's leverage and options are usually gone.

Waivers

Auditors often ask taxpayers to agree to waive the statute of limitations to "lock in" the audit period (frequently four years for income tax). For example, the auditor may want the taxpayer to sign a waiver for a few months so that the limitations period will not expire before the audit is completed. Generally, such a request is reasonable, but the waiver should be restricted to a specific date, tax, and issue. Limiting the waiver in this manner helps limit the scope of the audit, in addition to encouraging the auditor not to dawdle during the examination. Many states provide that whatever years are still open for the IRS are still open for the state.

Limits on time and distance

Taxpayers should try to get the auditor to commit to a time frame for the examination. In seeking to determine how long the audit will take, taxpayers might let the auditor know that, for example, they have other auditors and audits to schedule, as well as a business to run, and a life to live.

Also, consider isolating the auditors. That is, do not let them work at a desk next to the company's accounts payable clerk, one of the audit contacts, or the company president. Do not make it that easy for the auditor to pop her head in every five minutes or so with a "quick question." Specifically identifying who the auditor is to work with on particular issues, for example, their liaison, is important because it assures you that the information provided to the auditor is done so by informed competent professionals on your staff, rather than off-hand comments from someone who may not even work in the tax department.

Be professional

In dealing with auditors some interpersonal relationship rules should apply, such as the following:

- Be friendly, but do not be a friend. (Most of us probably have enough friends already.)
- Do not be an enemy. (We also have enough enemies already, and hostility does not pay.)
- Be cooperative without being a pushover. At the least, be nonconfrontational. Inevitably, the taxpayer and the auditor will disagree. Thus, starting with a professional demeanor is always a good strategy. (Yelling and screaming may come later, but once started, tends to discourage compromise.)
- Do not offer comments about fiscal reform, politics, the chances of a flat tax, or what you would do if you were in charge. An auditor who has been around for a while has heard it all. Keep the small talk limited to, for example, the weather, who won last week's big game, and the latest trend in body piercing.

Closing conference

Generally, the auditor will plan a closing conference. If not, the taxpayer should request one. In preparing for the closing conference, taxpayers should do the following:

- Review the assessments and the underlying working papers. Check for math or formula errors in the worksheets. Watch out for double-counting in the calculation of the factors, the treatment of dock sales, throwbacks, and the composition of business and nonbusiness income. Whenever possible, try to make adjustments at the audit level. It is almost always easier to get something removed at the audit level before the audit is turned in for processing, than afterward at appeal.
- Identify and review with the auditor the problem areas, and make sure that the positions taken by the auditor and the reasons for them are clear. Ask for explanations of the adjustments and substantiation for the positions taken, including relevant statutes, regulations, policy positions, case law, and so on.
- Discuss the billing process, protest procedures, and interest rates, and be sure that they are understood. If contemplating an appeal, this is where the process really starts. Procedural matters now become critical. Do not rely on the auditor or anyone else to get it right. Rather, get written copies of the various due dates, appeal procedures, and so on, directly from the statutes.
- Do not miss deadlines. When the buzzer sounds, the referee does not allow extra time to make that last score, and neither will the government.
- Finally, do not expect the auditor or taxing jurisdiction to just give in. Auditors are not paid to be easily intimidated. Further, the courts have stated more than once that government should constitutionally tax all that it can, and their resources are usually larger than the taxpayer's.

Conclusion

In considering all the ramifications of an audit, taxpayers and their advisors should keep things in perspective. Taxes and audits go back to the dawn of history. In fact, some of the earliest historical records in existence are written on clay tablets from the Sumerian civilization that flourished in Mesopotamia more than 4,000 years ago. Most of those writings deal with economic matters, largely the imposition of tax on grain, barley, and hops used in making beer. Taxpayers should keep that in mind the next time they sit down late at night with a pile of tax receipts and pop open a beer. They are participating in a long and respected historical tradition.

Tax Glossary

401(k) plan – A qualified retirement plan to which contributions from salary are made from pre-tax dollars.

Accelerated depreciation – Computation of depreciation to provide greater deductions in earlier years of equipment and other business or investment property.

Accounting method – Rules applied in determining when and how to report income and expenses on tax returns.

Accrual method – Method of accounting that reports income when it is earned, disregarding when it may be received, and expense when incurred, disregarding when it is actually paid.

Acquisition debt – Mortgage taken to buy, hold, or substantially improve main or second home that serves as security.

Active participation – Rental real estate activity involving property management at a level that permits deduction of losses.

Adjusted basis – Basis in property increased by some expenses (for example, by capital improvements) or decreased by some tax benefit (for example, by depreciation).

Adjusted gross income (AGI) – Gross income minus above-the-line deductions (such as deductions other than itemized deductions, the standard deduction, and personal and dependency exemptions).

Alimony – Payments for the support or maintenance of one's spouse pursuant to a judicial decree or written agreement related to divorce or separation.

Alternative minimum tax (AMT) – System comparing the tax results with and without the benefit of tax preference items for the purpose of preventing tax avoidance.

Amortization – Write-off of an intangible asset's cost over a number of years.

Applicable federal rate (AFR) – An interest rate determined by reference to the average market yield on U.S. government obligations. Used in Sec. 7872 to determine the treatment of loans with below-market interest rates.

At-risk rules – Limits on tax losses to business activities in which an individual taxpayer has an economic stake.

Backup withholding – Withholding for federal taxes on certain types of income (such as interest or dividend payments) by a payor that has not received required taxpayer identification number (TIN) information.

Bad debt – Uncollectible debt deductible as an ordinary loss if associated with a business and otherwise deductible as short-term capital loss.

Basis – Amount determined by a taxpayer's investment in property for purposes of determining gain or loss on the sale of property or in computing depreciation.

Cafeteria plan – Written plan allowing employees to choose among two or more benefits (consisting of cash and qualified benefits) and to pay for the benefits with pretax dollars. Must conform to Sec. 125 requirements.

Capital asset – Investments (such as stocks, bonds, and mutual funds) and personal property (such as home).

Capital gain/loss – Profit (net of losses) on the sale or exchange of a capital asset or Sec. 1231 property, subject to favorable tax rates, and loss on such sales or exchanges (net of gains) deductible against $3,000 of ordinary income.

Capitalization – Addition of cost or expense to the basis of property.

Carryovers (carryforwards) and carrybacks – Tax deductions and credits not fully used in one year are chargeable against prior or future tax years to reduce taxable income or taxes payable.

Conservation reserve program (CRP) – A voluntary program for soil, water, and wildlife conservation, wetland establishment and restoration and reforestation, administered by the U.S. Department of Agriculture.

Credit – Amount subtracted from income tax liability.

Deduction – Expense subtracted in computing adjusted gross income.

Defined benefit plan – Qualified retirement plan basing annual contributions on targeted benefit amounts.

Defined contribution plan – Qualified retirement plan with annual contributions based on a percentage of compensation.

Depletion – Deduction for the extent a natural resource is used.

Depreciation – Proportionate deduction based on the cost of business or investment property with a useful life (or recovery period) greater than one year.

Earned income – Wages, bonuses, vacation pay, and other remuneration, including self-employment income, for services rendered.

Earned income credit – Refundable credit available to low-income individuals.

Employee stock ownership plan (ESOP) – Defined contribution plan that is a stock bonus plan or a combined stock bonus and money purchase plan designed to invest primarily in qualifying employer securities.

Estimated tax – Quarterly payments of income tax liability by individuals, corporations, trusts, and estates.

Exemption – A deduction against net income based on taxpayer status (such as single, head of household, married filing jointly or separately, trusts, and estates).

Fair market value – The price that would be agreed upon by a willing seller and willing buyer, established by markets for publicly-traded stocks, or determined by appraisal.

Fiscal year – A 12-month taxable period ending on any date other than December 31.

Foreign tax – Income tax paid to a foreign country and deductible or creditable, at the taxpayer's election, against U.S. income tax.

Gift – Transfer of money or property without expectation of anything in return, and excludable from income by the recipient. A gift may still be affected by the unified estate and gift transfer tax applicable to the gift's maker.

Goodwill – A business asset, intangible in nature, adding a value beyond the business's tangible assets.

Gross income – Income from any and all sources, after any exclusions and before any deductions are taken into consideration.

Half-year convention – A depreciation rule assuming property other than real estate is placed in service in the middle of the tax year.

Head-of-household – An unmarried individual who provides and maintains a household for a qualifying dependent and therefore is subject to distinct tax rates.

Health savings account (HSA) – A trust operated exclusively for purposes of paying qualified medical expenses of the account beneficiary and thus providing for deductible contributions, tax-deferred earnings, and exclusion of tax on any monies withdrawn for medical purposes.

Holding period – The period of time a taxpayer holds onto property, therefore affecting tax treatment on its disposition.

Imputed interest – Income deemed attributable to deferred-payment transfers, such as below-market loans, for which no interest or unrealistically low interest is charged.

Incentive stock option (ISO) – An option to purchase stock in connection with an individual's employment, which defers tax liability until all of the stock acquired by means of the option is sold or exchanged.

Income in respect of a decedent (IRD) – Income earned by a person, but not paid until after his or her death.

Independent contractor – A self-employed individual whose work method or time is not controlled by an employer.

Indexing – Adjustments in deductions, credits, exemptions and exclusions, plan contributions, AGI limits, and so on, to reflect annual inflation figures.

Individual retirement account (IRA) – Tax-exempt trust created or organized in the U.S. for the exclusive benefit of an individual or the individual's beneficiaries.

Information returns– Statements of income and other items recognizable for tax purposes provided to the IRS and the taxpayer. Form W-2 and forms in the 1099 series, as well as Schedules K-1, are the prominent examples.

Installment method– Tax accounting method for reporting gain on a sale over the period of tax years during which payments are made, such as, over the payment period specified in an installment sale agreement.

Intangible property– Items such as patents, copyrights, and goodwill.

Inventory – Goods held for sale to customers, including materials used in the production of those goods.

Involuntary conversion – A forced disposition (for example, casualty, theft, condemnation) for which deferral of gain may be available.

Jeopardy – For tax purposes, a determination that payment of a tax deficiency may be assessed immediately as the most viable means of ensuring its payment.

Keogh plan – A qualified retirement plan available to self-employed persons.

Key employee – Officers, employees, and officers defined by the Internal Revenue Code for purposes of determining whether a plan is "top heavy."

Kiddie tax – Application of parents' maximum tax rate to unearned income of their child under age 19. Full-time students under 24 are also subject to the kiddie tax.

Lien – A charge upon property after a tax assessment has been made and until tax liability is satisfied.

Like-kind exchange – Tax-free exchange of business or investment property for property that is similar or related in service or use.

Listed property – Items subject to special restrictions on depreciation (for example, cars, computers, cell phones).

Lump-sum distribution – Distribution of an individual's entire interest in a qualified retirement plan within one tax year.

Marginal tax rate – The highest tax bracket applicable to an individual's income.

Material participation – The measurement of an individual's involvement in business operations for purposes of the passive activity loss rules.

Mid-month convention – Assumption, for purposes of computing depreciation, that all real property is placed in service in the middle of the month.

Mid-quarter convention – Assumption, for purposes of computing depreciation, that all property other than real property is placed in service in the middle of the quarter, when the basis of property placed in service in the final quarter exceeds a statutory percentage of the basis of all property placed in service during the year.

Minimum distribution – A retirement plan distribution, based on life expectancies, that an individual must take after age 70 ½ in order to avoid tax penalties.

Minimum funding requirements – Associated with defined benefit plans and certain other plans, such as money purchase plans, assuring the plan has enough assets to satisfy its current and anticipated liabilities.

Miscellaneous itemized deduction – Deductions for certain expenses (for example, unreimbursed employee expenses) limited to only the amount by which they exceed 2 percent of adjusted gross income.

Money purchase plan – Defined contribution plan in which the contributions by the employer are mandatory and established other than by reference to the employer's profits.

Net operating loss (NOL) – A business or casualty loss for which amounts exceeding the allowable deduction in the current tax year may be carried back two years to reduce previous tax liability and forward 20 years to cover any remaining unused loss deduction.

Nonresident alien – An individual who is neither a citizen nor a resident of the United States. Nonresidents are taxed on U.S. source income.

Original issue discount (OID) – The excess of face value over issue price set by a purchase agreement.

Passive activity loss (PAL) – Losses allowable only to the extent of income derived each year (such as by means of carryover) from rental property or business activities in which the taxpayer does not materially participate.

Passive foreign investment company (PFIC) – A foreign based corporation subject to strict tax rules which covers the treatment of investments in Sections 1291 through 1297.

Pass-through entities – Partnerships, LLCs, LLPs, S corporations, and trusts and estates whose income or loss is reported by the partner, member, shareholder, or beneficiary.

Personal holding company (PHC) – A corporation, usually closely-held, that exists to hold investments such as stocks, bonds, or personal service contracts and to time distributions of income in a manner that limits the owner(s) tax liability.

Qualified subchapter S trust (QSST) – A trust that qualifies specific requirements for eligibility as an S corporation shareholder.

Real estate investment trust (REIT) – A form of investment in which a trust holds real estate or mortgages and distributes income, in whole or in part, to the beneficiaries (such as investors).

Real estate mortgage investment conduit (REMIC) – Treated as a partnership, investors purchase interests in this entity which holds a fixed pool of mortgages.

Realized gain or loss – The difference between property's basis and the amount received upon its sale or exchange.

Recapture – The amount of a prior deduction or credit recognized as income or affecting its characterization (capital gain vs. ordinary income) when the property giving rise to the deduction or credit is disposed of.

Recognized gain or loss – The amount of realized gain or loss that must be included in taxable income.

Regulated investment company (RIC) – A corporation serving as a mutual fund that acts as investment agents for shareholders and customarily dealing in government and corporate securities.

Reorganization – Restructuring of corporations under specific Internal Revenue Code rules so as to result in nonrecognition of gain.

Resident alien – An individual who is a permanent resident, has substantial presence, or, under specific election rules is taxed as a U.S. citizen.

Roth IRA – Form of individual retirement account that produces, subject to holding period requirements, nontaxable earnings.

S corporation – A corporation that, upon satisfying requirements concerning its ownership, may elect to act as a pass-through entity.

Saver's credit – Term commonly used to describe Sec. 25B credit for qualified contributions to a retirement plan or via elective deferrals.

Sec. 1231 property – Depreciable business property eligible for capital gains treatment.

Sec. 1244 stock – Closely held stock whose sale may produce an ordinary, rather than capital, loss (subject to caps).

Split-dollar life insurance – Arrangement between an employer and employee under which the life insurance policy benefits are contractually split, and the costs (premiums) are also split.

Statutory employee – An insurance agent or other specified worker who is subject to social security taxes on wages but eligible to claim deductions available to the self-employed.

Stock bonus plan – A plan established and maintained to provide benefits similar to those of a profit-sharing plan, except the benefits must be distributable in stock of the employer company.

Tax preference items – Tax benefits deemed includable for purposes of the alternative minimum tax.

Tax shelter – A tax-favored investment, typically in the form of a partnership or joint venture, that is subject to scrutiny as tax-avoidance device.

Tentative tax – Income tax liability before taking into account certain credits, and AMT liability over the regular tax liability.

Transportation expense – The cost of transportation from one point to another.

Travel expense – Transportation, meals, and lodging costs incurred away from home and for trade or business purposes.

Unearned income – Income from investments (such as interest, dividends, and capital gains).

Uniform capitalization rules (UNICAP) – Rules requiring capitalization of property used in a business or income-producing activity (such as items used in producing inventory) and to certain property acquired for resale.

Unrelated business income (UBIT) – Exempt organization income produced by activities beyond the organization's exempt purposes and therefore taxable.

Wash sale – Sale of securities preceded or followed within 30 days by a purchase of substantially identical securities. Recognition of any loss on the sale is disallowed.

Index

MULTISTATE INCOME TAX

BY ANDREW JOHNSON, CPA

Solutions

Solutions

Chapter 1

Knowledge check solutions

1.

a. Incorrect. Volatility and complexity in defining nexus continues to grow as each state independently works on increasing its tax base.

b. Incorrect. Nexus issues are becoming increasingly complex.

c. Correct. States are using nexus as the means of increasing tax collections by finding the merest connections give rise to tax obligations.

d. Incorrect. Nexus volatility has not stopped and has only increased in light of most states' attempts to increase their tax base.

2.

a. Correct. Satisfying the federal due process and commerce clauses are at the base of any state's claim of nexus.

b. Incorrect. State laws defining nexus and imposing taxes are effective only if they do not exceed the bounds of the due process and commerce clauses of the U.S. Constitution.

c. Incorrect. Local taxing authorities must follow the bounds of the due process and commerce clauses of the U.S. Constitution.

d. Incorrect. The U.S. Constitution has commerce clauses that give the right to impose tax on out-of-state business.

3.

a. Incorrect. Due process requires rational relationships and the commerce clause requires fair apportionment.

b. Incorrect. The commerce clause imposes much more stringent requirements for state taxation of interstate commerce, in order to ensure that no state is imposing a burden on interstate commerce. Satisfying the due process clause's "minimal contacts" definition of nexus does not suffice for purposes of the commerce clause.

c. Correct. Due process is satisfied if a business has minimal contacts and there is a rational relationship between its income and the taxing state. The commerce clause, however, requires that nexus be substantial for the state to avoid a finding that its tax burdens interstate commerce.

d. Incorrect. Due process requires rational relationships and minimal contacts. Commerce clause requires substantial nexus and fair apportionment.

4.

a. Correct. The Commerce Clause requires substantial nexus instead of minimal nexus.
b. Incorrect. The Commerce Clause does require nondiscrimination.
c. Incorrect. The Commerce Clause does require fair apportionment.
d. Incorrect. The Commerce Clause does require some relation to services provided.

5.

a. Incorrect. The MTC's proposal provides $50,000 as the threshold for property ownership or payroll to define nexus.
b. Correct. The South Dakota law includes a minimum threshold of $100,000 in gross sales.
c. Incorrect. Under the MTC proposal there was a $500,000 in sales threshold, but the Wayfair decision will likely lower this proposal going forward.
d. Incorrect. This amount is a higher threshold than what was established by Wayfair.

6.

a. Incorrect. One transaction does not typically establish nexus.
b. Correct. Most states now have a threshold of 200 transactions.
c. Incorrect. Although this number would certain generate nexus, it is not the minimum amount of transactions that would do so.
d. Incorrect. This is amount that would definitely establish nexus, but it is not the lowest threshold.

7.

a. Incorrect. Public Law 86-272 applies only to net income taxes and the sale of tangible personal property.
b. Correct. Taxes measured by gross income or receipts are not covered by P.L. 86-272.
c. Incorrect. Public Law 86-272 applies only to net income taxes and the sale of tangible personal property.
d. Incorrect. Public Law 86-272 could help a business avoid income taxes.

Chapter 2

Knowledge check solutions

1.

   a. Correct. States that do a separate calculation of net operating losses usually begin with line 28 of Form 1120.

   b. Incorrect. Only the few states that merely allow the NOL as determined under federal law start out with line 30 of Form 1120.

   c. Incorrect. States that do a separate calculation of net operating losses usually begin with line 28 of Form 1120.

   d. Incorrect. Line 34 is the amount owed with the filing with the return.

2.

   a. Incorrect. Prior to enactment of the Worker, Homeownership, and Business Assistance Act of 2009, the federal tax code allowed a taxpayer to carry back an NOL for two years. California was not in conformity with this law.

   b. Incorrect. Many states, including California, have historically limited the use of carrybacks, or eliminated them entirely.

   c. Correct. Beginning in 2013 and in subsequent years, California allows 50%, then 75%, and finally 100% of NOL's to be carried back. California actually requires the NOL be carried back two years first, before allowing any excess NOL to be carried forward.

   d. Incorrect. For years beginning in 2013, California is phasing in the allowance of NOL carrybacks.

3.

   a. Incorrect. The U.S. Supreme Court ruled that Kentucky was not in violation of the Commerce Clause, and its participation in the bond market allowed it to make its bonds more marketable.

   b. Incorrect. The lower courts in Kentucky agreed with the taxpayers, holding that Kentucky's taxation of other states' bond interest was unconstitutional on its face, because it violated the Commerce Clause by affording more favorable taxation treatment to instate bonds than it did to out-of-state bonds.

   c. Correct. The U.S. Supreme Court found that Kentucky was motivated by legitimate political objectives apart from economic protectionism banned by the Commerce Clause, and that the state's participation in the municipal bond market did not favor Kentucky taxpayers over other taxpayers, but simply aided the state government in making its bonds more marketable.

   d. Incorrect. Kentucky bond interest income is not taxable to Kentucky residents. The court ruled that participation in the municipal bond market did not favor Kentucky taxpayers over other taxpayers.

4.

a. Incorrect. Alabama does allow for a subtraction for a portion of the federal income taxes paid.
b. Incorrect. Iowa does allow for a subtraction for a portion of the federal income taxes paid.
c. Incorrect. Louisiana does allow for a subtraction for a portion of the federal income taxes paid.
d. Correct. South Dakota is not a state that allows for a subtraction for the portion of income taxes paid.

5.

a. Incorrect. Federal taxable income would be overstated as the gain for federal taxable income would be higher than the gain for state purposes.
b. Incorrect. While a subtraction would need to be made, it is not because the federal taxable income is understated.
c. Correct. The federal taxable income would be overstated because the federal gain would be higher than the state gain and thus a subtraction would be warranted.
d. Incorrect. While the federal taxable income would be overstated, a subtraction would be needed instead of an addition.

Chapter 3

Knowledge check solutions

1.

a. Incorrect. There is neither an aggregation of a group's taxable items, or the ability to offset gains and losses among group members.
b. Correct. It is possible to reduce tax liabilities if the group can isolate high-profit centers in low-or no-tax states.
c. Incorrect. Each company with nexus is required to file a separate return.
d. Incorrect. Each company must file a separate return, and profits and losses are not combined or offset.

2.

a. Correct. The unity of operation test looks to such factors as central purchasing, advertising, accounting, and management.
b. Incorrect. The general system of operation is one of the factors considered in the unity of use test, not the unity of operation test.
c. Incorrect. Preparation of the affiliated groups tax return is considered in the unity of use test, not in the unity of operations test.
d. Incorrect. Unity of operation is evidenced by central purchasing, advertising, accounting and management divisions.

3.

a. Incorrect. Legal structure is irrelevant. It matters little for state tax purposes whether there is one corporation with various branches or separate corporations.
b. Correct. Because the unitary concept examines economic structure, it can apply equally to an affiliated group and to individual segments of a single corporation.
c. Incorrect. The control structure is irrelevant and does not aid in determining the unitary concept.
d. Incorrect. Tax rates are not relevant to the unitary concept.

4.

a. Incorrect. This amount is higher than the federal consolidated rules.
b. Incorrect. 90% is higher than the federal consolidated rules.
c. Correct. The federal consolidated rules require 80% stock ownership requirements.
d. Incorrect. This ownership requirement is not high enough for federal consolidated rules.

5.

a. Correct. Under the *Butler Brothers* decision, unity of ownership is one of the three unities that determine that a business is operating a unitary business. The other two unities are unity of operation and unity of use.
b. Incorrect response. The *Butler Brothers* decision did not address the issue of the intent of the business.
c. Incorrect. Under the *Butler Brothers* decision, unity of ownership is one of the three unities that determine that a business is operating a unitary business. The other two unities are unity of operation and unity of use.
d. Incorrect. The *Butler Brothers* decision does not focus on addresses of companies. It focuses on the unity of ownership.

6.

a. Correct. In *Edison*, the court determined that if the operations of a business in a state are dependent upon or contribute to the business operations outside the state, then the business may be taxed as a single economic unit. Examples of the relationship could include intercompany sales or loans.
b. Incorrect. The "factors of profitability test" is a test that was created by the U.S. Supreme Court in *Mobil Oil*.
c. Incorrect. In *Edison*, the court determined that if the operations of a business in a state are dependent upon or contribute to the business operations outside the state, then the business may be taxed as a single economic unit. Examples of the relationship could include intercompany sales or loans.
d. Incorrect. The *Edison* decision created the contribution or dependency test.

7.

a. Incorrect. The dependency or contribution test was created under the *Edison Stores* case.
b. Correct. The flow of value test was a result of the *Container* decision. The U.S. Supreme Court held that the unitary concept could be extended to include foreign subsidiaries, and there is the need for only a flow of value, not a flow of product.
c. Incorrect. The "factors of profitability test" is a test that was created by the U.S. Supreme Court in *Mobil Oil*.
d. Incorrect. The *Container* decision analyzed and discussed the flow of value test.

Chapter 4

Knowledge check solutions

1.

a. Incorrect. Currently, only 30 of the states have adopted the UDITPA. However, it is influential in those states in which it has not been adopted.
b. Correct. The function of the UDITPA is to promote uniformity among the states in the allocation and apportionment of multistate corporate income. The income to be apportioned must be business income.
c. Incorrect. UDIPTA is not mandatory. However, it is influential in those states in which it has not been adopted.
d. Incorrect. Currently 30 states have adopted the UDITPA.

2.

a. Incorrect. The income of a taxpayer is business income, unless it is clearly classifiable as nonbusiness income. This distinction is important, because for many states nonbusiness income is allocable to a specific state, while business income is subject to apportionment among two or more states.
b. Correct. The UDITPA defines business income as income arising from transactions and activity in the taxpayer's regular course of trade or business. It does not distinguish between income generated by tangible or intangible property.
c. Incorrect. The classification of income is not used in determining whether income is business or nonbusiness.
d. Incorrect. According to the UDITPA, business income includes income from tangible and intangible property if the acquisition, management and disposition of the property constitute integral parts of the taxpayer's regular trade or business operations.

3.

a. Correct. Many more states apportion intangible income than allocate it to the state of domicile.
b. Incorrect. Although some states allocate intangible income to the domiciliary state, many more find it apportionable.
c. Incorrect. Although some states allocate intangible income to the domiciliary state, there are more that find it apportionable.
d. Incorrect. This income is taxable and is generally apportioned amount the states in which the business operates.

Chapter 5

Knowledge check solutions

1.

a. Incorrect. MTC regulations are consistent with UDIPTA in valuing rental property at eight times its annual rent.
b. Incorrect. MTC regulations are consistent with UDIPTA. Rental property is valued at eight times its annual rent.
c. Correct. This is one area in which there is consistency. Both use a multiplier of eight in measuring the value of rental property.
d. Incorrect. Rental property is valued at eight times its annual rent.

2.

a. Correct. Compensation for the payroll factor is typically assigned to the state in which the unemployment compensation is reported.
b. Incorrect. Compensation for the payroll factor is not typically assigned to the state in which the most employees are situated. Also, the business's accounting methods are to be typically followed, although in some cases the business may use the cash method if the state requires the cash method for accounting for unemployment taxes.
c. Incorrect. Compensation for the payroll factor is typically assigned to the state in which the unemployment compensation is reported. The location of the home office is not a determining factor.
d. Incorrect. The location of the CEO is not a determining factor as the state in which unemployment is reported typically drives the payroll factor.

3.

a. Incorrect. Colorado does not treat nonemployees the same as employees for the payroll factor.
b. Incorrect. California does not treat nonemployees the same as employees for payroll factoring purposes.
c. Correct. Alabama held that if no difference exists between the generation of income by an employee or a nonemployee, then the nonemployee should be included in the payroll factor.
d. Incorrect. Independent contractors are not treated the same as employees for the payroll factor in New York.

4.

a. Incorrect. UDITPA defines a property's value as its cost, not its fair market value.
b. Correct. Both the UDITPA and the MTC define a property's value as its historical cost, not its FMV. Although property owned by a taxpayer is valued at its original cost, property rented by the taxpayer is valued at eight times the net annual rental.
c. Incorrect. UDITPA defines a property's value as its cost, not its net book value.
d. Incorrect. UDITPA defines a property's value as its cost, not its replacement value.

5.

a. Correct. Construction in progress is not usually found in the property factor.
b. Incorrect. Buildings are usually found in the property factor.
c. Incorrect. Machinery is usually found in the property factor.
d. Incorrect. Inventory is usually found in the property factor.

The AICPA publishes *CPA Letter Daily*, a free e-newsletter published each weekday. The newsletter, which covers the 10-12 most important stories in business, finance, and accounting, as well as AICPA information, was created to deliver news to CPAs and others who work with the accounting profession. Besides summarizing media articles, commentaries, and research results, the e-newsletter links to television broadcasts and videos and features reader polls. *CPA Letter Daily*'s editors scan hundreds of publications and websites, selecting the most relevant and important news so you don't have to. The newsletter arrives in your inbox early in the morning. To sign up, visit smartbrief.com/CPA.

Do you need high-quality technical assistance? The AICPA Auditing and Accounting Technical Hotline provides non-authoritative guidance on accounting, auditing, attestation, and compilation and review standards. The hotline can be reached at 877.242.7212.

Learn More

Continuing Professional Education

Thank you for selecting the American Institute of Certified Public Accountants as your continuing professional education provider. We have a diverse offering of CPE courses to help you expand your skillset and develop your competencies. Choose from hundreds of different titles spanning the major subject matter areas relevant to CPAs and CGMAs, including:

- Governmental and not-for-profit accounting, auditing, and updates
- Internal control and fraud
- Audits of employee benefit plans and 401(k) plans
- Individual and corporate tax updates
- A vast array of courses in other areas of accounting and auditing, controllership, management, consulting, taxation, and more!

Get your CPE when and where you want

- Self-study training options that includes on-demand, webcasts, and text formats with superior quality and a broad portfolio of topics, including bundled products like –
  - CPExpress® online learning for immediate access to hundreds of one- to four-credit hour online courses for just-in-time learning at a price that is right
  - Annual Webcast Pass offering live Q&A with experts and unlimited access to the scheduled lineup, all at an incredible discount.
- Staff training programs for audit, tax and preparation, compilation, and review
- Certificate programs offering comprehensive curriculums developed by practicing experts to build fundamental core competencies in specialized topics
- National conferences presented by recognized experts
- Affordable courses on-site at your organization – visit **aicpalearning.org/on-site** for more information.
- Seminars sponsored by your state society and led by top instructors. For a complete list, visit **aicpalearning.org/publicseminar**.

Take control of your career development

The AICPA's Competency and Learning website at **https://competency.aicpa.org** brings together a variety of learning resources and a self-assessment tool, enabling tracking and reporting of progress toward learning goals.

Visit www.AICPAStore.com to browse our CPE selections.